Family Favorites

Potluck Picks

Sunday Suppers

Make-ahead Meals

Hurry!
o get your
ree gift of
omestyle Casseroles,
etach and mail
his survey today!

We need your help!

Please take a moment to fill out and return the brief survey below.

To show our thanks, we'll send you a

free gift
of Homestyle Casseroles!

An exclusive collection of 67 family-favorite meals, with our compliments

heartfelt
homespun
comfort-foods

---

homestyle Casseroles
Customer Survey

Things that I like:

○ Gardening ○ Home improvement
○ Decorating ○ Crafts
○ Cooking/nutrition ○ Quilting
○ Health/fitness ○ Travel

How I got this book:

○ Discount store ○ Bookstore
○ Membership club ○ Internet
○ Home improvement ○ Gift
  store ○ Other _____

In the next 6 months I intend to:

○ Move ○ Landscape/improve garden
○ Redecorate ○ Get married/start a family
○ Remodel ○ Expand my spiritual life
○ Build ○ Start diet/fitness program

Yes!
○ I've completed your survey. Send me a **free gift** of Homestyle Casseroles! I'll mail this today because I know supplies are limited!

Yes!
○ I've completed your survey, but don't want to take advantage of this exclusive free-gift offer.

_____
Name *(Please print)*

_____
Address Apt. #

_____
City

_____
State ZIP

Please e-mail items of interest to me.

E-mail address: _____

Thank you for completing the survey!

FAMILY
Dinners

Grand Avenue Books
Des Moines, Iowa

Grand Avenue Books
An imprint of Meredith® Corporation

Big Book of Family Dinners

Contributing Editors: Sharyl Heiken, Rosemary Hutchinson
 (Spectrum Communication Services)
Senior Associate Art Director: Ken Carlson
Copy and Production Editor: Victoria Forlini
Contributing Designer: Patricia Seifert
Copy Chief: Terri Fredrickson
Editorial Operations Manager: Karen Schirm
Manager, Book Production: Rick von Holdt
Electronic Production Coordinator: Paula Forest
Editorial and Design Assistants: Kaye Chabot, Mary Lee Gavin, Patricia Loder

Grand Avenue Books

Editor In Chief: Linda Raglan Cunningham
Design Director: Matt Strelecki
Executive Editor, Grand Avenue Books: Dan Rosenberg

Publisher: James D. Blume
Executive Director, Marketing: Jeffrey Myers
Executive Director, New Business Development: Todd M. Davis
Executive Director, Sales: Ken Zagor
Director, Operations: George A. Susral
Director, Production: Douglas M. Johnston
Business Director: Jim Leonard

Vice President and General Manager: Douglas J. Guendel

Meredith Publishing Group

President, Publishing Group: Stephen M. Lacy
Vice President-Publishing Director: Bob Mate

Meredith Corporation

Chairman and Chief Executive Officer: William T. Kerr

Chairman of the Executive Committee: E.T. Meredith III

All of us at
Grand Avenue Books
are dedicated to
providing you with the
information you need to create
delicious foods. If for any reason
you are not satisfied with this
book, or if you have other
comments or suggestions, write
to us at: Grand Avenue Books,
Editorial Department LN-116,
1716 Locust Street,
Des Moines, IA 50309-3023

With the *Big Book of Family Dinners*, feeding your family can be as easy as it is satisfying. This extraordinary collection brings you time- and work-saving ideas for great-tasting meals. You'll find tempting meat, poultry, fish and seafood, and meatless main dishes as well as irresistible snacks, side dishes, and desserts that you can fit into even the most hectic family schedule. What's more, if you're cooking with better health in mind, there are calorie- and fat-trimmed recipes to please young and old alike. In addition, you'll find dozens of tips and practical suggestions to make home cooking simpler and faster. So go ahead— take advantage of the innovative ideas in the *Big Book of Family Dinners*, and treat your family to something new and delicious tonight.

Contents

Pizza Burgers Recipe, page 30

Meats

Tenderloins with Rosemary and Mushrooms

Serve these savory steaks with a packaged salad mix, steamed asparagus spears, and purchased dinner rolls for a speedy yet elegant meal.

INGREDIENTS

- 1 tablespoon margarine or butter
- 1 tablespoon cooking oil
- 4 beef tenderloin steaks, cut 1 inch thick
- 2 cups sliced fresh mushrooms
- 2 green onions, sliced (¼ cup)
- 1 tablespoon snipped fresh rosemary or 1 teaspoon dried rosemary, crushed
- ½ teaspoon bottled minced garlic or 1 clove garlic, minced
- ¼ teaspoon pepper
- ⅓ cup dry sherry, dry red wine, or beef broth
- Fresh rosemary sprigs (optional)

Sliced green onion adds a colorful accent to just about any dish.

When cutting the onions, slice all of the white bulb and about an inch or so of the green stem. One green onion should give you about 2 tablespoons of sliced onion.

Prep time: 15 minutes
Cooking time: 15 minutes

DIRECTIONS

1. In a large skillet melt margarine or butter. Stir in cooking oil. Trim any separable fat from steaks. Add steaks to skillet and cook over medium to medium-high heat for 10 to 12 minutes or to desired doneness, turning once. Transfer to a serving platter, reserving drippings in skillet. Keep steaks warm.

2. Stir mushrooms, green onions, rosemary, garlic, and pepper into reserved drippings. Cook and stir over medium-high heat for 3 to 4 minutes or until mushrooms are tender. Reduce heat.

3. Carefully stir in sherry, wine, or beef broth. Cook and stir about 1 minute more or until heated through. Spoon over steaks. If desired, garnish with fresh rosemary sprigs. Makes 4 servings.

NUTRITION FACTS PER SERVING:

249 calories
14 g total fat
4 g saturated fat
64 mg cholesterol
83 mg sodium
4 g carbohydrate
1 g fiber
23 g protein

Grilled Sirloin With Smoky Pepper Sauce

Chipotle chile peppers are actually smoked jalapeños; they have a smoky, slightly sweet, spicy flavor.

INGREDIENTS

- 12 dried tomato halves (not oil-packed)
- 1 to 3 dried chipotle chile peppers
- 1 cup boiling water
- 1 cup dry red or white wine, or 1 cup water plus ½ teaspoon instant beef bouillon granules
- ½ cup chopped onion
- 1 tablespoon brown sugar
- 1 tablespoon lime or lemon juice
- 2 cloves garlic, quartered
- ¼ teaspoon black pepper
- 12 ounces boneless beef top sirloin steak, cut 1 inch thick

Prep time: 40 minutes
Marinating time: 2 hours
Grilling time: 18 minutes

DIRECTIONS

1. For marinade, in a medium mixing bowl place dried tomatoes and chile peppers; add boiling water. Let stand about 30 minutes or until vegetables are softened. Drain, reserving liquid.

2. Cut up tomatoes; place in a food processor bowl or blender container. Wearing disposable plastic gloves, trim stems from chiles; scrape out seeds. Cut up chile peppers; add to tomatoes along with ¼ cup reserved soaking liquid, the wine or water and bouillon granules, onion, sugar, lime or lemon juice, garlic, and black pepper.

Cover and process or blend until nearly smooth. Place meat in a shallow glass bowl; pour marinade over meat. Cover and marinate in the refrigerator for 2 to 8 hours. Drain, reserving marinade.

3. Grill meat on the rack of an uncovered grill directly over medium coals for 18 to 22 minutes for medium doneness (160°), turning and brushing once with marinade halfway through grilling. (Or coat the unheated rack of a broiler pan with nonstick cooking spray. Place meat on rack and broil 3 to 4 inches from the heat for 20 to 22 minutes, turning and brushing once with marinade halfway through.)

4. Bring the remaining marinade to boiling. Boil gently, uncovered, for 1 minute. Pass with meat. Makes 4 servings.

NUTRITION FACTS PER SERVING:

- 240 calories
- 8 g total fat
- 3 g saturated fat
- 57 mg cholesterol
- 105 mg sodium
- 12 g carbohydrate
- 1 g fiber
- 21 g protein

Herbed Steak

Enjoy this delicious steak in the summertime.
For optimal flavor, use a vine-ripened tomato and fresh herbs.

INGREDIENTS

2 beef top loin steaks, cut
    ¾ inch thick
    (about 1¼ pounds total)

1 tablespoon margarine or butter

3 green onions, sliced (about
    ⅓ cup)

1½ teaspoons snipped fresh thyme
    or basil or ½ teaspoon dried
    thyme or basil, crushed

¼ teaspoon salt

⅛ teaspoon pepper

1 medium tomato, chopped
    (⅔ cup)

Fresh basil or thyme (optional)

Prep time: 10 minutes
Cooking time: 12 minutes

DIRECTIONS

1. Trim any separable fat from steaks. Cut each steak in half. In a large, heavy skillet cook steaks in hot margarine or butter over medium heat about 10 minutes or to desired doneness, turning once.

2. Remove steaks, reserving drippings in skillet. Keep steaks warm. Cook green onions, snipped or crushed thyme or basil, salt, and pepper in drippings for 1 to 2 minutes or until green onions are tender. Stir in tomato. Heat through. Spoon over steaks. If desired, garnish with additional fresh basil or thyme. Makes 4 servings.

NUTRITION FACTS PER SERVING:

207 calories
9 g total fat
3 g saturated fat
81 mg cholesterol
230 mg sodium
2 g carbohydrate
0 g fiber
28 g protein

INGREDIENTS

- 4 boneless beef top loin steaks, cut 1 inch thick (1½ to 2 pounds total)
- 6 cloves garlic, thinly sliced
- 2 medium onions, coarsely chopped
- 1 teaspoon olive oil
- 2 tablespoons cider vinegar
- 1 tablespoon honey
- 1 medium nectarine, chopped
- 2 teaspoons snipped fresh applemint, pineapplemint, or spearmint
- Fresh applemint, pineapplemint, or spearmint sprigs (optional)

Prep time: 25 minutes
Grilling time: 11 minutes

Garlic Steaks With Nectarine-Onion Relish

What's better than the smell of steak on the grill in the summertime? The aroma of garlic-studded beef on the grill. The mint-scented relish features one of summer's favorite fruits. Serve this steak with some crusty bread to soak up the delicious juices.

DIRECTIONS

1. Trim fat from steaks. With the point of a paring knife, make small slits in steaks. Insert half of the garlic into slits. Wrap steaks in plastic wrap; let stand at room temperature up to 20 minutes. (For more intense flavor, refrigerate up to 8 hours.) Sprinkle with salt and pepper.

2. Meanwhile, for relish, in a large nonstick skillet cook onions and remaining garlic in hot oil over medium heat about 10 minutes or until onions are a deep golden color (but not brown), stirring occasionally. Stir in vinegar and honey. Stir in nectarine and the snipped mint; heat relish through.

3. Grill steaks on the rack of an uncovered grill directly over medium coals until desired doneness, turning once halfway through cooking. [Allow 11 to 15 minutes for medium-rare (145°) or 14 to 18 minutes for medium (160°).] Serve the relish with steaks. If desired, garnish with mint sprigs. Makes 4 servings.

NUTRITION FACTS PER SERVING:

272 calories
9 g total fat
3 g saturated fat
97 mg cholesterol
108 mg sodium
13 g carbohydrate
1 g fiber
34 g protein

Beef with Cucumber Raita

In the oft-fiery cuisine of India, a respite is offered in the form of a raita, a simple, cooling salad made with yogurt and fruits or vegetables. Snipped mint makes this raita particularly flavorful and refreshing.

INGREDIENTS

- 1 8-ounce carton plain fat-free or low-fat yogurt
- ¼ cup coarsely shredded unpeeled cucumber
- 1 tablespoon finely chopped red or yellow onion
- 1 tablespoon snipped fresh mint
- ¼ teaspoon sugar
- 1 pound boneless beef top sirloin steak, cut 1 inch thick
- ½ teaspoon lemon-pepper seasoning
- Fresh mint leaves (optional)

Start to finish: 25 minutes

DIRECTIONS

1. For raita, in a small bowl combine yogurt, cucumber, onion, snipped mint, and sugar. Season to taste with salt and pepper; set aside.

2. Trim fat from steak. Sprinkle steak with lemon-pepper seasoning. Grill steak on the rack of an uncovered grill directly over medium coals until desired doneness, turning once halfway through cooking. [Allow 18 to 22 minutes for medium (160°).] [Or broil on the unheated rack of a broiler pan 3 to 4 inches from the heat, turning once halfway through. (Allow 20 to 22 minutes for medium (160°).]

3. Cut steak across the grain into thin slices. If desired, arrange steak slices on mint leaves. Top with raita. Makes 4 servings.

NUTRITION FACTS PER SERVING:

237 calories
10 g total fat
4 g saturated fat
77 mg cholesterol
235 mg sodium
5 g carbohydrate
0 g fiber
29 g protein

Sautéed Sirloin And Mushrooms

INGREDIENTS

1 to 1¼ pounds boneless beef sirloin steak, cut ½ inch thick

¾ teaspoon herb pepper or ¼ teaspoon garlic pepper

1 tablespoon margarine or butter

¾ cup beef broth

1 tablespoon hoisin sauce, teriyaki sauce, or Worcestershire sauce

1 small onion, cut into very thin wedges

½ of an 8-ounce package sliced fresh mushrooms (about 1½ cups)

Bottled hoisin sauce, traditionally an Asian condiment, gives the mushroom glaze a subtle, sweet-and-tangy flavor. Look for hoisin sauce with the Asian products in your grocery store or in an Asian market.

Prep time: 10 minutes
Cooking time: 20 minutes

DIRECTIONS

1. Cut steak into 4 serving-size pieces. Sprinkle with herb pepper or garlic pepper. In a 10-inch skillet cook steak in hot margarine or butter over medium heat for 8 to 10 minutes or to desired doneness, turning once. Remove steak from skillet. Keep steak warm.

2. For mushroom glaze, carefully add beef broth and hoisin, teriyaki, or Worcestershire sauce to skillet. Cook and stir until bubbly, scraping brown bits from the bottom of the pan. Stir in onion wedges and sliced mushrooms. Cook over medium-high heat about 8 minutes or until vegetables are tender and the glaze is reduced by half its volume (to 1 cup). Transfer warm steak to dinner plates and spoon glaze over. Makes 4 servings.

NUTRITION FACTS PER SERVING:

247 calories
13 g total fat
5 g saturated fat
76 mg cholesterol
410 mg sodium
3 g carbohydrate
1 g fiber
27 g protein

Italian Beef Skillet

For an alternative, serve the saucy beef mixture over panfried polenta instead of pasta.

INGREDIENTS

1 pound boneless beef round
   steak, trimmed of
   separable fat
   Nonstick cooking spray
2 cups sliced fresh mushrooms
1 cup chopped onion
1 cup coarsely chopped green
   sweet pepper
½ cup chopped celery
2 cloves garlic, minced
1 14½-ounce can tomatoes,
   undrained and cut up
½ teaspoon dried basil, crushed
¼ teaspoon dried oregano, crushed
¼ teaspoon crushed red pepper
8 ounces packaged dried spaghetti
2 tablespoons grated Parmesan
   cheese

Prep time: 35 minutes
Cooking time: 1¼ hours

DIRECTIONS

1. Cut meat into 5 serving-size pieces. Coat an unheated large skillet with cooking spray. Preheat over medium heat. Add meat to skillet; cook each piece on both sides until browned. Remove from skillet.

2. Add mushrooms, onion, sweet pepper, celery, and garlic to the skillet. Cook until vegetables are nearly tender. Stir in undrained tomatoes, basil, oregano, and crushed red pepper. Add meat to skillet, spooning vegetable mixture over the meat. Simmer, covered, about 1¼ hours or until meat is tender, stirring occasionally. Meanwhile, cook spaghetti according to package directions, except omit any oil and salt.

3. Transfer meat to a serving platter. Spoon the vegetable mixture over the meat. Serve with spaghetti. Sprinkle with Parmesan cheese. Makes 5 servings.

NUTRITION FACTS PER SERVING:

354 calories
6 g total fat
2 g saturated fat
60 mg cholesterol
255 mg sodium
43 g carbohydrate
2 g fiber
31 g protein

Beef Tenderloins With Wine Sauce

Had a great day at work and feel like celebrating? Serve these richly sauced steaks for dinner.

INGREDIENTS

4   beef tenderloin steaks, cut
    1 inch thick
½   teaspoon coarsely cracked black
    pepper
1   tablespoon margarine or butter
½   of a medium onion, chopped
    (¼ cup)
¼   cup beef broth
¼   cup dry red wine
1   teaspoon dried marjoram,
    crushed

Prep time: 10 minutes
Cooking time: 15 minutes

DIRECTIONS

1. Trim any separable fat from steaks. Press pepper onto both sides of steaks. In a large skillet cook steaks in hot margarine or butter over medium to medium-high heat for 10 to 12 minutes or to desired doneness, turning once. Transfer steaks to a serving platter, reserving drippings in skillet. Keep steaks warm while preparing the sauce.

2. For sauce, stir onion into reserved drippings in skillet. Cook for 3 to 4 minutes or until onion is tender. Remove from heat. Carefully add broth, wine, and marjoram to onion in skillet, stirring to scrape up any browned bits. Return to heat. Bring to boiling. Reduce heat. Boil gently, uncovered, about 2 minutes or until mixture is reduced to about ¼ cup. Serve sauce over steaks. Makes 4 servings.

NUTRITION FACTS PER SERVING:

315 calories
15 g total fat
5 g saturated fat
112 mg cholesterol
176 mg sodium
2 g carbohydrate
0 g fiber
38 g protein

Beef Steak with Red Onion Relish

A good steak can be part of a healthful diet. Choose a lean cut, such as sirloin, and trim off any separable fat.

INGREDIENTS

- 1 pound boneless beef sirloin steak, cut ¾ inch thick
- ¼ to 1 teaspoon coarsely ground black pepper
- 2 teaspoons cooking oil
- 1 large red onion, thinly sliced and separated into rings
- ¼ cup dry red wine
- ½ teaspoon dried sage, crushed
- ¼ teaspoon salt

Dry red wine boosts the flavor of hearty beef dishes like this one. When selecting a wine to use, opt for a dry red dinner wine, such as red burgundy, cabernet sauvignon, or chianti. If you prefer not to add dry red wine to a dish, beef broth makes a good substitute.

Start to finish: 25 minutes

DIRECTIONS

1. Trim any separable fat from steak. Cut the steak into 4 serving-size pieces, and rub both sides with the pepper. In a large nonstick skillet heat oil over medium-high heat. Add the steaks and cook about 8 minutes or until medium doneness (160°), turning once. Remove the steak from the skillet; reserve drippings. Keep steak warm.

2. In the skillet cook onion in drippings over medium heat for 5 to 7 minutes or until crisp-tender. Carefully add wine, sage, and salt. Cook 1 to 2 minutes or until most of the liquid is evaporated. Serve onion mixture with steak. Makes 4 servings.

NUTRITION FACTS PER SERVING:

246 calories
12 g total fat
4 g saturated fat
76 mg cholesterol
200 mg sodium
3 g carbohydrate
1 g fiber
26 g protein

Flank Steak with Spanish Rice

INGREDIENTS

1   14½-ounce can Mexican-style
    stewed tomatoes

1¾ cups water

    Several dashes bottled
    hot pepper sauce

1¼ cups long grain rice

1   to 1¼ pounds beef flank steak

1   teaspoon chili powder

½   teaspoon salt

¼   teaspoon ground cumin

¼   teaspoon ground black pepper

Dash ground cinnamon

Snipped fresh cilantro or parsley
(optional)

Summertime, or anytime, you can grill the flank steak instead of broiling it. Cook the meat directly over medium coals for 17 to 21 minutes total for medium doneness (160°), turning once. Flank steak is a lean cut of beef, so avoid overcooking it or it may become dry and tough.

Start to finish: 30 minutes

DIRECTIONS

1. In a 2-quart saucepan combine the stewed tomatoes, water, and hot pepper sauce. Bring to boiling. Stir in uncooked rice. Return to boiling; reduce heat. Cover and simmer for 20 minutes. Remove from heat; let stand for 5 minutes.

2. Meanwhile, trim any separable fat from steak. Combine chili powder, salt, cumin, black pepper, and cinnamon. Rub spice mixture into flank steak on both sides. Place steak on unheated rack of a broiler pan. Broil steak 3 to 4 inches from the heat for 6 minutes. Turn and broil until desired doneness. [Allow 9 to 12 minutes more for medium-rare (145°).]

3. To serve, thinly slice flank steak diagonally across the grain. Fluff rice with a fork. Serve steak slices over rice. If desired, sprinkle with cilantro or parsley. Makes 4 to 6 servings.

NUTRITION FACTS PER SERVING:

409 calories
9 g total fat
4 g saturated fat
53 mg cholesterol
698 mg sodium
54 g carbohydrate
1 g fiber
27 g protein

15

Mustard-Pepper Steak Sandwiches

Save calories by serving this sandwich open-face. Use a knife and fork for easier eating.

INGREDIENTS

2 tablespoons Dijon-style mustard

1 teaspoon brown sugar

1 clove garlic, minced

½ teaspoon coarsely cracked pepper

1 pound beef flank steak, trimmed of separable fat

3 hoagie rolls, split and toasted

1 cup shredded lettuce

Thinly sliced tomato

Dijon-style mustard (optional)

To mince garlic,

use a utility knife to cut the peeled clove into very tiny, irregularly shaped pieces. Or save time by substituting ½ teaspoon of bottled minced garlic.

Prep time: 10 minutes
Broiling time: 15 minutes

DIRECTIONS

1. In a small bowl stir together the 2 tablespoons mustard, the brown sugar, garlic, and pepper. Set aside.

2. Place the meat on the unheated rack of a broiler pan. Brush with some of the mustard mixture. Broil 3 to 4 inches from the heat for 15 to 18 minutes for medium doneness (160°), turning and brushing once with the remaining mustard mixture halfway through broiling.

3. To serve, thinly slice meat diagonally across the grain. Fill each hoagie roll with some of the lettuce and sliced tomato. Layer meat slices on each sandwich. If desired, serve with additional mustard. Makes 6 servings.

NUTRITION FACTS PER SERVING:

320 calories
8 g total fat
3 g saturated fat
35 mg cholesterol
554 mg sodium
40 g carbohydrate
2 g fiber
21 g protein

Barbecue-Sauced Beef Sandwiches

Serve half of these saucy sandwiches now and freeze the rest for later. When you're short on time or the shelves are bare, you'll have a ready-to-heat meal in the freezer.

INGREDIENTS

- 1 2-pound boneless beef round steak, cut ¾ to 1 inch thick and trimmed of separable fat
  Nonstick cooking spray
- 1 14½-ounce can tomatoes, undrained and cut up
- 1 cup chopped onion
- 1 cup chopped carrot
- 2 tablespoons Worcestershire sauce
- 2 tablespoons vinegar
- 1 tablespoon brown sugar
- 1 bay leaf
- 1 clove garlic, minced
- 2 teaspoons chili powder
- 1 teaspoon dried oregano, crushed
- ⅛ teaspoon pepper
- 8 hamburger buns, split and toasted

Prep time: 40 minutes
Cooking time: 2 hours

DIRECTIONS

1. Cut the meat into 4 to 6 pieces. Coat an unheated Dutch oven with cooking spray. Preheat over medium heat. Add half of the meat; cook each piece on both sides until browned. Remove meat. Repeat to brown remaining meat. Drain off fat. Return all meat to Dutch oven.

2. Add undrained tomatoes, onion, carrot, Worcestershire sauce, vinegar, brown sugar, bay leaf, garlic, chili powder, oregano, and pepper. Bring to boiling; reduce heat. Simmer, covered, for 2 to 2½ hours or until meat is tender.

3. Remove meat from sauce; shred meat. Return meat to sauce. If necessary, simmer, uncovered, for 5 to 10 minutes or until slightly thickened. Discard bay leaf. Serve on buns. Makes 8 servings.

NUTRITION FACTS PER SERVING:

319 calories
8 g total fat
2 g saturated fat
72 mg cholesterol
393 mg sodium
30 g carbohydrate
2 g fiber
31 g protein

Stash any leftover meat in the freezer for up to 6 months. To reheat, transfer the mixture to a saucepan; add 1 tablespoon water. Cook, covered, over medium-low heat until heated through, stirring occasionally to break up. (Allow 8 to 10 minutes for 1 or 2 servings; 25 to 30 minutes for 4 servings.)

Garlic-Mustard Steak Sandwiches

Another time, skip the hoagie rolls and serve these zesty steak strips with fresh tomato slices, corn on the cob, and a tossed green salad.

- 2 tablespoons Dijon-style mustard
- ½ teaspoon dried marjoram or thyme, crushed
- ½ teaspoon bottled minced garlic or 1 clove garlic, minced
- ¼ teaspoon coarsely ground black pepper
- 1 to 1½ pounds beef flank steak
- 4 to 6 hoagie rolls, split
  Dijon-style mustard (optional)

Coarsely ground pepper gives this hearty sandwich extra pizzazz. Look for it in the spice aisle of your supermarket. Or, grind whole black peppercorns with a pepper mill.

Prep time: 10 minutes
Broiling time: 15 minutes

DIRECTIONS

1. In a small mixing bowl combine the 2 tablespoons mustard, the marjoram or thyme, garlic, and pepper. Trim any separable fat from the steak. Brush both sides of the steak with the mustard mixture.

2. Place the steak on the unheated rack of a broiler pan. Broil 3 to 4 inches from the heat for 15 to 18 minutes for medium doneness (160°), turning once. Thinly slice steak diagonally across the grain. Serve steak strips in hoagie rolls. If desired, pass additional mustard. Makes 4 to 6 servings.

NUTRITION FACTS PER SERVING:

176 calories
9 g total fat
3 g saturated fat
53 mg cholesterol
255 mg sodium
1 g carbohydrate
0 g fiber
22 g protein

INGREDIENTS

- 12 ounces boneless beef sirloin, cut 1 inch thick and trimmed of separable fat
- 2 teaspoons finely shredded lemon peel
- ⅓ cup lemon juice
- 3 tablespoons olive oil or cooking oil
- 1 tablespoon honey
- 1½ teaspoons snipped fresh basil or ½ teaspoon dried basil, crushed

- 1 teaspoon coarsely cracked black pepper
- ¼ teaspoon garlic salt
- 8 ounces baby carrots, peeled, or packaged, peeled baby carrots
- 1 medium zucchini
  Hot cooked couscous or rice (optional)

Summer Vegetables and Beef Kabobs

A light lemon-basil marinade flavors the grilled steak and complements the summer vegetables.

Prep time: 20 minutes
Marinating time: 2 hours
Grilling time: 12 minutes

DIRECTIONS

1. Cut meat into 1-inch cubes. Place in a plastic bag set in a shallow bowl.

2. For marinade, stir together lemon peel, lemon juice, oil, honey, basil, pepper, and garlic salt. Pour half of the marinade over meat in bag. Close bag. Marinate in the refrigerator for 2 to 4 hours, turning bag occasionally. Cover and refrigerate remaining marinade.

3. Meanwhile, in a medium covered saucepan cook the carrots in a small amount of boiling water for 3 minutes. Drain. Cut zucchini in half lengthwise; cut into ½-inch-thick slices.

4. Drain meat, discarding marinade. On 8 long metal skewers, alternately thread meat, carrots, and zucchini slices.

5. Grill kabobs on the rack of an uncovered grill directly over medium coals for 12 to 14 minutes or until meat is of desired doneness, turning once and brushing often with reserved marinade. If desired, serve with hot couscous or rice. Makes 4 servings.

When threading the meat and
vegetables onto the skewers, leave about ¼ inch between pieces. This allows the food to cook evenly.

NUTRITION FACTS PER SERVING:

264 calories
15 g total fat
4 g saturated fat
57 mg cholesterol
170 mg sodium
12 g carbohydrate
2 g fiber
20 g protein

Ginger Beef Stir-Fry

When you crave steak, but don't want high fat and calories, try this stir-fry. Lean beef and crispy spring vegetables combine for a full-flavored dinner you can toss together in 30 minutes.

INGREDIENTS

- 8 ounces beef top round steak, trimmed of separable fat
- ½ cup beef broth
- 3 tablespoons reduced-sodium soy sauce
- 2½ teaspoons cornstarch
- 1 teaspoon sugar
- ½ teaspoon grated fresh ginger
  Nonstick cooking spray
- 12 ounces asparagus spears, trimmed and cut into 1-inch pieces (2 cups)
- 1½ cups sliced fresh mushrooms
- 1 cup small broccoli florets
- 4 green onions, bias-sliced into 1-inch lengths (½ cup)
- 1 tablespoon cooking oil
- 2 cups hot cooked rice

Assemble and prepare all of the ingredients before you start to stir-fry. If you like, you can even do this up to 24 hours ahead and chill each ingredient separately.

Start to finish: 30 minutes

DIRECTIONS

1. If desired, partially freeze meat. Thinly slice meat across the grain into bite-size strips. Set aside. For the sauce, in a small bowl stir together the beef broth, soy sauce, cornstarch, sugar, and ginger. Set aside.

2. Coat an unheated wok or large skillet with cooking spray. Preheat over medium-high heat. Add asparagus, mushrooms, broccoli, and green onions. Stir-fry for 3 to 4 minutes or until vegetables are crisp-tender. Remove from wok.

3. Add oil to hot wok. Add the meat; stir-fry for 2 to 3 minutes or until desired doneness. Push meat from center of wok. Stir sauce; add to center of wok. Cook and stir until thickened and bubbly.

4. Return vegetables to the wok. Stir all ingredients together to coat with sauce; heat through. Serve immediately with hot cooked rice. Makes 4 servings.

NUTRITION FACTS PER SERVING:

270 calories
7 g total fat
2 g saturated fat
36 mg cholesterol
541 mg sodium
32 g carbohydrate
4 g fiber
21 g protein

Pineapple Beef

Fresh ginger gives a pleasant pungency and crushed red pepper lends a hint of hotness to this bright, fresh-tasting stir-fry.

INGREDIENTS

12 ounces beef top round steak, trimmed of separable fat

1 8-ounce can pineapple slices (juice pack)

2 tablespoons reduced-sodium soy sauce

½ teaspoon grated fresh ginger or ⅛ teaspoon ground ginger

¼ teaspoon crushed red pepper

1 tablespoon cornstarch

Nonstick cooking spray

4 green onions, cut into ½-inch pieces

1 6-ounce package frozen pea pods

1 medium tomato, cut into wedges

2 cups hot cooked rice

Prep time: 15 minutes
Marinating time: 15 minutes
Cooking time: 5 minutes

DIRECTIONS

1. If desired, partially freeze meat. Thinly slice meat across the grain into bite-size strips. Drain pineapple, reserving juice. Cut pineapple slices into quarters. Set aside.

2. In a bowl stir together reserved pineapple juice, soy sauce, ginger, and crushed red pepper. Add the meat; stir until coated. Cover and marinate meat at room temperature for 15 minutes. Drain, reserving marinade. For sauce, stir cornstarch into reserved marinade. Set aside.

3. Coat an unheated large nonstick skillet or wok with cooking spray. Preheat over medium heat. Add meat and green onions. Stir-fry for 2 to 3 minutes or until meat is of desired doneness. Push from center of skillet.

4. Stir sauce; add to center of skillet. Cook and stir until thickened and bubbly. Add pineapple, pea pods, and tomato. Cook and stir for 2 minutes more. Serve immediately over hot cooked rice. Makes 4 servings.

NUTRITION FACTS PER SERVING:

304 calories
5 g total fat
1 g saturated fat
54 mg cholesterol
311 mg sodium
40 g carbohydrate
2 g fiber
25 g protein

21

Southwest Beef And Linguine Toss

A jar of picante sauce makes an easy yet flavor-packed sauce for this stir-fried dish.

INGREDIENTS

4 ounces packaged dried linguine

¾ pound beef top round steak

1 tablespoon cooking oil

2 teaspoons chili powder

½ teaspoon bottled minced garlic
or 1 clove garlic, minced

1 small onion, sliced and
separated into rings

1 red or green sweet pepper, cut
into strips

1 10-ounce package frozen whole
kernel corn

¼ cup picante sauce

Fresh cilantro (optional)

Chili powder (optional)

Start to finish: 25 minutes

DIRECTIONS

1. Cook linguine according to package directions. Drain. Rinse with warm water. Set aside.

2. Meanwhile, trim any separable fat from steak. Cut steak into thin, bite-size strips. Set aside.

3. Pour cooking oil into a wok or large skillet. (Add more oil as necessary during cooking.) Preheat over medium-high heat. Stir-fry the 2 teaspoons chili powder and garlic in hot oil for 15 seconds. Add onion; stir-fry for 1 minute. Add the red or green pepper; stir-fry for 1 to 2 minutes more or until vegetables are crisp-tender. Remove vegetables from wok.

4. Add the beef to the hot wok; stir-fry for 2 to 3 minutes or to desired doneness. Return vegetables to the wok. Stir in corn and picante sauce. Add the cooked linguine. Toss together to coat with sauce. Cook and stir until heated through. If desired, garnish with fresh cilantro and sprinkle with additional chili powder. Makes 4 servings.

NUTRITION FACTS PER SERVING:

351 calories
9 g total fat
2 g saturated fat
54 mg cholesterol
166 mg sodium
43 g carbohydrate
1 g fiber
27 g protein

Beef Pot Pie

INGREDIENTS

12 ounces boneless beef sirloin steak, trimmed of separable fat

Nonstick cooking spray

½ cup chopped onion

1 clove garlic, minced

1½ cups low-sodium vegetable juice

1 10-ounce package frozen mixed vegetables

¾ cup beef broth

1 teaspoon dried basil, crushed

½ teaspoon dried marjoram, crushed

¼ teaspoon pepper

1 cup all-purpose flour

3 tablespoons cornmeal

2 teaspoons sugar

1½ teaspoons baking powder

⅛ teaspoon salt

3 tablespoons shortening

⅓ cup fat-free milk

¼ cup plain fat-free yogurt

You can enjoy potpies again. This lean version uses a modest amount of meat and lots of vegetables. A made-from-scratch biscuit topper becomes the golden-brown crust.

Prep time: 45 minutes
Baking time: 15 minutes

DIRECTIONS

1. Cut meat into ¾-inch cubes. Coat an unheated large Dutch oven with cooking spray. Preheat over medium-high heat. Add meat and cook until brown. Remove the meat from Dutch oven.

2. Add onion and garlic to Dutch oven. Cook and stir until onion is tender. Stir in vegetable juice, frozen vegetables, beef broth, basil, marjoram, and pepper. Stir in meat. Bring to boiling; reduce heat. Simmer, covered, for 20 to 25 minutes or until vegetables are tender.

3. For topper, in a medium mixing bowl stir together the flour, cornmeal, sugar, baking powder, and salt. Cut in shortening until mixture resembles coarse crumbs. Stir together the milk and yogurt. Add to flour mixture. Stir just until moistened.

4. Spoon hot meat mixture into a 2-quart casserole. Immediately drop the topper in small mounds onto meat mixture. Bake in a 450° oven for 15 to 20 minutes or until topper is golden brown. Makes 5 servings.

Be sure the meat mixture in the casserole is hot before adding the biscuit topper. This ensures that the topper will cook through completely.

NUTRITION FACTS PER SERVING:

368 calories
14 g total fat
5 g saturated fat
46 mg cholesterol
368 mg sodium
38 g carbohydrate
2 g fiber
22 g protein

Roast Beef And Red Pepper Sandwiches

For this hearty meat and vegetable sandwich, use leftover roast beef or beef from the deli.

INGREDIENTS

⅓ cup light mayonnaise dressing
   or mayonnaise

⅓ cup Dijon-style mustard

2 to 4 tablespoons prepared
   horseradish

6 6- or 7-inch Italian bread shells
   (Boboli) or Italian flatbreads
   (focaccia)

¾ pound thinly sliced cooked lean
   roast beef

1 12-ounce jar roasted red sweet
   peppers, drained and cut into
   ¼-inch-wide strips

6 ounces thinly sliced Monterey
   Jack cheese

2 cups fresh watercress

2 cups fresh spinach

On-call sandwiches are ideal for busy days because they're ready when you are. To make these robust beef sandwiches ahead, assemble the ingredients, wrap the sandwiches in plastic wrap, and store them in the refrigerator for up to 24 hours.

Start to finish: 25 minutes

DIRECTIONS

1. In a small bowl combine mayonnaise dressing, mustard, and horseradish. Slice bread shells in half horizontally. Spread bottom of each bread shell with mustard mixture; layer with roast beef, roasted red sweet peppers, Monterey Jack cheese, watercress, and spinach. Top with bread tops.

2. To serve, slice each sandwich in half. Makes 12 servings (half sandwich per serving).

NUTRITION FACTS PER SERVING:

303 calories
14 g total fat
4 g saturated fat
41 mg cholesterol
656 mg sodium
27 g carbohydrate
2 g fiber
20 g protein

INGREDIENTS

- ¼ cup mayonnaise or salad dressing
- 2 tablespoons chutney, chopped
- ½ teaspoon curry powder
- ¼ cup chunky peanut butter
- 8 slices whole grain bread or rye bread
- ½ pound thinly sliced, cooked lean roast beef or pork
- 8 thin slices tomato
- 4 lettuce leaves

Curried Roast Beef Sandwiches

Chutney adds to the East Indian flavor of this sandwich. Look for it in your supermarket's condiment aisle. Commercial chutneys come in a variety of flavors—they often contain mangoes, tamarinds, raisins, and spices, and can be spicy-hot.

Start to finish: 15 minutes

DIRECTIONS

1. In a small mixing bowl stir together the mayonnaise or salad dressing, chutney, and curry powder. Set aside.

2. Spread peanut butter on 4 of the bread slices. Top with roast beef or pork. Spoon curry mixture over meat; top with tomato, lettuce, and remaining bread slices. Makes 4 servings.

NUTRITION FACTS PER SERVING:

467 calories
25 g total fat
5 g saturated fat
53 mg cholesterol
487 mg sodium
37 g carbohydrate
5 g fiber
28 g protein

A pasta salad side dish comes together quickly if you remember to cook extra pasta whenever you fix it as a main course. Store cooked pasta in your refrigerator for 3 days. Toss it with a bottled dressing and chopped vegetables for a high-carbohydrate accompaniment to this sandwich.

Beer-Braised Rump Roast with Cabbage

Beer, onion, brown sugar, and thyme give this tender roast a robust, well-rounded flavor.

INGREDIENTS

1 3-pound boneless beef round
   rump roast
   Nonstick cooking spray
1½ cups light beer (12 ounces)
1 cup water
1 medium onion, sliced
1 tablespoon brown sugar
1 teaspoon instant beef
   bouillon granules
1 bay leaf
½ teaspoon dried thyme, crushed
½ teaspoon salt-free seasoning
   blend
½ teaspoon pepper

1 medium head cabbage, cored
8 medium carrots, bias-sliced into
   1-inch pieces

Prep time: 20 minutes
Cooking time: 2 hours and 5 minutes

DIRECTIONS

1. Trim fat from meat. Coat a 4-quart Dutch oven with cooking spray. Preheat over medium-high heat. Brown the meat on all sides in hot Dutch oven.

2. Add the beer, water, onion, brown sugar, bouillon granules, bay leaf, thyme, seasoning blend, and pepper. Bring to boiling; reduce heat. Simmer, covered, about 1¾ hours or until meat is nearly tender. Cut cabbage into 10 wedges.

3. Add cabbage and carrots to meat. Cook, covered, about 20 minutes more or until cabbage and carrots are crisp-tender and meat is very tender. Remove bay leaf.

4. Transfer the meat and vegetables to a serving platter; cover and keep warm. Skim fat from pan juices. Thinly slice meat; pass meat and vegetables with pan juices. Makes 10 servings.

NUTRITION FACTS PER SERVING:

243 calories
7 g total fat
2 g saturated fat
86 mg cholesterol
180 mg sodium
9 g carbohydrate
2 g fiber
34 g protein

Cranberry Pot Roast

INGREDIENTS

- 1   2- to 2½-pound beef bottom round roast, trimmed of separable fat
- 2   teaspoons cooking oil
- 1   cup cranberry juice
- ½   cup beef broth
- ½   teaspoon dried thyme, crushed
- 1   16-ounce package frozen small whole onions
- ¼   cup packed brown sugar
- 2   cups cranberries
- 3   tablespoons cold water
- 2   tablespoons cornstarch

Although poultry most often comes to mind when you think of cranberries, the tart berry flavor also blends well with beef. Here, both cranberry juice and fresh berries flavor the gravy.

Prep time: 20 minutes
Baking time: 2 hours

DIRECTIONS

1. In a Dutch oven quickly brown meat in hot oil over medium-high heat, turning to brown on all sides. Remove from heat.

2. Pour cranberry juice and beef broth over the meat. Add the thyme. Bake, covered, in a 325° oven for 1 hour. Stir onions and brown sugar into the pan juices. Bake meat, covered, 1 to 1¼ hours more or until meat and onions are tender. Transfer the meat to a serving platter, reserving pan juices. Cover meat and keep warm.

3. Strain pan juices, reserving onions. Measure pan juices. If necessary, add enough water to measure 2 cups liquid. Return to Dutch oven. Stir in cranberries and onions. Bring to boiling. Stir together cold water and cornstarch. Stir into mixture in Dutch oven. Cook and stir until thickened and bubbly. Cook and stir for 2 minutes more. Serve over meat. Makes 10 servings.

NUTRITION FACTS PER SERVING:

205 calories
5 g total fat
2 g saturated fat
58 mg cholesterol
85 mg sodium
16 g carbohydrate
2 g fiber
22 g protein

27

Festive Taco Burgers

A flour tortilla has about the same number of calories as a hamburger bun, and it's twice the fun with these burgers.

INGREDIENTS

1 cup finely chopped tomato

¼ cup green or red taco sauce

2 tablespoons snipped
   fresh cilantro

5 7-inch flour tortillas

1 4-ounce can diced mild green
   chile peppers, drained

¼ cup fine dry bread crumbs

¼ cup finely chopped green onions

2 tablespoons fat-free milk

1 teaspoon dried oregano, crushed

½ teaspoon ground cumin

¼ teaspoon black pepper

⅛ teaspoon salt

1 pound extra-lean ground beef
   Nonstick cooking spray

1 cup shredded lettuce or
   red cabbage

The internal color is not a reliable doneness indicator when cooking ground meat patties.

The internal **color** is not a reliable doneness indicator when cooking ground meat patties. Regardless of color, a beef, pork, lamb, or veal burger cooked to an internal temperature of 160° is safe to eat. (Ground turkey and chicken burgers must be cooked to 165°.) Use an instant-read thermometer to check for doneness. If using a dial instant-read thermometer, insert it through the side of the burger to a depth of 2 to 3 inches.

Prep time: 20 minutes
Broiling time: 10 minutes

DIRECTIONS

1. In a medium mixing bowl stir together tomato, taco sauce, and cilantro. Cover and set aside. Wrap the tortillas in foil; heat in a 350° oven for 15 minutes. Remove from oven; do not open foil packet.

2. Meanwhile, in a large bowl stir together the chile peppers, bread crumbs, green onions, milk, oregano, cumin, pepper, and salt. Add meat; mix well. Shape mixture into 5 oval patties 4½ to 5 inches long and ½ inch thick.

3. Coat the unheated rack of a broiler pan with cooking spray; arrange patties on broiler pan. Broil patties 3 to 4 inches from heat for 10 to 12 minutes or until done

(160°), turning once halfway through broiling.

4. To serve, place a patty on each warm tortilla; spoon some of the shredded lettuce and tomato mixture over the patty. Wrap tortillas around patties. Makes 5 servings.

NUTRITION FACTS PER SERVING:

303 calories
12 g total fat
4 g saturated fat
57 mg cholesterol
456 mg sodium
27 g carbohydrate
1 g fiber
21 g protein

Sun-Dried Tomato Burgers

INGREDIENTS

1 pound lean ground beef

1 tablespoon finely chopped, drained, oil-packed dried tomatoes

1 teaspoon finely shredded lemon or lime peel

½ teaspoon salt

¼ teaspoon black pepper

¼ cup light mayonnaise dressing or salad dressing

2 tablespoons snipped fresh basil

1 fresh jalapeño pepper, seeded and finely chopped

4 onion hamburger buns

1 cup lightly packed arugula or spinach leaves

Burgers on the grill take on a whole new meaning when they're infused with fresh lemon, studded with dried tomatoes, and slathered with a basil mayonnaise dressing zipped up with a jalapeño pepper.

Prep time: 15 minutes
Grilling time: 10 minutes

DIRECTIONS

1. In a medium bowl combine the ground beef, tomatoes, lemon peel, salt, and black pepper; mix well.

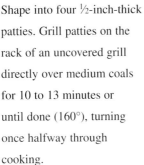

Shape into four ½-inch-thick patties. Grill patties on the rack of an uncovered grill directly over medium coals for 10 to 13 minutes or until done (160°), turning once halfway through cooking.

2. Meanwhile, in a small bowl combine mayonnaise dressing, basil, and jalapeño pepper. Toast buns, cut sides down, on grill rack next to burgers the last 1 to 2 minutes of grilling.

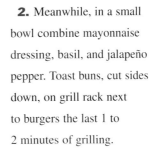

3. Place burgers on bottom halves of buns. Top with mayonnaise dressing mixture and arugula. Add bun tops. Makes 4 servings.

NUTRITION FACTS PER SERVING:

450 calories
20 g total fat
6 g saturated fat
71 mg cholesterol
784 mg sodium
40 g carbohydrate
2 g fiber
26 g protein

Warm summer evenings call for cooling drinks. Consider these:

• Sparkling water with fruit-juice cubes (orange, cranberry, mango, or papaya juice frozen in ice cube trays) and fresh mint.

• Spritzers made with sparkling water, cranberry juice, and a lime twist.

• Special iced teas, made with brewed green, herbal, or raspberry- or currant-flavored black tea.

29

Pizza Burgers

The beef is lean and the cheese is light, but the flavor comes on like a real heavyweight in the kid-pleasing burger arena.

INGREDIENTS

- 1 egg
- ¼ cup rolled oats
- 2 tablespoons catsup
- ¾ teaspoon dried Italian seasoning, crushed
- ¼ teaspoon garlic powder
- ¼ teaspoon onion powder
- ¼ teaspoon salt
- ¾ pound lean ground beef
- 4 ounces reduced-fat mozzarella cheese, sliced

   Lettuce leaves (optional)
- 4 whole wheat buns or kaiser rolls, split and toasted

   Tomato slices (optional)

   Catsup or other condiments (optional)

Prep time: 15 minutes
Broiling time: 13 minutes

DIRECTIONS

1. In a medium bowl stir together the egg, oats, 2 tablespoons catsup, dried Italian seasoning, garlic powder, onion powder, and salt. Add ground beef; mix well. Shape mixture into four ¾-inch-thick patties.

2. Place patties on the unheated rack of a broiler pan. Broil 3 to 4 inches from heat for 12 to 14 minutes or until done (160°), turning once. Top with cheese; broil about 1 minute more or until cheese is melted.

3. If desired, place lettuce on bottoms of toasted buns or rolls. Top with hot pizza burgers. If desired, add tomato slices and additional catsup or other condiments. Makes 4 servings.

NUTRITION FACTS PER SERVING:

370 calories
15 g total fat
7 g saturated fat
122 mg cholesterol
711 mg sodium
28 g carbohydrate
3 g fiber
30 g protein

Beefy Corn Bread

This meat pie with a Mexican flair boasts a ground beef-and-corn filling topped with corn bread, cheese, and salsa. Serve with a mixed greens salad.

INGREDIENTS

- 10 ounces extra-lean ground beef
- 1 teaspoon chili powder
- ¼ teaspoon ground cumin
- ½ cup loose-pack frozen whole kernel corn, thawed
- ¼ cup salsa
- ¾ cup all-purpose flour
- ¾ cup cornmeal
- 2 tablespoons sugar
- 2 teaspoons baking powder
- ½ teaspoon salt
- 2 beaten eggs
- ¾ cup fat-free milk
- 2 tablespoons cooking oil

- Nonstick cooking spray
- ½ cup shredded reduced-fat cheddar cheese (2 ounces)
- ⅓ cup salsa, heated
- Fresh cilantro (optional)
- Jalapeño pepper slices (optional)

Prep time: 25 minutes
Baking time: 20 minutes
Standing time: 5 minutes

DIRECTIONS

1. In a large skillet cook the ground beef, chili powder, and cumin until meat is brown. Drain off fat. Stir the corn and the ¼ cup salsa into the meat.

2. In a medium bowl stir together the flour, cornmeal, sugar, baking powder, and salt. In a small bowl combine the eggs, milk, and oil; add to the flour mixture, stirring just until moistened.

3. Coat a 2-quart rectangular baking dish with cooking spray. Spread half of the cornmeal mixture in dish. Spoon meat mixture over cornmeal mixture and sprinkle with half of the cheese. Spoon the remaining cornmeal mixture over cheese; spread to cover the meat layer.

4. Bake, uncovered, in a 375° oven about 20 minutes or until a wooden toothpick inserted near the center comes out clean. Sprinkle with remaining cheese. Let stand for 5 minutes. Serve with the ⅓ cup heated salsa. If desired, garnish with fresh cilantro and jalapeño pepper slices. Makes 6 servings.

NUTRITION FACTS PER SERVING:

335 calories
14 g total fat
4 g saturated fat
108 mg cholesterol
512 mg sodium
35 g carbohydrate
1 g fiber
18 g protein

31

Easy Shepherd's Pie

Frozen mashed potatoes make this hearty skillet supper extra-easy.

INGREDIENTS

1 28-ounce package frozen mashed potatoes

1¾ cups milk

1 10-ounce package (2 cups) frozen mixed vegetables

1 pound ground beef, uncooked ground turkey, or uncooked ground chicken

¼ cup water

1 teaspoon dried minced onion

1 10¾-ounce can condensed tomato soup or one 10¾-ounce can reduced-sodium condensed tomato soup

1 teaspoon Worcestershire sauce

¼ teaspoon dried thyme, crushed

½ cup shredded cheddar cheese (2 ounces)

This skillet meal is so easy that older kids can prepare it with minimal help from you. If your kids aren't old enough to handle cooking on the range top, let them prepare a tossed salad using packaged salad greens and bottled dressing.

Start to finish: 25 minutes

DIRECTIONS

1. Prepare the potatoes according to package directions using 4 cups of the frozen potatoes and the milk. Meanwhile, run cold water over frozen mixed vegetables to separate.

2. In a large skillet cook ground beef, turkey, or chicken over medium-high heat until meat is brown. Drain off fat.

3. Stir in vegetables, water, and onion. Bring to boiling; reduce heat. Cover and simmer for 5 to 10 minutes or until vegetables are tender. Stir in soup, Worcestershire sauce, and thyme. Return to boiling. Drop potatoes in mounds on top of the hot mixture. Sprinkle with cheese. Reduce heat. Cover and simmer about 5 minutes more or until heated through. Makes 6 servings.

NUTRITION FACTS PER SERVING:

342 calories
16 g total fat
7 g saturated fat
62 mg cholesterol
541 mg sodium
30 g carbohydrate
1 g fiber
19 g protein

Zippy Beef, Mac, And Cheese

The whole family will love this fast-fixin' one-dish meal.

INGREDIENTS

- 6 ounces packaged dried elbow macaroni or rotini (corkscrew macaroni) (about 1½ cups)
- ¾ pound lean ground beef, pork, or turkey
- 1 15-ounce can tomato sauce
- 1 14½-ounce can stewed tomatoes or Mexican-style stewed tomatoes
- 4 ounces American or sharp American cheese, cut into small cubes
- 1 tablespoon chili powder

    Shredded Parmesan cheese

Prep time: 20 minutes

Cooking time: 6 minutes

DIRECTIONS

1. In a 3-quart saucepan cook pasta according to package directions, except do not add salt.

2. Meanwhile, in a 10-inch skillet cook ground beef, pork, or turkey until meat is brown. Drain off fat.

3. Drain pasta; return it to the saucepan. Stir in cooked meat, tomato sauce, undrained stewed tomatoes, American cheese, and chili powder. Heat and stir over medium heat about 6 to 8 minutes or until heated through. Sprinkle Parmesan cheese on top of each serving. Makes 4 servings.

For a fresh, pretty salad, peel and cut up oranges and cut jicama into strips; arrange on a lettuce leaf and drizzle with an oil-and-vinegar dressing.

NUTRITION FACTS PER SERVING:

342 calories

15 g total fat

7 g saturated fat

55 mg cholesterol

957 mg sodium

32 g carbohydrate

2 g fiber

20 g protein

33

Beef and Vegetable Ragout

The earthy, elegant, and traditionally long-simmered French stew called ragout gets an update in taste and reduced preparation time. This version, flavored with port wine and filled with crisp, bright vegetables, can be on the table in 30 minutes.

INGREDIENTS

- 12 ounces beef tenderloin, cut into ¾-inch pieces
- 1 tablespoon olive oil or cooking oil
- 1½ cups sliced fresh shiitake or button mushrooms (4 ounces)
- 1 medium onion, chopped
- 2 cloves garlic, minced
- 3 tablespoons all-purpose flour
- ½ teaspoon salt
- ¼ teaspoon pepper
- 1 14-ounce can beef broth
- ¼ cup port wine or dry sherry
- 2 cups sugar snap peas, strings and tips removed, or one 10-ounce package frozen sugar snap peas, thawed
- 1 cup cherry tomatoes, halved
- Hot cooked wide noodles or bow-tie pasta (optional)

There's a reason

stews and casseroles have remained time-honored traditions at the table. The one-pot meal can stand alone, if necessary. All of the elements of the meal are in one place, so there aren't three pots to watch and wash. For casual entertaining, the one-pot meal is ideal. This hearty and flavorful dish can be made ahead and simply reheated while the noodles are cooking (just add the snap peas right before serving so they stay crisp and green). Serve with some crusty bread or corn bread and a salad, if you like, and your company fare is finished.

Start to finish: 30 minutes

DIRECTIONS

1. In a large nonstick skillet cook and stir meat in hot oil for 2 to 3 minutes or until meat is desired doneness. Remove meat; set aside. In the same skillet cook the mushrooms, onion, and garlic until tender.

2. Stir in the flour, salt, and pepper. Add the beef broth and wine. Cook and stir until thickened and bubbly. Stir in the sugar snap peas. Cook and stir for 2 to 3 minutes more or until peas are tender. Stir in meat and tomatoes; heat through. If desired, serve meat mixture over noodles. Makes 4 servings.

NUTRITION FACTS PER SERVING:

252 calories
9 g total fat
3 g saturated fat
48 mg cholesterol
647 mg sodium
17 g carbohydrate
3 g fiber
21 g protein

INGREDIENTS

- 8 ounces boneless beef
     sirloin steak
- 2 teaspoons olive oil
- 1 large shallot, sliced
- 4 cups water
- 1 cup unsweetened apple juice
- 2 carrots, cut into thin strips
- ⅓ cup long grain rice
- 1 tablespoon grated fresh ginger
- 3 cloves garlic, minced
- 1 teaspoon instant beef
     bouillon granules
- 2 cups coarsely chopped broccoli

- 1 to 2 tablespoons reduced-
     sodium teriyaki sauce
- 1 tablespoon dry sherry (optional)

Teriyaki Beef Soup

Cut up the beef and vegetables the evening before to get this soup on the table even faster. The next day, you'll be able to toss the whole meal together in the time it takes to cook the rice.

Start to finish: 40 minutes

DIRECTIONS

1. Trim fat from meat. Cut meat into bite-size strips. In a large saucepan heat olive oil over medium-high heat. Add the meat and shallot. Cook and stir for 2 to 3 minutes or until meat is desired doneness. Remove meat mixture with a slotted spoon.

2. In the same saucepan combine the water, apple juice, carrots, uncooked rice, ginger, garlic, and bouillon granules. Bring to boiling; reduce heat. Simmer, covered, about 15 minutes or until the carrots are tender.

3. Stir in the broccoli and meat mixture. Simmer, covered, for 3 minutes. Stir in the teriyaki sauce and dry sherry (if desired). Makes 5 servings.

NUTRITION FACTS PER SERVING:

197 calories
6 g total fat
2 g saturated fat
30 mg cholesterol
382 mg sodium
22 g carbohydrate
2 g fiber
13 g protein

Beef and Fruit Salad

For an exotic presentation, serve the fruit mixture in a kiwano (kee-WAH-noh) shell. Also called "horned melon," the kiwano has a jellylike pulp with a tart, yet sweet flavor likened to a combination of banana and cucumber.

INGREDIENTS

- 12 ounces boneless beef sirloin steak, cut 1 inch thick
- 1/3 cup reduced-sodium teriyaki sauce or soy sauce
- 1/4 cup lemon juice
- 1/4 cup water
- 2 teaspoons toasted sesame oil
- 1/8 teaspoon bottled hot pepper sauce
- 3 cups shredded napa cabbage
- 1 cup torn or shredded sorrel or spinach
- 2 cups fresh fruit (choose from sliced plums, nectarines, or kiwi fruit; halved seedless grapes or strawberries; raspberries; and/or blueberries)
- 2 kiwanos (optional)

To serve the fruit in kiwano shells, cut each kiwano in half crosswise. Scoop out the pulp.

Prep time: 20 minutes
Marinating time: 30 minutes
Grilling time: 14 minutes

DIRECTIONS

1. Trim fat from meat. Place meat in a plastic bag set in a shallow dish. For marinade, combine the teriyaki sauce, lemon juice, water, sesame oil, and hot pepper sauce. Reserve 1/3 cup for dressing. Pour remaining marinade over meat; close bag. Marinate at room temperature up to 30 minutes, turning bag occasionally. (Or, marinate in the refrigerator for up to 8 hours.)

2. Drain meat, reserving marinade. Grill meat on the rack of an uncovered grill directly over medium coals to desired doneness, turning once and brushing occasionally with marinade up to the last 5 minutes of grilling. [Allow 14 to 18 minutes for medium-rare (145°) or 18 to 22 minutes for medium (160°).] Discard any remaining marinade.

3. To serve, divide the cabbage and sorrel among 4 dinner plates. Thinly slice meat diagonally. Arrange meat and fruit on top of greens. (Or, if desired, serve the fruit in kiwano shells.) Drizzle with the dressing (and, if desired, the pulp of the kiwano fruit). Makes 4 servings.

NUTRITION FACTS PER SERVING:

248 calories
10 g total fat
3 g saturated fat
57 mg cholesterol
307 mg sodium
19 g carbohydrate
2 g fiber
22 g protein

INGREDIENTS

- **6** to 8 whole tiny new potatoes
- **4** cups torn mixed salad greens
- **1** medium cucumber, halved lengthwise and sliced
- **4** radishes, sliced
- **4** ounces very thinly sliced cooked roast beef or turkey
- **2** small tomatoes, cut into wedges
- **½** cup low-calorie creamy cucumber or ranch salad dressing
- **1** teaspoon snipped fresh dill or ¼ teaspoon dried dill

Beef and New Potato Salad

No need to peel the potatoes. Leaving the skin on the potatoes hastens preparation, adds color, and provides a little extra fiber to these salads.

Start to finish: 30 minutes

DIRECTIONS

1. Scrub the new potatoes; cut into quarters.

2. In a medium saucepan cook the potatoes in a small amount of lightly salted boiling water for 10 to 15 minutes or until tender. Drain. Rinse with cold water. Drain again.

3. In a mixing bowl gently toss together greens, cucumber, and radishes. Add potatoes. Gently toss. Arrange on 4 plates. Roll up the beef or turkey slices and arrange on top of greens mixture. Place a few tomato wedges to the side of each salad.

4. Combine salad dressing and dill. Drizzle over salads. Makes 4 servings.

Give the cucumber slices

a ruffled edge if you like. Before halving and slicing, draw the tines of a fork lengthwise down the cucumber. Repeat scoring all around the vegetable.

NUTRITION FACTS PER SERVING:

197 calories
7 g total fat
1 g saturated fat
25 mg cholesterol
494 mg sodium
20 g carbohydrate
3 g fiber
12 g protein

Veal Scaloppine

Serve this fat- and calorie-trimmed classic with hot cooked broccoli and whole-wheat dinner rolls.

INGREDIENTS

12 ounces boneless veal leg round steak, veal leg sirloin steak, or beef top round steak, cut ¼ inch thick and trimmed of separable fat

Salt and pepper

½ cup chopped onion

¼ cup water

2 cloves garlic, minced

1 14½-ounce can tomatoes, undrained and cut up

3 tablespoons dry white wine

1 tablespoon snipped fresh oregano or 1 teaspoon dried oregano, crushed

1 tablespoon capers, drained (optional)

⅛ teaspoon pepper

Nonstick cooking spray

2 cups hot cooked noodles

Start to finish: 30 minutes

DIRECTIONS

1. Cut meat into 8 pieces. Place each piece of meat between 2 pieces of plastic wrap. Working from center to edges, pound with flat side of a meat mallet to about ⅛-inch thickness. Remove plastic wrap. Sprinkle meat lightly with salt and pepper. Set aside.

2. For sauce, in a medium covered saucepan combine the onion, water, and garlic. Cook until onion is tender. Stir in undrained tomatoes, wine, oregano, capers (if desired), and pepper. Bring to boiling; reduce heat. Simmer, uncovered, about 15 minutes or until desired consistency. Keep warm.

3. Meanwhile, coat an unheated large skillet with cooking spray. Preheat over medium-high heat. Cook meat, half at a time, for 2 to 4 minutes or until desired doneness, turning once. Transfer meat to a serving platter. Keep warm.

4. To serve, spoon the sauce over meat. Serve with hot cooked noodles. Makes 4 servings.

NUTRITION FACTS PER SERVING:

246 calories
5 g total fat
1 g saturated fat
94 mg cholesterol
216 mg sodium
25 g carbohydrate
3 g fiber
23 g protein

Veal Scaloppine with Marsala Skillet

INGREDIENTS

- 1½ cups fresh mushrooms (such as crimini, porcini, morel, shiitake, or button), quartered, halved, or sliced
- 2 green onions, sliced (¼ cup)
- 4 teaspoons margarine or butter
- ½ pound veal leg round steak or veal sirloin steak or 2 skinless, boneless chicken breast halves (½ pound total)
- ⅛ teaspoon salt
- ⅛ teaspoon pepper
- ⅓ cup dry marsala or dry sherry
- ¼ cup chicken broth
- 1 tablespoon snipped fresh parsley

Chicken breasts make an inexpensive substitute for traditional veal, if you prefer. Serve with steamed Italian flat beans or whole green beans.

Start to finish: 15 minutes

DIRECTIONS

1. In a 12-inch skillet cook mushrooms and green onions in 2 teaspoons of the hot margarine for 4 to 5 minutes or until tender. Remove from skillet, reserving drippings. Set aside.

2. Meanwhile, cut veal into 2 serving-size pieces. Place each piece of veal or chicken breast half between 2 sheets of plastic wrap. Working from center to edges, pound lightly with the flat side of a meat mallet to about ⅛-inch thickness. Remove the plastic wrap.

3. Sprinkle meat with salt and pepper. In the same skillet cook veal or chicken in the remaining hot margarine over medium-high heat for 2 minutes or until no longer pink, turning once. Transfer to dinner plates. Keep warm.

4. Add marsala or sherry and chicken broth to drippings in skillet. Bring to boiling. Boil mixture gently, uncovered, about 1 minute, scraping up any browned bits. Return mushroom mixture to skillet; add parsley. Heat through. To serve, spoon the mushroom mixture over meat. Serve immediately. Makes 2 servings.

NUTRITION FACTS PER SERVING:

283 calories
12 g total fat
3 g saturated fat
92 mg cholesterol
384 mg sodium
6 g carbohydrate
1 g fiber
27 g protein

39

Jamaican Pork Chops with Melon Salsa

The jerk cooks of Jamaica may use dry rubs or wet marinades, but the central ingredient in all jerk seasoning is allspice (along with fiery Scotch bonnet chilies and thyme), which grows in abundance on the sunny island.

INGREDIENTS

- 1 cup chopped honeydew melon
- 1 cup chopped cantaloupe
- 1 tablespoon snipped fresh mint
- 1 tablespoon honey
- 4 boneless pork top loin chops, cut ¾ to 1 inch thick
- 4 teaspoons purchased or homemade Jamaican jerk seasoning (see box below)

Star anise and/or fresh mint sprigs (optional)

For homemade Jamaican jerk

seasoning, combine 1 teaspoon crushed red pepper; ½ teaspoon ground allspice; ¼ teaspoon curry powder; ¼ teaspoon coarsely ground black pepper; ⅛ teaspoon dried thyme, crushed; ⅛ teaspoon ground red pepper; and ⅛ teaspoon ground ginger.

Prep time: 15 minutes
Grilling time: 12 minutes

DIRECTIONS

1. For salsa, in a medium bowl combine honeydew, cantaloupe, snipped mint, and honey. Cover and refrigerate until ready to serve.

2. Trim fat from chops. Rub both sides of the chops with Jamaican jerk seasoning. Grill chops on the rack of an uncovered grill directly over medium coals for 12 to 15 minutes or until chops are slightly pink in center and juices run clear (160°). Serve the salsa with chops. If desired, garnish with star anise and/or mint sprigs. Makes 4 servings.

NUTRITION FACTS PER SERVING:

189 calories
8 g total fat
3 g saturated fat
51 mg cholesterol
231 mg sodium
13 g carbohydrate
1 g fiber
17 g protein

Southwest Pork Chops with Corn Salsa

In late summer, when corn is at its sweetest and tomatoes are at their juiciest, these meaty pork chops crowned with a colorful, chunky salsa are unsurpassed for the freshest tastes of the season's best.

INGREDIENTS

¼ cup white wine vinegar

3 tablespoons snipped fresh cilantro

1 teaspoon olive oil

1 cup fresh or frozen whole kernel corn

3 roma tomatoes, chopped

½ cup thinly sliced green onions

1 small fresh jalapeño pepper, seeded and minced

4 center-cut pork loin chops, cut ¾ inch thick

Cactus leaves (optional)

Fresh cilantro sprigs (optional)

Prep time: 20 minutes
Grilling time: 10 minutes

DIRECTIONS

1. For sauce, in a small bowl combine 3 tablespoons of the vinegar, 1 tablespoon of the snipped cilantro, and the olive oil. For salsa, in a covered small saucepan cook fresh corn in a small amount of boiling water for 2 to 3 minutes or until corn is crisp-tender; drain. Or, thaw corn, if frozen. In a medium bowl combine the corn, tomatoes, green onions, jalapeño pepper, remaining vinegar, and remaining snipped cilantro. Set aside.

2. Trim fat from chops. Grill chops on the rack of an uncovered grill directly over medium coals for 10 to 12 minutes or until chops are slightly pink in center and juices run clear (160°), turning once and brushing occasionally with sauce up to the last 5 minutes of grilling. If desired, arrange chops on cactus leaves and garnish with cilantro sprigs. Serve with salsa. Makes 4 servings.

NUTRITION FACTS PER SERVING:

201 calories
9 g total fat
3 g saturated fat
51 mg cholesterol
51 mg sodium
14 g carbohydrate
2 g fiber
18 g protein

Peppered Pork With Chive Sauce

For pork that's juicy and tender, cook it just until the center of the meat is slightly pink and the juices run clear. It's safe to eat slightly pink pork loin.

INGREDIENTS

4 boneless pork top loin chops, cut ¾ inch thick

1 teaspoon coarsely ground tricolored peppercorns or coarsely ground black pepper

2 teaspoons cooking oil

¼ cup water

3 tablespoons dry sherry or chicken broth

1 3-ounce package cream cheese with chives, cut up

Snipped fresh chives (optional)

While the chops cook, steam or microwave quartered new potatoes and green beans, then drizzle with lemon juice. Serve glasses of apple cider with dinner.

Start to finish: 20 minutes

DIRECTIONS

1. Trim any separable fat from pork chops. Sprinkle both sides of pork chops with pepper, rubbing it lightly into the pork. In a 10-inch skillet cook pork in hot oil for 8 to 10 minutes or until pork is slightly pink in center and juices run clear (160°), turning once. Remove pork from skillet. Keep warm.

2. For sauce, carefully add the water to the hot skillet. Add sherry or broth to skillet and heat until bubbly. Add the cream cheese. Using a wire whisk, heat and whisk over medium heat until the cream cheese is melted. Serve sauce over pork. If desired, sprinkle with snipped chives. Makes 4 servings.

NUTRITION FACTS PER SERVING:

291 calories
20 g total fat
8 g saturated fat
92 mg cholesterol
117 mg sodium
2 g carbohydrate
0 g fiber
23 g protein

Pork with Pear, Fennel, and Cabbage

INGREDIENTS

- 2 medium fennel bulbs
- 4 boneless pork top loin chops, cut 1½ inches thick (America's Cut)
-    Salt
-    Pepper
- 1 small onion, sliced
- 1 tablespoon olive oil
- ½ of a small head cabbage, coarsely chopped (about 2½ cups)
- ½ cup pear nectar or apple juice
- ¼ cup balsamic vinegar
- ½ teaspoon caraway seed
- ½ teaspoon dried thyme, crushed
- ¼ teaspoon salt
- ¼ teaspoon pepper
- ⅛ teaspoon ground nutmeg
-    Pear nectar or apple juice
- 2 tablespoons cold water
- 1 tablespoon cornstarch
- 1 large pear, cored and sliced

Fennel bulbs are sold with stalks attached. The vegetable has a celerylike texture, and the stalks have feathery green tops or leaves. The stalks should be crisp, and the leaves, bright green and fresh-looking.

Start to finish: 30 minutes

DIRECTIONS

1. Trim fennel; cut into thin wedges. Trim any separable fat from pork. Season pork with salt and pepper. In a 10-inch skillet cook the chops and onion in hot oil about 8 minutes or until browned, turning once. Drain off fat.

2. Arrange the fennel and cabbage on top of meat. In a small bowl stir together the ½ cup pear nectar or apple juice, the vinegar, caraway seed, thyme, the ¼ teaspoon salt, ¼ teaspoon pepper, and the nutmeg; pour into skillet. Cover and simmer for 12 to 15 minutes or until pork is slightly pink in center and juices run clear (160°). Use a slotted spoon to transfer pork and vegetables to a serving platter. Keep warm.

3. For sauce, measure the pan juices. If necessary, add enough additional pear nectar or apple juice to pan juices to make 1¼ cups liquid; return to skillet. Blend together the water and cornstarch; stir into juices. Cook and stir over medium heat until thickened and bubbly. Stir in pear slices; heat through. Spoon pear slices and sauce over pork and vegetables. Makes 4 servings.

To keep the chops and vegetables warm, cover the serving platter with foil. Or, if you prefer, use a heatproof platter and place the foil-covered platter in an oven on low heat.

NUTRITION FACTS PER SERVING:

- 334 calories
- 15 g total fat
- 4 g saturated fat
- 77 mg cholesterol
- 229 mg sodium
- 25 g carbohydrate
- 2 g fiber
- 26 g protein

43

Pork Chops in Creamy Vegetable Sauce

This cream sauce combines reduced-fat soup and fat-free sour cream, providing a seemingly high-fat richness that won't give away its real secret.

INGREDIENTS

Nonstick cooking spray

6 pork rib chops, cut ½ inch thick and trimmed of separable fat (about 1¾ pounds total)

1½ cups sliced fresh mushrooms

1 medium green or red sweet pepper, cut into thin strips

1 10¾-ounce can condensed reduced-fat and reduced-sodium cream of mushroom soup

½ cup fat-free dairy sour cream

¼ cup fat-free milk

1 teaspoon paprika

1 medium tomato, seeded and chopped

Hot cooked noodles or rice (optional)

Start to finish: 25 minutes

DIRECTIONS

1. Coat an unheated 12-inch skillet with cooking spray. Preheat over medium heat. Add pork chops; cook for 6 minutes. Turn chops; add mushrooms and sweet pepper. Cook about 6 minutes more or until meat is slightly pink in center and juices run clear (160°). Remove the chops and vegetables.

2. For sauce, in a small mixing bowl stir together the soup, sour cream, milk, and paprika. Stir the mixture into skillet; bring to boiling.

3. Return the chops and vegetables to skillet. Cook, covered, for 5 minutes. Add the tomato. Cook for 1 to 2 minutes more or until heated through. If desired, serve with hot cooked noodles. Makes 6 servings.

NUTRITION FACTS PER SERVING:

193 calories
9 g total fat
3 g saturated fat
50 mg cholesterol
264 mg sodium
11 g carbohydrate
1 g fiber
17 g protein

Peppered Pork Chops and Pilaf

Roasted red pepper comes in both mild and hot forms. For this recipe, be sure to select roasted red sweet pepper. Look for it in the produce section of your supermarket or in the canned vegetable aisle.

INGREDIENTS

4   boneless pork top loin chops, cut ¾ inch thick

1   tablespoon herb-pepper seasoning

2   tablespoons olive oil

2   cups cut-up salad-bar vegetables (such as sweet peppers, carrots, mushrooms, onion, and/or broccoli)

1   14-ounce can chicken broth

2   cups quick-cooking brown rice

¼   cup chopped roasted red sweet pepper

Fresh herb sprigs (optional)

Start to finish: 25 minutes

DIRECTIONS

1. Sprinkle both sides of pork chops with 2 teaspoons of the herb-pepper seasoning. In a large skillet cook chops in 1 tablespoon of the oil for 5 minutes. Turn pork chops. Cook for 5 to 7 minutes more or until the meat is slightly pink in center and juices run clear (160°).

2. Meanwhile, cut vegetables into bite-size pieces. In a saucepan heat the remaining olive oil. Add vegetables and cook for 2 minutes. Carefully add broth. Bring to boiling. Stir in uncooked rice, roasted sweet pepper, and remaining herb-pepper seasoning. Return to boiling; reduce heat. Cover and simmer for 5 minutes. Remove from heat. Let stand 5 minutes. Serve chops with rice. If desired, garnish with fresh herbs. Makes 4 servings.

NUTRITION FACTS PER SERVING:

431 calories
20 g total fat
5 g saturated fat
77 mg cholesterol
408 mg sodium
34 g carbohydrate
5 g fiber
31 g protein

If you don't have chicken broth on hand, substitute chicken bouillon and water instead. To make the equivalent of a 14-ounce can of broth, combine 2 teaspoons of bouillon granules or 2 bouillon cubes with 1¾ cups of boiling water.

Easy Moo-Shu-Style Pork

For an attractive garnish, save some of the shredded carrot from the coleslaw mix.

INGREDIENTS

8   7-inch flour tortillas

3   tablespoons cold water

2   tablespoons soy sauce

1   tablespoon cornstarch

2   teaspoons toasted sesame oil

1   teaspoon sugar

¼   teaspoon bottled minced garlic

¾   pound pork tenderloin or
    pork loin

1   tablespoon cooking oil

3   cups packaged shredded
    cabbage with carrot
    (coleslaw mix)

⅓   cup hoisin sauce

    Shredded carrot (optional)

Toasted sesame oil is a reddish-brown oil made from toasted sesame seed. Look for it in the Oriental food section of the supermarket. Use it sparingly; a little goes a long way.

Start to finish: 20 minutes

DIRECTIONS

1. Wrap tortillas in foil. Warm in a 350° oven for 10 minutes. Meanwhile, for sauce, in a small mixing bowl stir together the water, soy sauce, cornstarch, sesame oil, sugar, and garlic. Set aside.

2. Trim any separable fat from pork. Cut pork into thin bite-size strips. Pour cooking oil into a wok or large skillet. (Add more oil as necessary during cooking.) Preheat over medium-high heat. Add the pork strips and stir-fry for 2 to 3 minutes or until meat is slightly pink in center.

3. Push meat from the center of the wok. Stir sauce; add to the center of the wok. Cook and stir until thickened and bubbly. Cook and stir for 2 minutes more. Add shredded cabbage with carrot to skillet. Stir to coat with sauce.

4. Spread one side of each warm tortilla with some of the hoisin sauce. Spoon about ½ cup of the pork mixture onto the center of each tortilla. Fold the bottom edge up over filling. Fold the sides to the center, overlapping edges. Secure with toothpicks. If desired, garnish with carrot. Makes 4 servings.

NUTRITION FACTS PER SERVING:

435 calories
14 g total fat
3 g saturated fat
60 mg cholesterol
2,266 mg sodium
49 g carbohydrate
1 g fiber
27 g protein

INGREDIENTS

- 1 pound pork tenderloin
- Salt
- Pepper
- Nonstick cooking spray
- ¾ cup cranberry juice or apple juice
- 2 teaspoons spicy brown mustard
- 1 teaspoon cornstarch
- 1 cup sweet cherries (such as Rainier or Bing), halved and pitted, or 1 cup frozen unsweetened pitted dark sweet cherries, thawed

Pork Medallions With Cherry Sauce

During the autumn months, pork is often prepared with fruit such as prunes or apples. These quick-seared medallions cloaked in a delightful sweet cherry sauce provide a whole new reason—and season—to pair pork with fruit.

Start to finish: 20 minutes

DIRECTIONS

1. Trim fat from meat. Cut meat into 1-inch slices. Place each slice between 2 pieces of plastic wrap. Using the heel of your hand, press slice into a ½-inch-thick medallion. Remove the plastic wrap. Sprinkle lightly with salt and freshly ground pepper.

2. Coat an unheated large nonstick skillet with cooking spray. Heat skillet over medium-high heat. Add meat; cook about 6 minutes or until meat is slightly pink in center, turning once halfway through cooking. Transfer meat to a serving platter; cover and keep warm.

3. Combine the cranberry juice, mustard, and cornstarch; add to skillet. Cook and stir until thickened and bubbly. Cook and stir for 2 minutes more. Stir in cherries. Serve over meat. Makes 4 servings.

NUTRITION FACTS PER SERVING:

197 calories
5 g total fat
2 g saturated fat
81 mg cholesterol
127 mg sodium
12 g carbohydrate
0 g fiber
26 g protein

Sweet-and-Sour Pork Kabobs

Try pork tenderloin or loin chops for these kabobs. They're both boneless, lean cuts. Serve the kabobs with couscous, which adds 57 calories per ½ cup serving.

INGREDIENTS

- 2 medium carrots, bias-sliced into 1-inch pieces
- 1 8-ounce can pineapple slices (juice pack)
- ⅓ cup wine vinegar
- 2 tablespoons reduced-sodium soy sauce
- 1 tablespoon cooking oil
- 2 teaspoons cornstarch
- 1 teaspoon sugar
- 1 clove garlic, minced
- 2 small green and/or red sweet peppers, cut into 1-inch cubes
- 12 ounces lean boneless pork, cut into 1-inch pieces
- Hot cooked couscous (optional)

Prep time: 35 minutes
Grilling time: 12 minutes

DIRECTIONS

1. In a covered saucepan cook carrots in a small amount of boiling water for 8 minutes; drain well. Drain pineapple, reserving juice. Cut pineapple slices into quarters; set aside.

2. For sauce, in a saucepan combine reserved pineapple juice, vinegar, soy sauce, oil, cornstarch, sugar, and garlic. Cook and stir until thickened and bubbly. Cook and stir for 2 minutes more.

3. On 8 short or 4 long metal skewers, alternately thread the carrots, pineapple, sweet peppers, and meat, leaving about ¼ inch between pieces. Brush with the sauce.

4. Grill kabobs on the rack of an uncovered grill directly over medium coals for 12 to 14 minutes or until meat is slightly pink in center, turning once and brushing frequently with sauce during the first half of grilling. (Or broil the kabobs on the unheated rack of a broiler pan 4 to 5 inches from the heat for 12 to 14 minutes, turning once and brushing frequently with sauce during the first half of broiling.) If desired, serve the kabobs over hot cooked couscous. Makes 4 servings.

NUTRITION FACTS PER SERVING:

- 203 calories
- 9 g total fat
- 2 g saturated fat
- 38 mg cholesterol
- 318 mg sodium
- 19 g carbohydrate
- 2 g fiber
- 14 g protein

Pork and Noodle Skillet Dinner

Strips of boneless chicken breast or thighs taste equally delicious in this creamy one-dish meal.

INGREDIENTS

- ¾ pound lean boneless pork
- 1 medium onion, chopped (½ cup)
- 1 tablespoon cooking oil
- 3 cups frozen loose-pack broccoli, cauliflower, and carrots
- 4 ounces packaged dried medium noodles or curly medium noodles (3 cups)
- 1 10¾-ounce can reduced-sodium condensed cream of celery soup
- 1 cup reduced-sodium chicken broth
- ¾ cup water
- ½ teaspoon dried marjoram or thyme, crushed
- ¼ teaspoon pepper

Prep time: 15 minutes
Cooking time: 12 minutes

DIRECTIONS

1. Trim any separable fat from pork. Cut pork into thin bite-size strips. In a 12-inch skillet cook and stir pork and onion in hot oil over medium-high heat for 3 to 4 minutes or until pork is slightly pink in center.

2. Stir in the frozen vegetables, uncooked noodles, soup, broth, water, marjoram or thyme, and pepper. Bring to boiling; reduce heat. Cover and simmer for 12 to 15 minutes or until noodles are tender, stirring occasionally. Makes 4 servings.

Reduced-sodium chicken broth is available in cans. If you can't find it at your supermarket, substitute regular chicken broth. Keep in mind, however, the amount of sodium will increase by one-third.

NUTRITION FACTS PER SERVING:

317 calories
12 g total fat
3 g saturated fat
64 mg cholesterol
531 mg sodium
33 g carbohydrate
3 g fiber
19 g protein

49

Italian Pork Sandwiches

For added pizzazz, cook the pork as directed, then cook some chopped onion and chopped green sweet pepper in the skillet. Stir in the Italian cooking sauce and continue as directed.

INGREDIENTS

¾ **pound pork tenderloin**

¼ **cup seasoned fine dry bread crumbs**

1 **tablespoon margarine or butter**

½ **cup Italian cooking sauce, spaghetti sauce, or pizza sauce**

4 **kaiser rolls or hamburger buns, split**

2 **tablespoons grated Parmesan cheese**

Toast the kaiser rolls or hamburger buns, if you like, by arranging the split rolls or buns, cut sides up, on the unheated rack of a broiler pan. Broil 4 inches from the heat for 1 to 2 minutes or until cut surfaces are golden brown. Check the rolls often to prevent overbrowning.

Start to finish: 15 minutes

DIRECTIONS

1. Trim any separable fat from pork. Cut pork crosswise into 4 slices. Place each slice of pork between 2 sheets of plastic wrap. Working from center to edges, pound with the flat side of a meat mallet to ¼-inch thickness.

2. Place seasoned bread crumbs in a shallow bowl. Dip each pork slice into the bread crumbs, coating lightly.

3. In a large skillet cook 2 of the pork slices in hot margarine or butter for 6 to 8 minutes or until pork is slightly pink in center, turning once. Remove. Keep warm. Repeat with remaining pork, adding more margarine or butter if necessary.

4. Add Italian cooking sauce, spaghetti sauce, or pizza sauce to skillet. Cook and stir until heated through. Place each pork slice on the bottom of a roll or bun. Spoon some sauce over each. Sprinkle each sandwich with Parmesan cheese; add tops of rolls or buns. Makes 4 servings.

NUTRITION FACTS PER SERVING:

605 calories
13 g total fat
4 g saturated fat
70 mg cholesterol
1,279 mg sodium
86 g carbohydrate
17 g fiber
34 g protein

50

INGREDIENTS

12	ounces pork tenderloin
1/8	teaspoon pepper
6	cups shredded cabbage
1	large onion, sliced
2/3	cup shredded carrot
1/3	cup water
2	tablespoons vinegar
1	teaspoon dillseed, crushed
1/4	teaspoon salt
1/8	teaspoon pepper

Roast Pork and Cabbage

Dillseed refers to the small, hard, dried seeds of the dill plant. Compared to the leaves from the plant, the seeds have a stronger, slightly pungent flavor.

Prep time: 15 minutes
Roasting time: 25 minutes

DIRECTIONS

1. Trim fat from meat. Sprinkle the meat with 1/8 teaspoon pepper. Place the meat on a rack in a shallow roasting pan. Insert a meat thermometer. Roast, uncovered, in a 425° oven for 25 to 35 minutes or until the thermometer registers 160°.

2. Meanwhile, in a large saucepan combine the cabbage, onion, carrot, water, vinegar, dillseed, salt, and 1/8 teaspoon pepper. Bring to boiling; reduce heat. Simmer, covered, for 8 to 10 minutes or just until the vegetables are tender.

3. Slice the meat and serve with the vegetables. Makes 4 servings.

NUTRITION FACTS PER SERVING:

166 calories
4 g total fat
1 g saturated fat
60 mg cholesterol
224 mg sodium
14 g carbohydrate
7 g fiber
21 g protein

Mustard-Orange Pork Tenderloin

Roast a mixture of vegetables, such as cut-up red onions, baby carrots, and chunks of zucchini, alongside the meat. Just spray the vegetables with olive-oil-flavored nonstick coating before placing them in the pan around the meat.

INGREDIENTS

- 12 ounces pork tenderloin
- ½ cup apricot preserves or orange marmalade
- 3 tablespoons Dijon-style mustard
  Nonstick cooking spray
- 2 cups sliced fresh mushrooms
- ½ cup sliced green onions
- 2 tablespoons orange juice

Prep time: 10 minutes
Cooking time: 25 minutes

DIRECTIONS

1. Trim any fat from meat. Place the meat in a shallow roasting pan. Insert a meat thermometer. Roast, uncovered, in a 425° oven for 10 minutes.

2. Meanwhile, in a small mixing bowl stir together the preserves and mustard. Spoon half of the mustard mixture over the meat; set remaining mixture aside. Roast for 15 to 25 minutes more or until thermometer registers 160°. Cover meat with foil and let stand for 10 minutes before carving.

3. Coat a medium saucepan with cooking spray. Preheat saucepan over medium heat. Add the mushrooms and green onions. Cook and stir for 2 to 3 minutes or until mushrooms are tender. Stir in remaining mustard mixture and orange juice. Cook and stir until heated through. To serve, thinly slice meat. Spoon mushroom mixture over meat. Makes 4 servings.

NUTRITION FACTS PER SERVING:

240 calories
4 g total fat
1 g saturated fat
60 mg cholesterol
334 mg sodium
32 g carbohydrate
3 g fiber
21 g protein

Pork Lo Mein

INGREDIENTS

- 12 ounces lean ground pork
- 2 cups sliced fresh mushrooms
- 1 cup shredded or biased-sliced carrot
- ½ cup red and/or green sweet pepper cut into bite-size strips
- 2 cloves garlic, minced
- 1 tablespoon cornstarch
- 1 cup reduced-sodium chicken broth
- 1 tablespoon reduced-sodium soy sauce
- 1 teaspoon grated fresh ginger
- ¼ teaspoon crushed red pepper
- ¼ teaspoon curry powder
- 4 ounces packaged dried thin spaghetti, broken, or linguine, cooked and drained (2 cups cooked)
- 1 cup fresh bean sprouts
- ½ cup sliced green onions
  Sliced green onion (optional)

If you prefer, use lean boneless pork, thinly sliced into bite-size strips, instead of the ground pork. Boneless loin chops work well.

Start to finish: 35 minutes

DIRECTIONS

1. In a large skillet cook the meat, mushrooms, carrot, sweet pepper, and garlic until meat is brown and vegetables are tender. Drain off fat.

2. Stir cornstarch into meat mixture. Stir in broth, soy sauce, ginger, crushed red pepper, and curry powder. Cook and stir until thickened and bubbly. Cook and stir for 2 minutes more.

3. Stir in cooked pasta, bean sprouts, and the ½ cup green onions; heat through. If desired, garnish with additional green onion. Makes 4 servings.

NUTRITION FACTS PER SERVING:

269 calories
7 g total fat
0 g saturated fat
40 mg cholesterol
350 mg sodium
34 g carbohydrate
3 g fiber
17g protein

To cook boneless pork,

heat 1 teaspoon cooking oil in the large skillet. Add the meat strips. Stir-fry for 2 to 3 minutes or until slightly pink in center. Remove from skillet. Cook the mushrooms, carrot, sweet pepper, and garlic as directed. Return meat to skillet and continue as directed.

Ham with Sweet Potatoes And Apples

Although it's hard to beat fresh vegetables of any kind, canned vegetables help out in a pinch. By using canned sweet potatoes, you'll cut your preparation time to just 10 minutes.

INGREDIENTS

- 4 medium sweet potatoes or one 18-ounce can sweet potatoes, drained
- 2 ½-inch-thick slices lower-fat, lower-sodium cooked ham, trimmed of separable fat (about 12 ounces)
- 2 medium apples
- 1 teaspoon finely shredded orange peel
- ¾ cup orange juice
- 2 teaspoons cornstarch
- 1 teaspoon reduced-sodium soy sauce
- 1 teaspoon grated fresh ginger
- 1 clove garlic, minced
  Snipped fresh parsley (optional)

Prep time: 30 minutes
Baking time: 25 minutes

DIRECTIONS

1. Peel and quarter fresh sweet potatoes. In a large covered saucepan cook the potatoes in a small amount of boiling water about 15 minutes or until almost tender. Drain.

2. Cut each ham slice in half. Core apples and cut each apple into 8 wedges. Arrange fresh or drained canned sweet potatoes and the apple wedges in a 2-quart rectangular baking dish. Arrange ham slices on top of the sweet potatoes and apples.

3. In a small saucepan combine orange peel, orange juice, cornstarch, soy sauce, ginger, and garlic. Cook and stir until thickened and bubbly. Pour over ham.

4. Bake, covered, in a 375° oven for 15 minutes. Uncover and bake about 10 minutes more or until potatoes and apples are just tender. If desired, sprinkle with fresh parsley. Makes 4 servings.

NUTRITION FACTS PER SERVING:

266 calories
3 g total fat
1 g saturated fat
36 mg cholesterol
986 mg sodium
44 g carbohydrate
6 g fiber
18 g protein

INGREDIENTS

- 6 packaged dried lasagna noodles
  (4 ounces)
- 1 10-ounce package frozen
  chopped spinach
- 2 cups fat-free milk
- ¼ cup chopped onion
- 3 tablespoons cornstarch
- 1½ cups diced lower-fat,
  lower-sodium cooked ham
  (about 8 ounces)

- ½ teaspoon dried Italian seasoning,
  crushed
- 1 cup low-fat cottage cheese
- 1 cup shredded mozzarella cheese
  (4 ounces)

Spinach and Ham Lasagna

Deviate from the traditional red-sauced lasagna. This luscious lasagna is layered with spinach, ham, cheese, and a lightened "cream" sauce. Ham adds a tasty smoky flavor.

Prep time: 40 minutes
Baking time: 30 minutes
Standing time: 10 minutes

DIRECTIONS

1. Cook the lasagna noodles according to package directions, except omit oil. Drain. Rinse with cold water; drain again. Set aside.

2. Meanwhile, cook the spinach according to package directions; drain well. Set spinach aside.

3. For sauce, in a medium saucepan combine the milk, onion, and cornstarch. Cook and stir until thickened and bubbly. Cook and stir for 2 minutes more.

4. Spread 2 tablespoons of the sauce evenly on the bottom of a 2-quart rectangular baking dish. Stir ham and Italian seasoning into remaining sauce. Arrange 3 lasagna noodles in the dish. Spread with one-third of the remaining sauce. Layer the spinach on top. Layer another one-third of the sauce, the cottage cheese, and half of the mozzarella cheese over the spinach. Place remaining noodles on top. Top with the remaining sauce and mozzarella cheese.

5. Bake, uncovered, in a 375° oven for 30 to 35 minutes or until heated through. Let stand 10 minutes before serving. Makes 6 servings.

NUTRITION FACTS PER SERVING:

241 calories
5 g total fat
2 g saturated fat
30 mg cholesterol
724 mg sodium
26 g carbohydrate
0 g fiber
22 g protein

Ham and Potato Skillet

Fat-free sour cream becomes the base for a creamy, rich-tasting sauce in this family-style dish. For the best herb flavor, use fresh herbs when you can. You can substitute another fresh herb for the dill.

INGREDIENTS

1   pound small potatoes

1   cup water

8   ounces fresh green beans, cut into 1-inch pieces, or one 9-ounce package frozen cut green beans

1   8-ounce carton fat-free dairy sour cream

2   tablespoons all-purpose flour

2   teaspoons prepared mustard

¾   teaspoon snipped fresh dill or ¼ teaspoon dried dill

⅛   teaspoon pepper

1½ cups cubed lower-fat, lower-sodium cooked ham (about 8 ounces)

Tomato slices (optional)

Fresh dill (optional)

Start to finish: 30 minutes

DIRECTIONS

1. Scrub and slice potatoes; halve any large slices.

2. In a large skillet bring the water to boiling. Add the potatoes and fresh green beans (if using). Cover and cook about 15 minutes or until potatoes and beans are tender. (If using frozen beans, cook potatoes for 10 minutes; add beans. Return to boiling. Cook for 5 minutes more.) Drain well; return to skillet.

3. Meanwhile, in a small saucepan stir together the sour cream, flour, mustard, the snipped dill or dried dill, and the pepper. Cook and stir until thickened and bubbly.

Pour over vegetables in skillet. Stir in ham. Heat through. If desired, garnish with tomato slices and additional fresh dill. Makes 4 servings.

NUTRITION FACTS PER SERVING:

254 calories
2 g total fat
1 g saturated fat
24 mg cholesterol
698 mg sodium
41 g carbohydrate
3 g fiber
18 g protein

Ham and Swiss Pizza

INGREDIENTS

- 1 green sweet pepper, cut into
    bite-size strips
- 1 small onion, sliced and
    separated into rings
- 1 tablespoon olive oil or
    cooking oil
- 1 tablespoon Dijon-style mustard
    or coarse brown mustard
- ½ teaspoon caraway seed, crushed
- 1 12-inch Italian bread shell
    (Boboli)
- 6 ounces cooked ham, cut into
    thin strips
- 1 cup cherry tomatoes, halved
- 1 cup shredded Swiss cheese
    (4 ounces)

In this simple recipe, traditional sandwich ingredients reconfigure into a family-pleasing pizza.

Prep time: 20 minutes
Baking time: 8 minutes

DIRECTIONS

1. In a large skillet cook green pepper and onion in hot oil for 2 to 3 minutes or until tender. Stir in mustard and caraway seed. Set aside.

2. Place bread shell on a lightly greased baking sheet. Top with pepper-onion mixture, ham, and cherry tomatoes. Sprinkle with Swiss cheese. Bake in a 400° oven about 8 minutes or until cheese melts and pizza is heated through. Makes 4 servings.

For bite-size pieces in no time, cut the pepper into strips about ¼ inch thick. Then gather the pepper strips together and cut them into lengths 1 to 1½ inches long.

NUTRITION FACTS PER SERVING:

529 calories
21 g total fat
6 g saturated fat
53 mg cholesterol
1,305 mg sodium
57 g carbohydrate
3 g fiber
31 g protein

Grilled Italian Sausage with Sweet And Sour Peppers

Sicilians love sweet and sour flavors and toss super-sweet raisins into their delicious meat and fish dishes with culinary abandon. Here, grilled Italian sausage is presented on a bed of tangy, yet sweet grilled vegetables. For more Italian goodness, serve with grilled purchased polenta.

INGREDIENTS

- 3 tablespoons slivered almonds
- ¼ cup raisins
- 3 tablespoons red wine vinegar
- 2 tablespoons sugar
- ¼ teaspoon salt
- ⅛ teaspoon black pepper
- 6 uncooked sweet Italian sausage links
- 1 tablespoon olive oil
- 2 green sweet peppers, cut into 1-inch-wide strips
- 2 red sweet peppers, cut into 1-inch-wide strips
- 1 medium red onion, thickly sliced

Prep time: 20 minutes
Grilling time: 10 minutes

DIRECTIONS

1. In a small nonstick skillet cook and stir almonds for 1 to 2 minutes or until golden brown. Stir in raisins. Remove skillet from heat. Let stand for 1 minute. Carefully stir in vinegar, sugar, salt, and pepper. Return to heat; cook and stir just until the sugar dissolves.

2. Prick the sausage links several times with a fork. Drizzle oil over sweet pepper strips and onion slices. Grill sausage and vegetables on the rack of an uncovered grill directly over medium coals for 10 to 15 minutes or until sausage is cooked through (160°) and vegetables are tender, turning once halfway through cooking.

3. In a large bowl toss vegetables with the almond mixture; spoon onto a serving platter. Arrange sausage on top of vegetable mixture. Makes 6 servings.

NUTRITION FACTS PER SERVING:

276 calories
19 g total fat
6 g saturated fat
59 mg cholesterol
604 mg sodium
15 g carbohydrate
1 g fiber
13 g protein

Bow Ties with Sausage and Sweet Peppers

You will be amazed that so few ingredients generate so much flavor.

INGREDIENTS

- 8 ounces packaged dried large bow-tie pasta
- ¾ pound hot Italian sausage links
- 2 medium red sweet peppers, cut into ¾-inch pieces
- ½ cup vegetable broth or beef broth
- ¼ teaspoon coarsely ground black pepper
- ¼ cup snipped fresh Italian parsley

Start to finish: 25 minutes

DIRECTIONS

1. Cook pasta according to package directions; drain. Return pasta to saucepan.

2. Meanwhile, cut the sausage into 1-inch-thick pieces. In a large skillet cook the sausage and sweet peppers over medium-high heat until sausage is brown. Drain off fat.

3. Stir the broth and black pepper into the skillet. Bring to boiling; reduce heat. Simmer, uncovered, for 5 minutes. Remove from heat. Pour over pasta; add parsley. Toss gently to coat. Transfer to a warm serving dish. Makes 4 servings.

If red sweet peppers aren't available, use yellow or green sweet peppers instead.

NUTRITION FACTS PER SERVING:

397 calories
18 g total fat
6 g saturated fat
94 mg cholesterol
713 mg sodium
38 g carbohydrate
3 g fiber
24 g protein

59

Sausage, Beans, And Greens

Escarole, a type of endive, is typically used in salads, but it makes a great addition to this one-pot dish.

INGREDIENTS

½   pound hot or mild Italian sausage links, bias-sliced into ½-inch pieces

1   medium onion, chopped (½ cup)

2   19-ounce cans white kidney beans (cannellini), rinsed and drained

¾   cup reduced-sodium chicken broth

¼   cup dry white wine or reduced-sodium chicken broth

2   tablespoons snipped fresh thyme or 1 teaspoon dried thyme, crushed

2   cups torn escarole or fresh spinach

¼   cup shredded Parmesan cheese (optional)

Cannellini beans are white Italian
kidney beans. They're found in the canned vegetable section of the supermarket or in the Italian food aisle. If you can't find them, substitute navy beans or Great Northern beans.

Start to finish: 25 minutes

DIRECTIONS

1. In a large saucepan cook sausage and onion over medium heat for 5 minutes or until onion is tender. Drain off fat. Add beans, the ¾ cup chicken broth, the ¼ cup wine or chicken broth, and the thyme. Bring to boiling; reduce heat. Cover and simmer for 5 minutes. Stir in escarole or fresh spinach; heat through.

2. To serve, ladle mixture into serving bowls. If desired, sprinkle with Parmesan cheese. Makes 4 servings.

NUTRITION FACTS PER SERVING:

309 calories
12 g total fat
4 g saturated fat
32 mg cholesterol
921 mg sodium
39 g carbohydrate
13 g fiber
24 g protein

Nuevo Pork 'n' Beans

INGREDIENTS

- 6 ounces spicy chorizo or bulk Italian sausage
- 1 16-ounce can fat-free refried beans
- 1 4½-ounce can diced green chile peppers, drained
- 3 8-inch-long pieces baguette-style French bread, split lengthwise and toasted
- ½ of a medium red sweet pepper, cut into thin strips
- ½ of a medium green sweet pepper, cut into thin strips
- ½ cup shredded reduced-fat Monterey Jack cheese (2 ounces)

Add a Mexican accent to a knife-and-fork sandwich by corralling a can of refried beans, chorizo sausage, and cheese.

Prep time: 20 minutes
Broiling time: 1 minute

DIRECTIONS

1. Remove casings from sausage, if present. In a skillet crumble sausage; cook over medium heat until brown. Drain sausage in a colander; wipe skillet with paper towels. Return sausage to skillet.

2. Stir in refried beans and chile peppers; heat through. Spread sausage-bean mixture on bottom halves of bread; arrange bread on unheated rack of a broiler pan. Top with sweet pepper strips; sprinkle with cheese. Broil 4 inches from heat for 1 to 2 minutes or until cheese melts. Place toasted bread tops over filling; cut each portion in half crosswise. Makes 6 servings.

Chorizo is a spicy Mexican pork sausage that's available in bulk or link form. Look for it in larger supermarkets or in Mexican specialty food shops.

NUTRITION FACTS PER SERVING:

311 calories
15 g total fat
6 g saturated fat
7 mg cholesterol
865 mg sodium
53 g carbohydrate
4 g fiber
20 g protein

Thai Cobb Salad

Hit a home run with this refreshing mix of meat, cubed avocado, roasted peanuts, and spicy ginger-soy dressing. Leftover grilled meats work admirably, or deli-sliced meats can pinch-hit.

INGREDIENTS

½ cup bottled fat-free Italian salad dressing

1 tablespoon soy sauce

1 to 1½ teaspoons grated fresh ginger

¼ to ½ teaspoon crushed red pepper

8 cups torn mixed salad greens

1½ cups coarsely chopped cooked pork, beef, or chicken (8 ounces)

1 avocado, halved, seeded, peeled, and cut into ½-inch pieces

1 cup coarsely shredded carrots

¼ cup coarsely snipped fresh cilantro

2 green onions, thinly sliced (¼ cup)

¼ cup honey-roasted peanuts (optional)

To carry through with the Asian flavors, include Chinese cabbage as part of the mixed greens.

Start to finish: 25 minutes

DIRECTIONS

1. For dressing, in a large bowl combine salad dressing, soy sauce, fresh ginger, and crushed red pepper. Add salad greens; toss lightly to coat.

2. Divide salad greens among 4 dinner plates. Top each with meat, avocado, carrots, cilantro, green onions, and, if desired, peanuts. Makes 4 servings.

NUTRITION FACTS PER SERVING:

255 calories
15 g total fat
4 g saturated fat
52 mg cholesterol
743 mg sodium
11 g carbohydrate
4 g fiber
19 g protein

INGREDIENTS

- 1 cup frozen peas and carrots or frozen mixed vegetables
- ½ cup packaged dried orzo, tripolini, tiny tube macaroni, or tiny star macaroni
- 6 ounces lower-fat, lower-sodium cooked ham, cut into ½-inch cubes (about 1 cup)
- 4 green onions, sliced
- ½ cup light dairy sour cream
- 2 tablespoons reduced-calorie ranch salad dressing
- 1 teaspoon snipped fresh dill or ¼ teaspoon dried dill

- 2 medium tomatoes, sliced
- 1 green sweet pepper, cut into half rings
  Lettuce leaves

Ham and Orzo Salad

Use any tiny pasta you have on hand for this salad. Orzo, shown in the photograph, looks like grains of rice; tripolini resembles tiny bow ties.

Prep time: 35 minutes
Chilling time: 4 hours

DIRECTIONS

1. In a medium saucepan bring a large amount of water to boiling. Add the frozen vegetables and the pasta. Return to boiling. Boil, uncovered, for 5 to 8 minutes or until pasta and vegetables are tender. Immediately drain mixture in a colander. Rinse with cold water. Drain again.

2. In a medium mixing bowl stir together the pasta mixture, ham, and green onions. In a small mixing bowl stir together the sour cream, salad dressing, and dill. Pour the sour cream mixture over the pasta mixture.

Toss until well coated. Cover and chill for 4 to 8 hours.

3. To serve, arrange the tomato slices and sweet pepper on 4 lettuce-lined plates. Stir the pasta mixture; spoon onto the plates. Makes 4 servings.

NUTRITION FACTS PER SERVING:

224 calories
6 g total fat
1 g saturated fat
22 mg cholesterol
597 mg sodium
31 g carbohydrate
3 g fiber
15 g protein

Tuscan Lamb Chop Skillet

Tuscans, once disparaged by the rest of Italy as "bean eaters" because of their love of the legume, now wear that mantle with pride. Here, healthful white beans are flavored with rosemary and garlic, then topped with lamb chops.

INGREDIENTS

8 lamb rib chops, cut 1 inch thick
   (about 1½ pounds total)

2 teaspoons olive oil

3 cloves garlic, minced

1 19-ounce can white kidney
   (cannellini) beans, rinsed and
   drained

1 8-ounce can Italian-style stewed
   tomatoes, undrained

1 tablespoon balsamic vinegar

2 teaspoons snipped fresh
   rosemary

   Fresh rosemary sprigs (optional)

Start to finish: 18 minutes

DIRECTIONS

1. Trim fat from chops. In a large skillet cook chops in hot oil over medium heat until desired doneness, turning once halfway through cooking. (Allow 7 to 9 minutes for medium.) Remove chops from skillet; keep warm.

2. Stir garlic into drippings in skillet. Cook and stir for 1 minute. Stir in beans, undrained tomatoes, vinegar, and snipped rosemary. Bring to boiling; reduce heat. Simmer, uncovered, for 3 minutes.

3. Spoon bean mixture onto 4 dinner plates; arrange 2 chops on each serving. If desired, garnish with rosemary sprigs. Makes 4 servings.

NUTRITION FACTS PER SERVING:

272 calories
9 g total fat
3 g saturated fat
67 mg cholesterol
466 mg sodium
24 g carbohydrate
6 g fiber
30 g protein

INGREDIENTS

- 3 tablespoons apple jelly
- 1 green onion, thinly sliced
- 1 tablespoon soy sauce
- 2 teaspoons lemon juice
- ⅛ teaspoon curry powder
- Dash ground cinnamon
- Dash ground red pepper
- 2 small red and/or green apples, cut crosswise into ¼-inch slices
- Lemon juice
- 8 lamb loin chops, cut 1 inch thick (about 2 pounds total)
- Hot cooked couscous (optional)
- 1 tablespoon small fresh mint leaves

Apple-Glazed Lamb Chops

Lamb chops make an elegant quick-to-fix dish, and these cinnamon- and apple-spiced chops are the ultimate company fare. Add a side of couscous tossed with fresh mint and finish with a scoop of sorbet for a weekday dinner with friends.

Prep time: 15 minutes
Grilling time: 12 minutes

DIRECTIONS

1. For glaze, in a small saucepan combine apple jelly, green onion, soy sauce, lemon juice, curry powder, cinnamon, and red pepper. Cook and stir over medium heat until bubbly. Remove from heat. Remove seeds from apple slices. Brush apples with lemon juice. Set aside.

2. Trim fat from chops. Grill chops on the rack of an uncovered grill directly over medium coals until desired doneness, turning and brushing once with glaze halfway through cooking.

[Allow 12 to 14 minutes for medium-rare (145°) or 15 to 17 minutes for medium (160°).] Place apples on grill rack next to chops the last 5 minutes of grilling, turning and brushing once with glaze halfway through cooking.

3. If desired, serve chops and apples with couscous. Sprinkle with mint leaves. Makes 4 servings.

NUTRITION FACTS PER SERVING:

385 calories
14 g total fat
5 g saturated fat
133 mg cholesterol
378 mg sodium
20 g carbohydrate
1 g fiber
43 g protein

Grilled Lambburger Roll-Ups

Here's perfect alfresco food for friends! Spinach, seasoned lamb, and hummus are rolled up in soft cracker bread and cut into eye-catching spirals. For dessert, offer Red Wine-Marinated Peaches (page 246) with coffee or mint tea.

INGREDIENTS

1 **beaten egg**

3 **tablespoons fine dry bread crumbs**

2 **tablespoons snipped fresh oregano**

1 **tablespoon water**

2 **cloves garlic, minced**

¾ **teaspoon salt**

½ **teaspoon freshly ground pepper**

1 **pound lean ground lamb**

2 **14- to 15-inch soft cracker bread rounds or four 7- to 8-inch flour tortillas**

⅓ **cup prepared hummus (garbanzo bean spread)**

4 **cups torn spinach or red-tipped leaf lettuce**

¼ **cup crumbled feta cheese**

3 **tablespoons sliced pitted kalamata or ripe olives**

Start to finish: 30 minutes

DIRECTIONS

1. In a large bowl combine egg, bread crumbs, oregano, water, garlic, salt, and pepper. Add ground lamb; mix well. Form mixture into eight 4-inch-long logs.

2. Grill meat on the rack of an uncovered grill directly over medium coals for 14 to 18 minutes or until meat is done (160°), turning once halfway through cooking. (Or, place in a shallow baking pan. Bake in a 400° oven for 12 to 14 minutes.)

3. Meanwhile, spread the cracker bread or tortillas with hummus. Sprinkle with spinach, feta cheese, and olives. If using cracker bread, place 4 meat pieces, end to end, near an edge of each piece. Starting from edge closest to meat, roll up into a spiral. Slice each roll-up diagonally in fourths. (If using tortillas, place 2 meat pieces, end to end, on each tortilla. Roll up. Slice each roll-up diagonally in half.) Makes 4 servings.

NUTRITION FACTS PER SERVING:

625 calories
26 g total fat
9 g saturated fat
135 mg cholesterol
1,225 mg sodium
64 g carbohydrate
2 g fiber
34 g protein

The Ultimate Sloppy Joe

Chilly days bring requests for comfort foods such as sloppy joes. Dress up this favorite loose-meat sandwich with feta cheese, bulgur, and crispy romaine.

INGREDIENTS

- 1 pound lean ground lamb or ground beef
- 1 medium onion, chopped (½ cup)
- 1 15-ounce can tomato sauce
- ⅓ cup bulgur
- 1 teaspoon dried oregano, crushed
- 2 cups chopped romaine
- 6 kaiser rolls, split and toasted
- 2 ounces feta cheese with tomato and basil or plain feta cheese

Start to finish: 20 minutes

DIRECTIONS

1. In a 10-inch skillet cook ground lamb or beef and onion until meat is brown. Drain off fat. Stir in tomato sauce, bulgur, and oregano. Bring to boiling; reduce heat. Simmer, uncovered, about 10 minutes or until mixture is desired consistency, stirring occasionally.

2. Arrange romaine on bottom halves of rolls. Spoon meat mixture on top. Crumble feta cheese over the meat. Cover with top halves of rolls. Makes 6 servings.

NUTRITION FACTS PER SERVING:

396 calories
15 g total fat
6 g saturated fat
59 mg cholesterol
889 mg sodium
43 g carbohydrate
3 g fiber
22 g protein

Fashion a colorful relish

platter from your pantry and refrigerator using ingredients such as cut-up vegetables, pickles, olives, and cubed cheese.

For another simple side dish, warm chunky applesauce with a dash of ground nutmeg, cinnamon, or apple pie spice.

Greek-Style Pasta Skillet

Lamb, cinnamon, and feta cheese add a Greek twist to this one-dish macaroni meal.

INGREDIENTS

¾ pound ground lamb or ground beef

1 medium onion, chopped (½ cup)

1 14½-ounce can diced tomatoes, undrained

1 5½-ounce can tomato juice

½ cup water

½ teaspoon instant beef bouillon granules

½ teaspoon ground cinnamon

⅛ teaspoon garlic powder

1 cup packaged dried medium shell macaroni or elbow macaroni

1 cup frozen loose-pack cut green beans

½ cup crumbled feta cheese (2 ounces)

Feta cheese has a wonderfully

sharp, salty flavor. This soft, white, crumbly cheese can be made from cow, sheep, or goat milk. It's available in chunks or already crumbled.

Prep time: 15 minutes
Cooking time: 15 minutes

DIRECTIONS

1. In a large skillet cook ground lamb or beef and onion until meat is brown. Drain off fat. Stir in undrained tomatoes, tomato juice, water, beef bouillon granules, cinnamon, and garlic powder. Bring to boiling.

2. Stir uncooked macaroni and green beans into meat mixture. Return to boiling; reduce heat. Cover and simmer about 15 minutes or until macaroni and green beans are tender. Sprinkle with feta cheese. Makes 4 servings.

NUTRITION FACTS PER SERVING:

362 calories
16 g total fat
7 g saturated fat
70 mg cholesterol
647 mg sodium
33 g carbohydrate
2 g fiber
22 g protein

Greek-Style Salad

INGREDIENTS

- 12 ounces boneless lamb leg center slice or beef top round steak, cut 1 inch thick
- 1 teaspoon finely shredded lemon peel
- ¼ cup lemon juice
- 1 tablespoon snipped fresh oregano or 1 teaspoon dried oregano, crushed
- 1 tablespoon olive oil or salad oil
- 1 tablespoon water
- 1 clove garlic, minced
- ¼ teaspoon salt
- ¼ teaspoon pepper
- 6 cups torn fresh spinach and/or romaine leaves
- 1 medium cucumber, thinly sliced
- ¼ cup chopped red onion
- 4 pitted ripe olives, halved
- 2 tablespoons crumbled feta cheese
- 2 small pita bread rounds, cut into wedges and toasted

Preparation is easy—make the dressing and arrange the salad ingredients on serving plates while the meat broils.

Start to finish: 18 minutes

DIRECTIONS

1. Trim fat from meat. Place meat on the unheated rack of a broiler pan. Broil 3 to 4 inches from heat 12 to 15 minutes or until desired doneness, turning meat once.

2. Meanwhile, for the dressing, in a screw-top jar combine the lemon peel, lemon juice, oregano, oil, water, garlic, salt, and pepper. Cover jar and shake well. Set aside.

3. Divide spinach and/or romaine leaves among 4 plates. Cut the broiled meat across the grain into thin, bite-size strips. Arrange warm sliced meat, cucumber, onion, olives, and feta cheese on top of greens. Drizzle dressing over salads. Serve with toasted pita bread wedges. Makes 4 servings.

NUTRITION FACTS PER SERVING:

269 calories
11 g total fat
4 g saturated fat
50 mg cholesterol
504 mg sodium
25 g carbohydrate
3 g fiber
21 g protein

69

Rosemary Chicken Recipe, page 84

Poultry

Chicken with Mushroom Sauce

For a colorful sauce, use half of a green and half of a red sweet pepper. Then accent the dish with a colorful sprinkling of fresh edible flowers.

INGREDIENTS

Nonstick cooking spray

4 small skinless, boneless chicken breast halves (about 12 ounces total)

1 teaspoon olive oil

2 cups sliced fresh mushrooms

1 medium red or green sweet pepper, cut into ¾-inch cubes

1 clove garlic, minced

½ cup reduced-sodium chicken broth

Salt and pepper

½ cup fat-free dairy sour cream

1 tablespoon all-purpose flour

⅛ teaspoon black pepper

1 tablespoon dry sherry (optional)

2 cups hot cooked white or brown rice

Snipped fresh parsley

Fresh chives (optional)

Edible flowers (optional)

Choose unsprayed edible flowers, such as nasturtiums, pansies, dianthus, or daylilies, from your own garden or supermarket produce section. Avoid blossoms from florist shops—they're usually treated with chemicals.

Start to finish: 30 minutes

DIRECTIONS

1. Coat an unheated large nonstick skillet with cooking spray. Preheat skillet over medium heat. Cook chicken for 3 to 5 minutes or until browned, turning once. Remove chicken from skillet.

2. Add oil to hot skillet. Cook the mushrooms, sweet pepper, and garlic in hot oil until tender. Remove vegetables; keep warm. Carefully stir broth into skillet. Return chicken to skillet. Sprinkle lightly with salt and black pepper. Bring to boiling; reduce heat. Simmer, covered, for 5 to 7 minutes or until chicken is tender and no longer pink (170°). Transfer chicken to a platter; keep warm.

3. For sauce, in a bowl stir or whisk together the sour cream, flour, and the ⅛ teaspoon black pepper until smooth. If desired, stir in sherry. Stir into mixture in skillet. Cook and stir until bubbly. Cook and stir 1 minute more. Serve chicken, vegetables, and sauce over hot cooked rice tossed with parsley. If desired, garnish with chives and flowers. Makes 4 servings.

NUTRITION FACTS PER SERVING:

259 calories
4 g total fat
1 g saturated fat
45 mg cholesterol
176 mg sodium
32 g carbohydrate
1 g fiber
22 g protein

Spicy Chicken And Star Fruit

INGREDIENTS

- 2 tablespoons balsamic vinegar or red wine vinegar
- 1 tablespoon olive oil
- ½ teaspoon dried rosemary, crushed
- ¼ teaspoon ground cumin
- ⅛ teaspoon ground coriander
- ⅛ teaspoon black pepper
  Dash ground red pepper
- 2 star fruit (carambola), sliced
- 8 green onions, cut into 2-inch pieces, and/or 4 small purple boiling onions, cut into wedges
- 4 medium skinless, boneless chicken breast halves (about 1 pound total)
- 2 cups hot cooked rice
- 1 teaspoon finely shredded orange peel (optional)
- 2 tablespoons peach or apricot preserves, melted (optional)

It's a match made in heaven. The celestial star fruit, also called carambola, is a fitting addition to this chicken dish that's a little bit Italian (balsamic vinegar, olive oil, and rosemary) and a little bit Indian (cumin, coriander, and hot red pepper).

Prep time: 15 minutes
Grilling time: 12 minutes

DIRECTIONS

1. In a small bowl combine vinegar, olive oil, rosemary, cumin, coriander, black pepper, and red pepper. On eight 6-inch skewers alternately thread star fruit and green onions. Set aside.

2. Grill chicken on the lightly greased rack of an uncovered grill directly over medium coals for 12 to 15 minutes or until chicken is tender and no longer pink (170°), turning and brushing once with the vinegar mixture halfway through cooking. Place kabobs on grill rack next to chicken the last 5 minutes of grilling, turning and brushing once with vinegar mixture halfway through cooking.

3. To serve, if desired, toss the hot cooked rice with orange peel. Serve chicken and kabobs over rice. If desired, drizzle with preserves. Makes 4 servings.

NUTRITION FACTS PER SERVING:

286 calories
7 g total fat
1 g saturated fat
59 mg cholesterol
57 mg sodium
30 g carbohydrate
1 g fiber
24 g protein

Chicken and Prosciutto Roll-Ups

This pretty dish takes the Italian technique braciola—thin slices of meat wrapped around savories such as Italian ham, cheese, artichokes, spinach, and herbs—and applies it to chicken. Serve the attractive spirals with spinach fettuccine.

INGREDIENTS

¼ cup dry white wine

2 teaspoons snipped fresh thyme or ½ teaspoon dried thyme, crushed

4 medium skinless, boneless chicken breast halves (about 1 pound total)

4 thin slices prosciutto (Italian ham), trimmed of fat

2 ounces fontina cheese, thinly sliced

½ of a 7-ounce jar roasted red sweet peppers, cut into thin strips (about ½ cup)

Fresh thyme sprigs (optional)

Prep time: 25 minutes
Grilling time: 15 minutes

DIRECTIONS

1. For sauce, in a small bowl combine the wine and the 2 teaspoons fresh or ½ teaspoon dried thyme. Set aside.

2. Place a chicken piece between 2 pieces of plastic wrap. Using the flat side of a meat mallet, pound chicken lightly into a rectangle about ⅛ inch thick. Remove plastic wrap. Repeat with remaining chicken pieces.

3. Place a slice of the prosciutto and one-fourth of the cheese on each chicken piece. Arrange one-fourth of the roasted peppers on cheese near bottom edge of chicken. Starting from bottom edge, roll up into a spiral; secure with wooden toothpicks. (At this point, chicken may be individually wrapped in plastic wrap and refrigerated up to 4 hours.)

4. Grill chicken on the lightly greased rack of an uncovered grill directly over medium coals for 15 to 17 minutes or until chicken is tender and no longer pink, turning to cook evenly and brushing twice with sauce up to the last 5 minutes of grilling. If desired, garnish with thyme sprigs. Makes 4 servings.

NUTRITION FACTS PER SERVING:

214 calories
9 g total fat
4 g saturated fat
76 mg cholesterol
294 mg sodium
2 g carbohydrate
0 g fiber
27 g protein

Chicken with Peach Salsa

INGREDIENTS

2   tablespoons lime juice

4   teaspoons teriyaki sauce
    or soy sauce

4   medium skinless, boneless
    chicken breast halves
    (about 1 pound total)

1   medium peach, peeled, pitted,
    and chopped, or ½ of a
    medium papaya, peeled,
    seeded, and chopped
    (about 1 cup)

1   small tomato, chopped

2   tablespoons sliced green onion

1   tablespoon lime juice

1   teaspoon grated ginger or
    ¼ teaspoon ground ginger

¼   teaspoon bottled minced garlic
    or ⅛ teaspoon garlic powder

Hot cooked rice (optional)

Fresh thyme (optional)

If fresh peaches or papayas aren't in season, thaw and chop 1 cup frozen peach slices.

Prep time: 20 minutes
Marinating time: 30 minutes
Broiling time: 12 minutes

DIRECTIONS

1. In a small bowl stir together the 2 tablespoons lime juice and the teriyaki or soy sauce. Brush chicken with lime juice mixture. Cover and marinate at room temperature for 30 minutes or in the refrigerator for up to 2 hours.

2. For salsa, in a medium mixing bowl stir together the peach or papaya, tomato, green onion, the 1 tablespoon lime juice, the ginger, and garlic or garlic powder. Cover and let stand at room temperature for 30 minutes or chill for up to 2 hours.

3. Place chicken on the unheated rack of a broiler pan. Broil 4 to 5 inches from the heat for 12 to 15 minutes or until tender and no longer pink (170°), turning once. Serve chicken with salsa. If desired, serve over hot cooked rice and garnish with thyme. Makes 4 servings.

NUTRITION FACTS PER SERVING:

146 calories
3 g total fat
1 g saturated fat
59 mg cholesterol
287 mg sodium
6 g carbohydrate
1 g fiber
22 g protein

Margarita Chicken

The classic margarita flavors of lime and tequila are a delicious complement to chicken.

INGREDIENTS

½ teaspoon finely shredded
   lime peel
¼ cup lime juice
2 tablespoons tequila
2 tablespoons honey
1 tablespoon cooking oil
2 teaspoons cornstarch
¼ teaspoon garlic salt
¼ teaspoon coarsely ground
   black pepper
4 medium skinless, boneless
   chicken breast halves
   (about 1 pound total)
4 flour tortillas, warmed

1 medium tomato, cut into
   8 wedges
1 medium avocado, seeded,
   peeled, and cut up
Lime slices, cut in half (optional)

For soft, warm tortillas, wrap them in foil and heat in a 350° oven about 10 minutes. Or, micro-cook each unwrapped tortilla for 10 to 20 seconds on 100% power (high).

Prep time: 15 minutes
Broiling time: 12 minutes

DIRECTIONS

1. For glaze, in a small saucepan stir together lime peel, lime juice, tequila, honey, cooking oil, cornstarch, garlic salt, and pepper. Cook and stir over medium heat until thickened and bubbly. Cook and stir for 2 minutes more.

2. Place chicken on the unheated rack of a broiler pan. Broil 4 to 5 inches from the heat for 12 to 15 minutes or until chicken is tender and no longer pink (170°), turning once after half of the broiling time and brushing with some of the glaze during the last 5 minutes.

3. Arrange chicken, warmed tortillas, tomato, and avocado on 4 dinner plates. Drizzle chicken with the remaining glaze. If desired, garnish with lime slices. Makes 4 servings.

NUTRITION FACTS PER SERVING:

415 calories
16 g total fat
3 g saturated fat
59 mg cholesterol
356 mg sodium
39 g carbohydrate
3 g fiber
26 g protein

Chicken with Honey-Cranberry Sauce

A can of red cranberry sauce sweetened with honey and spiced with ginger makes a flavorful addition to quick-cooked chicken breasts.

INGREDIENTS

4 medium skinless, boneless
    chicken breast halves
    (about 1 pound total)

1 tablespoon margarine or butter

½ of a 16-ounce can (1 cup) whole
    cranberry sauce

2 tablespoons honey

½ teaspoon ground ginger

Prep time: 10 minutes
Cooking time: 10 minutes

DIRECTIONS

1. In a large skillet cook chicken in hot margarine or butter over medium heat about 10 minutes or until chicken is tender and no longer pink (170°), turning once. Remove chicken from skillet, reserving drippings in skillet. Keep warm.

2. Stir cranberry sauce, honey, and ginger into the reserved drippings in the skillet. Cook and stir until heated through. Spoon over chicken. Makes 4 servings.

To keep chicken warm while you prepare the honey-cranberry sauce, place the pieces on a serving platter and cover the platter with foil.

NUTRITION FACTS PER SERVING:

284 calories
6 g total fat
1 g saturated fat
59 mg cholesterol
108 mg sodium
36 g carbohydrate
1 g fiber
22 g protein

Lemon Chicken

This delectable chicken dish boasts the flavor of the restaurant favorite of the same name—without the mess of deep frying.

INGREDIENTS

- 4 medium skinless, boneless chicken breast halves (about 1 pound total)
- ⅓ cup all-purpose flour
- ¼ teaspoon pepper
- 2 tablespoons margarine or butter
- 1 cup chicken broth
- ¼ cup lemon juice
- 1 tablespoon cornstarch
- 2 green onions, sliced (¼ cup)
  Lemon slices, cut in half (optional)
  Hot cooked couscous (optional)
  Cooked artichoke halves (optional)

Quick-cooking

COUSCOUS is the perfect main-dish accompaniment for time-pressured cooks. Simply pour boiling water over the couscous; let stand for 5 minutes. Fluff couscous with a fork, and it's ready to eat.

Start to finish: 25 minutes

DIRECTIONS

1. Place each chicken breast half, boned side up, between 2 sheets of plastic wrap. Working from the center to the edges, pound lightly with the flat side of a meat mallet to ¼-inch thickness. Remove plastic wrap. In a shallow dish stir together flour and pepper. Lightly coat each piece of chicken with flour mixture.

2. In a large skillet cook chicken in hot margarine or butter over medium heat for 4 to 6 minutes or until chicken is tender and no longer pink, turning once. Remove chicken from skillet. Keep warm.

3. For sauce, in a small mixing bowl stir together the chicken broth, lemon juice, and cornstarch. Add to skillet. Cook and stir over medium heat until thickened and bubbly. Cook and stir for 2 minutes more. Stir in green onions. If desired, top

chicken with lemon slices. Serve chicken with sauce and, if desired, hot cooked couscous. If desired, garnish with artichoke halves. Makes 4 servings.

NUTRITION FACTS PER SERVING:

226 calories
9 g total fat
2 g saturated fat
60 mg cholesterol
315 mg sodium
10 g carbohydrate
0 g fiber
24 g protein

Marinated Chicken Breasts With Mozzarella

Marinated yet quick-to-fix—it's possible when you start with purchased marinated chicken breasts.

INGREDIENTS

- 1 6-ounce package long grain and wild rice pilaf mix
- 2 green onions, thinly sliced (¼ cup)
- ½ cup water
- 1 cup broccoli florets
- 4 Italian-style or butter-garlic marinated boneless chicken breast halves
- 2 teaspoons olive oil
- 1 medium tomato, halved and thinly sliced
- 2 slices part-skim mozzarella cheese, halved (3 ounces)

Start to finish: 25 minutes

DIRECTIONS

1. Prepare rice according to package directions, adding green onions the last 5 minutes of cooking. In a saucepan bring the water to boiling; add broccoli. Cover and cook for 3 minutes or until crisp-tender; drain and set aside.

2. In a large cast-iron skillet cook chicken breasts in hot oil over medium heat 8 to 10 minutes or until chicken is tender and no longer pink (170°), turning once. Overlap halved tomato slices on top of chicken.

Spoon the cooked broccoli over tomato slices; cover each with a half-slice of cheese. Broil 3 to 4 inches from the heat for 1 minute or until cheese is melted and bubbly. Serve over hot rice. Makes 4 servings.

NUTRITION FACTS PER SERVING:

377 calories
12 g total fat
4 g saturated fat
22 mg cholesterol
1,532 mg sodium
38 g carbohydrate
2 g fiber
31 g protein

Cut preparation time even more by using precut broccoli florets from your supermarket's salad bar or produce section.

Sesame Chicken

The appealing nutty flavor of these quick-to-fix chicken breasts comes from both sesame seed and toasted sesame oil.

INGREDIENTS

½ cup all-purpose flour

1½ teaspoons lemon-pepper seasoning

¾ teaspoon salt

⅓ cup sesame seed

2 cups sliced fresh shiitake or button mushrooms

¼ cup finely chopped onion

2 teaspoons olive oil

1½ cups milk

1 tablespoon Dijon-style mustard

1 tablespoon snipped fresh parsley

6 medium skinless, boneless chicken breast halves (about 1½ pounds total)

⅓ cup milk

1 tablespoon olive oil

1 teaspoon toasted sesame oil

Start to finish: 30 minutes

DIRECTIONS

1. In a shallow bowl stir together flour, lemon-pepper seasoning, and salt. Reserve 2 tablespoons flour mixture. Stir the sesame seed into the remaining flour mixture. Set aside.

2. For sauce, in a medium saucepan cook mushrooms and onion in the 2 teaspoons olive oil until tender. Stir the reserved 2 tablespoons flour mixture into mushroom mixture until combined. Add the 1½ cups milk all at once. Cook and stir until thickened and bubbly. Cook and stir 1 minute more. Stir in the mustard and parsley. Keep sauce warm.

3. Meanwhile, dip chicken in the ⅓ cup milk; roll in sesame-seed-and-flour mixture. In a 12-inch skillet heat 1 tablespoon olive oil and the sesame oil over medium-high heat. Cook chicken in hot oil about 6 minutes or until chicken is tender and no longer pink (170°), turning once. Serve sauce with chicken. Makes 6 servings.

NUTRITION FACTS PER SERVING:

362 calories
14 g total fat
3 g saturated fat
65 mg cholesterol
702 mg sodium
30 g carbohydrate
2 g fiber
30 g protein

Molasses-Orange Glazed Chicken

INGREDIENTS

- 2 tablespoons frozen orange juice concentrate, thawed
- 2 tablespoons molasses
- ¼ teaspoon onion powder
- 4 medium skinless, boneless chicken breast halves (about 1 pound total) or 8 small skinless, boneless chicken thighs

  Salt

  Pepper

  Hot cooked spinach fettuccine or plain fettuccine (optional)

  Orange peel strips (optional)

This easy glaze gives the chicken a golden color and a sweet citrus flavor.

Prep time: 5 minutes
Broiling time: 12 minutes

DIRECTIONS

1. For glaze, in a small mixing bowl stir together the orange juice concentrate, molasses, and onion powder.

2. Season chicken with salt and pepper. Place on the unheated rack of a broiler pan. Broil 4 to 5 inches from the heat for 6 minutes. Brush with some of the glaze. Turn chicken; brush with the remaining glaze. Broil for 6 to 9 minutes more or until chicken is tender and no longer pink (170°). If desired, serve with fettuccine and garnish with orange peel strips. Makes 4 servings.

For the orange peel strips, use a vegetable peeler to cut thin strips of peel from the surface of an orange. Make sure to remove only the orange part of the peel.

NUTRITION FACTS PER SERVING:

160 calories
3 g total fat
1 g saturated fat
59 mg cholesterol
56 mg sodium
10 g carbohydrate
0 g fiber
22 g protein

Thyme Chicken Marsala

For a party meal, accompany this elegant chicken entrée with a loaf of crusty French bread and your favorite dessert.

INGREDIENTS

- 2 medium skinless, boneless chicken breast halves (about ½ pound total)
- 1 tablespoon all-purpose flour
- 2 tablespoons olive oil
- 1 medium carrot, cut into thin bite-size strips
- 1 small red or yellow sweet pepper, cut into thin bite-size strips
- 1 teaspoon bottled minced garlic or 2 cloves garlic, minced
- ¼ teaspoon salt
- ¼ teaspoon ground black pepper
- ⅓ cup dry marsala
- 1 tablespoon snipped fresh thyme or ¼ teaspoon dried thyme, crushed
- Hot cooked linguine or other pasta (optional)

Marsala is a rich Sicilian wine that is available in both sweet and dry varieties. Sweet marsala makes a delicious after-dinner wine and dry marsala often is served as an aperitif or used in dishes such as this chicken entrée.

Prep time: 15 minutes
Cooking time: 13 minutes

DIRECTIONS

1. Place each chicken piece, boned side up, between 2 sheets of plastic wrap. Working from the center to the edges, pound lightly with the flat side of a meat mallet to ¼-inch thickness. Remove plastic wrap. Coat breasts lightly with the flour; shake off excess. Set aside.

2. In a large skillet heat 1 tablespoon of the oil. Add the carrot strips and cook for 3 minutes. Add the pepper strips, garlic, salt, and black pepper to the skillet. Cook and stir about 5 minutes or until crisp-tender. Arrange on 2 dinner plates. Cover and keep warm.

3. In the same skillet heat the remaining oil over medium heat. Add the chicken and cook for 4 to 6 minutes or until chicken is tender and no longer pink, turning once. Place chicken

on top of vegetables.

4. Add the marsala and thyme to the skillet. Cook and stir for 1 minute, scraping up any browned bits from skillet. Pour mixture over chicken. If desired, serve with linguine or other pasta. Makes 2 servings.

NUTRITION FACTS PER SERVING:

311 calories
17 g total fat
3 g saturated fat
59 mg cholesterol
350 mg sodium
10 g carbohydrate
2 g fiber
23 g protein

Chicken With Grapes

For a delicious dinner entrée, begin with fruit juice plus a few simple ingredients. Red and green grapes add a light sweetness and a pretty color.

INGREDIENTS

- Nonstick cooking spray
- 4 small skinless, boneless chicken breast halves (about 12 ounces total)
- ½ cup white grape juice, apple juice, or apple cider
- 1 teaspoon instant chicken bouillon granules
- 1 teaspoon cornstarch
- 1 cup seedless green and/or red grapes, halved
- Hot cooked linguine (optional)
- Fresh herb, such as oregano or thyme (optional)

Start to finish: 20 minutes

DIRECTIONS

1. Coat an unheated large skillet with cooking spray. Preheat over medium to medium-high heat. Add chicken. Cook chicken for 8 to 10 minutes or until tender and no longer pink (170°), turning to brown evenly. Remove chicken from skillet; keep warm.

2. Combine the grape or apple juice or cider, chicken bouillon granules, and cornstarch. Add to the skillet. Cook and stir until thickened and bubbly. Cook and stir for 2 minutes more. Stir in the halved grapes; heat through. Serve the sauce over chicken. If desired, serve chicken with hot cooked linguine and garnish with fresh herb. Makes 4 servings.

NUTRITION FACTS PER SERVING:

143 calories
3 g total fat
1 g saturated fat
45 mg cholesterol
258 mg sodium
13 g carbohydrate
0 g fiber
17 g protein

Rosemary Chicken

You may have to fend off the neighbors once they get a whiff of this aromatic grilled chicken. Better yet, invite them to join your family for a backyard picnic.

INGREDIENTS

2 to 2½ pounds meaty chicken pieces (breasts, thighs, and drumsticks)

½ cup dry white wine

2 tablespoons olive oil

4 cloves garlic, minced

4 teaspoons snipped fresh rosemary

1 tablespoon finely shredded lemon peel

¼ teaspoon salt

¼ teaspoon pepper

Fresh rosemary (optional)

Prep time: 15 minutes
Marinating time: 6 hours
Grilling time: 35 minutes

DIRECTIONS

1. If desired, skin chicken. Place chicken in a plastic bag set in a shallow dish.

2. For marinade, in a blender container or food processor bowl combine wine, oil, garlic, snipped rosemary, lemon peel, salt, and pepper. Cover and blend or process about 15 seconds or until well combined. Pour over chicken. Close bag. Marinate in the refrigerator for 6 hours or overnight, turning bag occasionally.

3. Drain chicken, reserving marinade. Place the chicken, bone side up, on the rack of an uncovered grill directly over medium coals. Grill for 35 to 45 minutes or until chicken is tender and no longer pink (170° for breasts; 180° for thighs and drumsticks), turning and brushing once with marinade halfway through grilling.

4. Discard any remaining marinade. Transfer chicken to a serving platter. If desired, garnish with additional rosemary. Makes 6 servings.

NUTRITION FACTS PER SERVING:

192 calories
10 g total fat
3 g saturated fat
69 mg cholesterol
93 mg sodium
0 g carbohydrate
0 g fiber
22 g protein

INGREDIENTS

Nonstick cooking spray

4 chicken thighs, skinned

    (about 1½ pounds total)

1 cup chopped onion

¾ cup chopped carrot

¾ cup water

½ cup pearl barley

1 teaspoon instant chicken

    bouillon granules

1 clove garlic, minced

½ teaspoon poultry seasoning

2 tablespoons snipped fresh

    parsley

Chicken and Barley Bake

Replace your high-fat chicken noodle casserole with this updated one-dish meal. It's low in calories and fat, and it's economical, too. Barley supplies more fiber than noodles or rice.

NUTRITION FACTS PER SERVING:

219 calories

7 g total fat

2 g saturated fat

49 mg cholesterol

284 mg sodium

23 g carbohydrate

5 g fiber

17 g protein

Prep time: 20 minutes

Baking time: 1 hour

Standing time: 10 minutes

DIRECTIONS

1. Coat an unheated large skillet with cooking spray. Preheat over medium heat. Add chicken and cook for 10 minutes, turning to brown evenly. Remove the chicken from skillet.

2. In the same skillet combine the onion, carrot, water, barley, bouillon granules, garlic, and poultry seasoning. Bring to boiling.

3. Pour hot barley mixture into a 1½-quart casserole. Arrange the chicken thighs on top of mixture.

4. Bake, covered, in a 350° oven about 1 hour or

until barley and chicken are tender and chicken is no longer pink (180°). Let stand, covered, for 10 minutes before serving. Sprinkle with parsley. Makes 4 servings.

Pearl barley is the most readily available form of the cereal grain barley. It has the outer hull removed and has been polished or "pearled." Pearl barley is sold in regular and quick-cooking forms; be sure to use the regular barley for this recipe.

Chicken with Golden Raisins And Pine Nuts

Pine nuts, also called pignoli, are frequently used in Italian pasta sauces, pesto, rice dishes, and cookies.

INGREDIENTS

1   medium onion, cut into thin slivers

2   cloves garlic, minced

1   tablespoon olive oil

1½   pounds meaty chicken pieces (breasts, thighs, and drumsticks), skinned

½   cup white wine vinegar

¼   teaspoon salt

⅛   teaspoon pepper

1   cup reduced-sodium chicken broth

½   cup golden raisins

2   teaspoons snipped fresh thyme or ½ teaspoon dried thyme, crushed

1   teaspoon snipped fresh rosemary or ¼ teaspoon dried rosemary, crushed

1   tablespoon cold water

1½   teaspoons cornstarch

2   tablespoons pine nuts, toasted Fresh rosemary (optional)

To prevent pine nuts from turning rancid quickly at room temperature, refrigerate the nuts in an airtight container for up to 2 months or freeze them for up to 6 months.

Prep time: 20 minutes
Cooking time: 45 minutes

DIRECTIONS

1. In a large nonstick skillet cook onion and garlic in hot oil over medium heat for 1 minute. Add chicken pieces to skillet and cook for 10 to 15 minutes or until lightly browned, turning to brown evenly. Drain well.

2. Add the vinegar, salt, and pepper to skillet. Bring to boiling. Cook, uncovered, over high heat about 5 minutes or until vinegar is nearly evaporated, turning chicken once. Carefully add broth, raisins, thyme, and rosemary to the skillet. Bring to boiling; reduce heat. Simmer, covered, for 30 to 35 minutes or until chicken is tender and no longer pink (170° for breasts; 180° for thighs and drumsticks).

3. To serve, transfer the chicken to a serving platter. Combine cold water and cornstarch. Add to skillet. Cook and stir until thickened and bubbly. Cook and stir for 2 minutes more. Spoon some of the sauce over chicken; pass remainder. Sprinkle chicken with pine nuts. If desired, garnish with additional fresh rosemary. Makes 4 servings.

NUTRITION FACTS PER SERVING:

269 calories
10 g total fat
2 g saturated fat
71 mg cholesterol
334 mg sodium
22 g carbohydrate
1 g fiber
24 g protein

Chicken and Pasta Primavera

Here's a homespun dish that should appeal to your whole family. You can use spaghetti or any fun-shaped pasta.

INGREDIENTS

- 2 to 2½ pounds meaty chicken pieces (breasts, thighs, and drumsticks)
- 4 cups vegetables, peeled, trimmed, and cut into 1-inch pieces (carrots, celery, zucchini, and/or yellow summer squash)
- 1 medium onion, cut into wedges
- 2 tablespoons Dijon-style mustard
- 1 tablespoon olive oil
- 2 large cloves garlic, minced
- 1 teaspoon dried oregano, crushed
- ½ teaspoon dried thyme, crushed
- ½ teaspoon celery salt
- ¼ teaspoon pepper
- ⅛ teaspoon salt
- 6 ounces packaged dried spaghetti, linguine, or farfalle (bow ties)
- Freshly shredded Parmesan cheese (optional)

Prep time: 20 minutes
Baking time: 1 hour

DIRECTIONS

1. If desired, skin chicken. Set aside.

2. In a 13×9×2-inch baking pan combine vegetables and onion. In a bowl stir together mustard and oil. Drizzle about 2 tablespoons of the oil mixture over vegetables. Sprinkle with garlic, oregano, thyme, celery salt, pepper, and salt. Toss to coat.

3. Arrange the chicken pieces, bone sides down, on top of vegetables. Brush chicken with the remaining mustard mixture.

4. Bake, uncovered, in a 350° oven about 1 hour or until chicken is tender and no longer pink (170° for breasts; 180° for thighs and drumsticks). Just before removing chicken from the oven, cook pasta according to package directions. Drain well. Transfer the chicken to a serving platter; cover and keep warm.

5. In a large serving bowl combine the pasta and the vegetables and juices from the pan, tossing to combine. If desired, sprinkle with Parmesan cheese. Serve pasta and vegetable mixture with chicken. Makes 6 servings.

To retain the full flavor of pasta, just cook it enough to maintain a firm texture. This texture is sometimes described as chewy or al dente.

NUTRITION FACTS PER SERVING:

329 calories
12 g total fat
3 g saturated fat
69 mg cholesterol
410 mg sodium
27 g carbohydrate
2 g fiber
27 g protein

Herb Roasted Chicken

The best way to cut back on fat and calories with poultry is to remove the skin. However, leaving the skin on during roasting helps keep the meat moist. Simply remove the skin when carving or leave it on your plate.

INGREDIENTS

¼ cup snipped fresh herbs (such as basil, rosemary, marjoram, or sage) or 4 teaspoons dried mixed herbs, crushed

¼ teaspoon salt

¼ teaspoon pepper

1 3-pound whole broiler-fryer chicken

2 cups ½-inch-long carrot pieces

1 cup pearl onions, peeled

2 teaspoons olive oil

1 10-ounce package frozen peas, thawed

Fresh rosemary (optional)

Prep time: 20 minutes
Roasting time: 1¼ hours

DIRECTIONS

1. For herb rub, combine the herbs, salt, and pepper. Rinse chicken; pat dry with paper towels. Loosen skin on chicken breast. Using your fingers, carefully spread half of the herb rub under the skin. Skewer neck skin to back; tie legs to tail. Twist wings under back.

2. Place chicken, breast side up, on a rack in a shallow roasting pan. If desired, insert a meat thermometer into center of an inside thigh muscle. Roast, uncovered, in a 375° oven for 30 minutes.

3. In a 1½-quart casserole combine carrots and onions. Toss with the remaining herb rub and the olive oil. Cover; place in oven. Roast about 45 minutes more or until chicken is no longer pink, juices run clear (the meat thermometer, if using, should register 180°), and vegetables are tender, adding peas to the casserole the last 15 minutes of roasting. If desired, garnish with fresh rosemary. Makes 6 servings.

NUTRITION FACTS PER SERVING:

293 calories
14 g total fat
4 g saturated fat
79 mg cholesterol
230 mg sodium
13 g carbohydrate
4 g fiber
27 g protein

INGREDIENTS

⅓ cup bottled hoisin sauce

1 to 1½ teaspoons five-spice
      powder

   Orange juice

1 1½- to 2-pound hot deli-cooked
      rotisserie chicken

2 3-ounce packages ramen noodles

   Fresh red chile peppers, sliced
      (optional)

   Steamed pea pods (optional)

   Orange slices (optional)

Five-Spice Chicken

The skin of this chicken should have a dark, lacquered look and give off a rich, spicy aroma.

Prep time: 15 minutes
Baking time: 15 minutes

DIRECTIONS

1. In a small bowl stir together the hoisin sauce, five-spice powder, and enough orange juice (1 to 2 tablespoons) to thin mixture for brushing. Brush about half of the mixture over entire chicken. Place chicken on a rack in a shallow roasting pan.

2. Bake, uncovered, in a 400° oven for 15 to 18 minutes or until heated through and glazed. Stir 1 to 2 tablespoons additional orange juice into remaining hoisin mixture until easy to drizzle. Place in a small saucepan; heat through.

3. Discard seasoning packets from ramen noodles. Cook and drain noodles according to package directions.

4. To serve, carve the chicken. Arrange chicken slices and ramen noodles on 4 dinner plates. Spoon half of the sauce over the chicken; pass the remaining sauce. If desired, garnish with fresh chile peppers. If desired, serve with pea pods and orange slices. Makes 4 servings.

NUTRITION FACTS PER SERVING:

317 calories
16 g total fat
4 g saturated fat
125 mg cholesterol
926 mg sodium
20 g carbohydrate
1 g fiber
24 g protein

You can find five-spice powder in
Asian specialty stores or most supermarkets. Or to prepare your own, in a spice grinder or blender combine 3 tablespoons ground cinnamon, 6 star anise or 2 teaspoons anise seed, 1½ teaspoons fennel seed, 1½ teaspoons whole Szechwan peppers or whole black peppercorns, and ¾ teaspoon ground cloves. Cover and grind spices to a fine powder. Store in a tightly covered container for up to 2 months. Makes about ¼ cup.

Fruit and Chicken Kabobs

Bring the fresh style and bold flavors of the Caribbean to your backyard grill with these easy fruit-and-chicken kabobs, steeped in a sweet-and-fiery marinade.

INGREDIENTS

- 1 pound skinless, boneless chicken breast halves
- 3 tablespoons reduced-sodium soy sauce
- 4 teaspoons honey
- 4 teaspoons red wine vinegar
- ½ teaspoon curry powder
- ½ teaspoon ground allspice
- ¼ teaspoon bottled hot pepper sauce
- 1 medium red onion, cut into 1-inch wedges
- 1 nectarine, pitted and cut into 1-inch pieces, or 1 papaya, peeled, seeded, and cut into 1-inch pieces
- 2 cups hot cooked rice
- Snipped fresh parsley

Prep time: 30 minutes
Marinating time: 4 hours
Grilling time: 12 minutes

DIRECTIONS

1. Cut chicken into 1-inch pieces. Place chicken pieces in a plastic bag set in a shallow dish.

2. For marinade, in a small bowl stir together soy sauce, honey, vinegar, curry powder, allspice, and hot pepper sauce. Pour over chicken. Close bag. Marinate in the refrigerator for 4 hours, turning bag occasionally. Drain chicken, reserving the marinade.

3. In a saucepan cook the onion in a small amount of boiling water for 3 minutes; drain. On eight 6-inch metal skewers, alternately thread the chicken, nectarine or papaya pieces, and partially cooked onion.

4. Grill kabobs on the rack of an uncovered grill directly over medium coals for 12 to 14 minutes or until chicken is tender and no longer pink, turning skewers occasionally. Place marinade in a small saucepan. Bring to boiling. Boil gently, uncovered, for 1 minute. Pour marinade through a strainer, reserving the liquid.

5. Before serving, brush kabobs with the strained marinade. Serve kabobs with hot cooked rice tossed with parsley. Pass any remaining marinade. Makes 4 servings.

NUTRITION FACTS PER SERVING:

374 calories
4 g total fat
1 g saturated fat
59 mg cholesterol
462 mg sodium
54 g carbohydrate
9 g fiber
30 g protein

INGREDIENTS

- 12 ounces skinless, boneless chicken breast halves
- ¼ cup orange juice
- 2 tablespoons reduced-sodium soy sauce
- 2 teaspoons rice vinegar
- 1 teaspoon ground ginger
- 1 teaspoon toasted sesame oil
- ⅛ teaspoon crushed red pepper
- 2 teaspoons cornstarch
- 6 8-inch flour tortillas
- Nonstick cooking spray
- 2 small carrots, cut into bite-size strips
- 1 cup sliced fresh mushrooms
- ½ cup thinly sliced green onions
- ½ cup sliced bamboo shoots
- 1 to 2 teaspoons cooking oil
- 2 cups shredded leaf lettuce
- ¼ cup sweet-and-sour duck sauce

Moo Shu Chicken

Flour tortillas make an easy substitute for the pancake wrappers traditionally used in this Chinese-style burrito. If you like, use hoisin sauce in place of the duck sauce.

Prep time: 15 minutes
Marinating time: 1 hour
Cooking time: 7 minutes

DIRECTIONS

1. Cut chicken into bite-size strips. Place chicken in a plastic bag set in a deep bowl. For marinade, in a small bowl combine orange juice, soy sauce, vinegar, ginger, sesame oil, and red pepper. Pour over chicken. Close bag. Marinate in refrigerator for 1 to 2 hours, turning bag frequently. Drain chicken, reserving marinade. Stir the cornstarch into reserved marinade. Set aside.

2. Wrap tortillas in foil. Heat in a 350° oven for 10 minutes. Meanwhile, coat an unheated large nonstick skillet with cooking spray. Preheat over medium-high heat. Add the carrots, mushrooms, green onions, and bamboo shoots; stir-fry for 2 minutes. Remove from skillet. Add oil to hot skillet. Add chicken; stir-fry for 2 to 3 minutes or until no longer pink. Push the chicken from center of skillet. Stir sauce; add to center of skillet. Cook and stir until bubbly. Return vegetables to skillet. Add lettuce. Stir ingredients to coat; heat through.

3. To serve, spread tortillas with duck sauce. Divide chicken mixture among tortillas; fold tortillas over filling. Makes 6 servings.

NUTRITION FACTS PER SERVING:

208 calories
6 g total fat
1 g saturated fat
30 mg cholesterol
371 mg sodium
25 g carbohydrate
2 g fiber
14 g protein

Chicken Tacos

If you don't have any leftover chicken to use, buy frozen chopped cooked chicken at your supermarket.

INGREDIENTS

Nonstick cooking spray

1 cup chopped onion

1 clove garlic, minced

2 cups chopped cooked chicken

1 8-ounce can tomato sauce

1 4-ounce can diced green chile peppers, drained

12 taco shells

2 cups shredded lettuce

1 medium tomato, seeded and chopped

½ cup finely shredded reduced-fat cheddar cheese and/or Monterey Jack cheese (2 ounces)

Start to finish: 30 minutes

DIRECTIONS

1. Coat an unheated large skillet with cooking spray. Preheat over medium heat. Add the onion and garlic; cook until onion is tender.

2. Stir in the chicken, tomato sauce, and chile peppers. Heat through.

3. Divide chicken mixture among taco shells. Top with lettuce, tomato, and cheese. Makes 6 servings.

NUTRITION FACTS PER SERVING:

276 calories
12 g total fat
3 g saturated fat
52 mg cholesterol
502 mg sodium
23 g carbohydrate
2 g fiber
21 g protein

INGREDIENTS

12	ounces skinless, boneless chicken breast halves
2	beaten egg whites
1	tablespoon honey
2	cups cornflakes, crushed
¼	teaspoon pepper
¼	cup honey
4	teaspoons prepared mustard or Dijon-style mustard
¼	teaspoon garlic powder

Chicken Fingers With Honey Sauce

Serve your favorite barbecue sauce as a quick alternative to the honey sauce.

Prep time: 15 minutes
Baking time: 11 minutes

DIRECTIONS

1. Cut the chicken breast into strips about 3 inches long and ¾ inch wide.

2. In a small mixing bowl combine the egg whites and the 1 tablespoon honey. In a shallow bowl combine the cornflake crumbs and pepper. Dip chicken strips into the egg white mixture, then roll in the crumb mixture to coat.

3. Place in a single layer on an ungreased baking sheet. Bake chicken in a 450° oven for 11 to 13 minutes or until no longer pink.

4. Meanwhile, for sauce, in a small bowl stir together the ¼ cup honey, the mustard, and garlic powder. Serve with chicken. Makes 4 servings.

NUTRITION FACTS PER SERVING:

230 calories
2 g total fat
1 g saturated fat
45 mg cholesterol
275 mg sodium
31 g carbohydrate
1 g fiber
19 g protein

93

Stroganoff-Style Chicken

Chicken replaces the usual beef in this rich-tasting dish. Named after a 19th-century Russian diplomat, traditional stroganoff contains butter and sour cream. Here, low-fat sour cream helps pare down the fat and calories.

INGREDIENTS

- 12 ounces skinless, boneless chicken breast halves
- Nonstick cooking spray
- 2 cups sliced fresh mushrooms
- ½ cup chopped onion
- 2 teaspoons cooking oil (optional)
- 1 8-ounce carton light dairy sour cream
- 2 tablespoons all-purpose flour
- 1 teaspoon paprika
- ¼ teaspoon salt
- ½ cup reduced-sodium chicken broth
- 3¾ cups hot cooked noodles

Start to finish: 25 minutes

DIRECTIONS

1. Cut chicken into 1-inch pieces. Coat an unheated large skillet with cooking spray. Preheat over medium heat. Add the mushrooms and onion; cook until onion is nearly tender.

2. If needed, add the oil to skillet. Add the chicken pieces and cook for 3 to 4 minutes or until chicken is tender and no longer pink.

3. In a small bowl stir together the sour cream, flour, paprika, and salt; stir in chicken broth. Add to skillet. Cook and stir until slightly thickened and bubbly. Cook and stir for 1 minute more. Serve over hot cooked noodles. Makes 5 servings.

NUTRITION FACTS PER SERVING:

308 calories
7 g total fat
2 g saturated fat
79 mg cholesterol
257 mg sodium
39 g carbohydrate
3 g fiber
23 g protein

INGREDIENTS

1 **pound fresh tomatillos, husked and chopped, or one 18-ounce can tomatillos, rinsed, drained, and cut up**	**Nonstick cooking spray**
1½ **cups chopped onion**	⅔ **cup low-sodium tomato juice**
¼ **cup firmly packed fresh cilantro leaves or fresh parsley sprigs**	12 **6-inch corn tortillas**
1 **4-ounce can diced green chile peppers, drained**	⅔ **cup shredded reduced-fat Monterey Jack cheese**
¼ **teaspoon ground cumin**	
¼ **teaspoon pepper**	
1 **cup chopped tomato**	
3 **cups shredded cooked chicken or turkey (1 pound)**	

Green-and-Red Chicken Enchiladas

Although tomatillos are not related to tomatoes, their texture is like that of a firm tomato (with lots of seeds) and their flavor is rather acidic with hints of lemon and apple. Look for firm tomatillos with tight-fitting, dry husks.

Prep time: 25 minutes
Baking time: 35 minutes

DIRECTIONS

1. In a blender container or food processor bowl combine the tomatillos, 1 cup of the onion, the cilantro or parsley, chile peppers, cumin, and pepper. Cover and blend or process until pureed. Set the mixture aside.

2. In a nonstick skillet cook tomato and the remaining onion for 3 minutes. Stir in chicken and 1 cup of the tomatillo mixture; heat through. Coat a 3-quart rectangular baking dish with cooking spray. Set aside.

3. To assemble enchiladas, pour the tomato juice into a shallow dish. Dip a tortilla in tomato juice, coating both sides. Place tortilla on a work surface. Spoon about 3 tablespoons of the chicken mixture down center of tortilla; roll up. Place, seam side down, in prepared baking dish. Repeat with remaining juice, tortillas, and chicken mixture. Spoon the remaining tomatillo mixture over the enchiladas.

4. Bake, covered, in a 350° oven about 30 minutes or until heated through. Sprinkle with cheese; bake about 5 minutes more or until the cheese melts. Makes 6 servings.

NUTRITION FACTS PER SERVING:

375 calories
13 g total fat
4 g saturated fat
67 mg cholesterol
313 mg sodium
35 g carbohydrate
2 g fiber
30 g protein

95

Quick Chicken Fajitas

Splurge by offering sour cream, guacamole, and chopped fresh jalapeño peppers—in addition to salsa—as toppers for the fajitas.

INGREDIENTS

8   7-inch flour tortillas
1   tablespoon lime juice or lemon juice
½   teaspoon ground cumin
½   teaspoon ground coriander
¼   teaspoon dried oregano, crushed
¾   pound skinless, boneless chicken breast halves or turkey breast tenderloin, thinly sliced into bite-size pieces
¼   cup clear Italian salad dressing (not reduced-oil dressing)
1   small red and/or green sweet pepper, cut into strips
1   small onion, halved and sliced
¼   cup frozen guacamole dip, thawed (optional)
    Salsa

After a Tex-Mex meal, serve Almost-Fried Ice Cream:
Scoop your favorite ice cream into a shallow pan and place the balls, covered, in the freezer until firm. Stir together 1½ cups almond cluster multigrain cereal, coarsely crushed, and 2 teaspoons melted margarine. Roll ice cream scoops in cereal mixture; return to freezer until ready to serve. To serve, drizzle honey over ice cream and sprinkle with cinnamon.

Start to finish: 20 minutes

DIRECTIONS

1. Wrap tortillas in foil; heat in a 350° oven for 10 to 15 minutes or until heated through. [Or, wrap in paper towels or waxed paper and heat in a microwave oven on 100% power (high) for 15 to 20 seconds.]

2. Meanwhile, in a medium bowl combine lime juice, cumin, coriander, and oregano. Stir in chicken.

3. Pour salad dressing into a large skillet. Preheat over medium-high heat. Add chicken mixture. Stir-fry for 2 minutes. With a slotted spoon, remove chicken from skillet. Add sweet pepper and onion to skillet; stir-fry for 2 to 3 minutes or until crisp-tender. Return chicken to skillet; heat through.

4. Spoon mixture onto warm tortillas; roll up. If desired, top with guacamole dip. Top with salsa. Makes 4 servings.

NUTRITION FACTS PER SERVING:

425 calories
17 g total fat
4 g saturated fat
51 mg cholesterol
600 mg sodium
45 g carbohydrate
1 g fiber
23 g protein

INGREDIENTS

1½ cups quick-cooking rice

¾ pound skinless, boneless chicken
    breasts

2 tablespoons cooking oil

1 medium onion, chopped (½ cup)

1 to 2 teaspoons curry powder

3 tablespoons all-purpose flour

1 cup chicken broth

1 5½-ounce can tomato juice

1 11-ounce can mandarin orange
    sections, drained, or one
    8-ounce can pineapple
    tidbits, drained

½ cup raisins, chopped cashews,
    chopped peanuts, coconut,
    and/or chopped banana
    Fresh chives with flowers
    (optional)

Chicken Curry

Cooking the curry powder with the onion mellows the flavor yet retains the spiciness of this dish.

Start to finish: 20 minutes

DIRECTIONS

1. Cook rice according to package directions. Meanwhile, cut chicken into ¾-inch pieces.

2. In a large skillet heat 1 tablespoon of the oil over medium heat. Add chicken to hot oil; cook and stir for 2 to 3 minutes or until no longer pink. Remove chicken from the skillet, reserving drippings. Set aside.

3. Add the remaining oil to the reserved drippings in skillet. Cook the onion and curry powder in the oil-drippings mixture until onion is tender. Stir in flour. Stir in chicken broth and tomato juice. Cook and stir over medium heat until thickened and bubbly. Cook and stir for 1 minute more.

4. Return chicken to skillet. Gently stir in orange sections or pineapple. Cook until heated through. Serve over the hot cooked rice. Serve with raisins, cashews, peanuts, coconut, and/or banana. If desired, garnish with fresh chives. Makes 4 servings.

NUTRITION FACTS PER SERVING:

423 calories
10 g total fat
2 g saturated fat
45 mg cholesterol
385 mg sodium
62 g carbohydrate
2 g fiber
22 g protein

Mango Chicken

To complement this Caribbean-style dish, cook your rice with a bit of fresh ginger and chopped mint.

INGREDIENTS

½ cup reduced-sodium chicken broth

2 teaspoons finely shredded lime peel or orange peel

2 tablespoons lime juice

2 teaspoons brown sugar

2 teaspoons curry powder

1 teaspoon cornstarch

12 ounces skinless, boneless chicken breast halves or thighs

2 teaspoons peanut oil or cooking oil

2 cloves garlic, minced

1 cup sliced red onion

2 cups chopped, peeled mango or papaya

2 cups hot cooked rice

Lime peel strips (optional)

Start to finish: 30 minutes

DIRECTIONS

1. For sauce, in a small bowl stir together the broth, shredded lime or orange peel, lime juice, brown sugar, curry powder, and cornstarch; set aside. Cut chicken into bite-size strips; set aside.

2. In a large wok or 12-inch skillet heat oil over medium-high heat. Add garlic; stir-fry for 30 seconds. Add onion slices; stir-fry for 3 minutes. Remove onion mixture from wok. Add chicken; stir-fry for 2 to 3 minutes or until chicken is no longer pink. Push chicken from center of wok.

3. Stir sauce; add to center of wok. Cook and stir until thickened and bubbly. Return onion mixture to the wok. Add mango or papaya. Cook and stir about 2 minutes or until heated through. Serve immediately over rice. If desired, garnish with lime peel strips. Makes 4 servings.

NUTRITION FACTS PER SERVING:

301 calories
5 g total fat
1 g saturated fat
45 mg cholesterol
125 mg sodium
44 g carbohydrate
3 g fiber
20 g protein

INGREDIENTS

12 ounces skinless, boneless
   chicken breast halves

3 tablespoons reduced-sodium
   soy sauce

1 tablespoon dry sherry

¼ cup reduced-sodium
   chicken broth

1 teaspoon cornstarch

¼ teaspoon black pepper
   Nonstick cooking spray

1 medium onion, cut into wedges

1 medium green sweet pepper,
   thinly sliced

1 medium red sweet pepper,
   thinly sliced

1½ cups sliced fresh mushrooms

2 teaspoons cooking oil

1 teaspoon grated fresh ginger

½ of an 8-ounce can bamboo
   shoots, drained (about
   ½ cup)

2 cups hot cooked brown rice

Chicken and Sweet Pepper Stir-Fry

Dress up this simple stir-fry by using a variety of exotic mushrooms. Many kinds are available in larger grocery stores. Try chanterelle, shiitake (use only the caps), or straw mushrooms.

Prep time: 20 minutes
Marinating time: 30 minutes
Cooking time: 12 minutes

DIRECTIONS

1. Cut chicken into ½-inch pieces. Place the chicken in a medium bowl; stir in soy sauce and sherry. Cover and marinate at room temperature for 30 minutes. Drain the chicken, reserving marinade. Stir the chicken broth, cornstarch, and black pepper into the reserved marinade. Set aside.

2. Coat an unheated nonstick wok or large skillet with cooking spray. Preheat wok over medium-high heat. Add onion; stir-fry for 2 minutes. Add sweet peppers; stir-fry for 2 minutes. Add mushrooms; stir-fry about 2 minutes more or until vegetables are crisp-tender. Remove from wok.

3. Add the oil to hot wok. Add ginger; stir-fry for 15 seconds. Add the chicken; stir-fry for 2 to 3 minutes or until no longer pink. Push from center of wok. Stir sauce; add to center of wok. Cook and stir until slightly thickened and bubbly. Return the cooked vegetables. Add the bamboo shoots. Cook and stir for 2 minutes more. Serve immediately with rice. Makes 4 servings.

Don't overload your wok or skillet.

When too much of any item is added at once, the food stews rather than fries. Add no more than 12 ounces of poultry or meat. If your recipe calls for more, stir-fry half at a time.

NUTRITION FACTS PER SERVING:

258 calories
5 g total fat
1 g saturated fat
45 mg cholesterol
480 mg sodium
30 g carbohydrate
1 g fiber
21 g protein

99

Chicken with Peppers and Potatoes

This dish is packed with the flavor of fresh herbs and roasted sweet peppers. If you like, substitute Greek kalamata olives packed in vinegar, not oil, for the ripe olives.

INGREDIENTS

12 ounces skinless, boneless chicken breast halves

Nonstick cooking spray

2 cups diced potatoes

1 7-ounce jar roasted red sweet peppers, drained and diced

½ cup reduced-sodium chicken broth

4½ teaspoons snipped fresh basil or 1½ teaspoons dried basil, crushed

4½ teaspoons snipped fresh oregano or 1½ teaspoons dried oregano, crushed

⅛ teaspoon salt

⅛ teaspoon black pepper

2 tablespoons sliced pitted ripe olives

Fresh oregano (optional)

Start to finish: 30 minutes

DIRECTIONS

1. Cut chicken into 1-inch pieces. Coat an unheated large skillet with cooking spray. Preheat skillet over medium-high heat. Add chicken pieces. Cook and stir for 4 to 5 minutes or until tender and no longer pink. Remove chicken from skillet. Set aside.

2. Add uncooked potatoes, sweet peppers, chicken broth, basil, oregano, salt, and black pepper to the skillet. Bring to boiling; reduce heat. Simmer, covered, about 7 minutes or until potatoes are just tender.

3. Stir in the chicken and olives. Heat through. If desired, garnish with additional fresh oregano. Makes 4 servings.

NUTRITION FACTS PER SERVING:

183 calories
4 g total fat
1 g saturated fat
45 mg cholesterol
213 mg sodium
20 g carbohydrate
2 g fiber
19 g protein

INGREDIENTS

- 2 **tablespoons oyster-flavored sauce**
- 1 **tablespoon fish sauce or soy sauce**
- 1 **tablespoon brown sugar**
- 2 **teaspoons cornstarch**
- ⅓ **cup water**
- ¾ **pound skinless, boneless chicken breast halves**
- 2 **tablespoons cooking oil**
- 1 **medium onion, sliced**
- 2 **to 4 fresh red chile peppers, seeded and cut into thin strips**
- ½ **teaspoon bottled minced garlic or 1 clove garlic, minced**
- ½ **cup unsalted or lightly salted roasted cashews**
- **Hot cooked rice**

Spicy Stir-Fried Chicken with Cashews

Pick up some fortune cookies to accompany this dynamite dish. Maybe you'll get a great fortune to go along with the guaranteed great meal.

Start to finish: 25 minutes

DIRECTIONS

1. For sauce, in a small bowl stir together the oyster-flavored sauce, fish sauce or soy sauce, brown sugar, and cornstarch. Stir in water. Cut chicken into bite-size strips. Set aside.

2. Pour cooking oil into a wok or large skillet. Preheat over medium-high heat. Add onion and stir-fry 1 minute. Add chile peppers and garlic and stir-fry 1 to 2 minutes more or until onion is crisp-tender. Remove with slotted spoon and set aside.

3. Add chicken to wok. Stir-fry 2 to 3 minutes or until no longer pink. Push chicken from center of wok. Stir sauce; add to skillet. Cook and stir until thickened and bubbly. Return onion, chile peppers, and garlic to skillet. Cook and stir 1 minute more. Stir in cashews. Serve over rice. Makes 4 servings.

NUTRITION FACTS PER SERVING:

444 calories
18 g total fat
3 g saturated fat
47 mg cholesterol
549 mg sodium
48 g carbohydrate
2 g fiber
23 g protein

Chicken and Dumplings

You won't have to forego Mom's chicken and dumplings again. Skinning the chicken before you cook it keeps the calories and fat in check, making it kinder to your waistline.

INGREDIENTS

- 4 chicken thighs (about 1½ pounds total), skinned
- 2½ cups water
- 1 cup sliced carrots
- 1 cup sliced celery
- ½ cup chopped onion
- 2 teaspoons instant chicken bouillon granules
- ¾ teaspoon snipped fresh sage or ¼ teaspoon dried sage, crushed
- 2 tablespoons cold water
- 4 teaspoons cornstarch
- 1 recipe Dumplings

Prep time: 30 minutes
Cooking time: 45 minutes

DIRECTIONS

1. In a large saucepan combine chicken, the 2½ cups water, the carrots, celery, onion, bouillon granules, and sage. Bring to boiling; reduce heat. Simmer, covered, for 35 minutes.

2. Remove chicken from saucepan; set aside. Skim fat from broth.

3. Stir together the 2 tablespoons cold water and the cornstarch. Stir into broth in saucepan. Cook and stir until thickened and bubbly. Return chicken to saucepan.

4. Meanwhile, prepare the Dumplings. Drop the dumpling mixture from a tablespoon into 8 mounds directly on top of the bubbling chicken mixture. Cover tightly and simmer about 10 minutes (do not lift cover) or until a wooden toothpick inserted in a dumpling comes out clean. To serve, ladle the chicken mixture and dumplings into bowls. Makes 4 servings.

Dumplings: In a medium mixing bowl stir together 1 cup all-purpose flour, 1 tablespoon snipped fresh parsley, 2 teaspoons baking powder, and ⅛ teaspoon salt. In a small bowl combine 1 beaten egg, ¼ cup fat-free milk, and 2 tablespoons cooking oil. Stir egg mixture into the flour mixture with a fork just until moistened.

NUTRITION FACTS PER SERVING:

341 calories
14 g total fat
3 g saturated fat
103 mg cholesterol
808 mg sodium
33 g carbohydrate
3 g fiber
20 g protein

INGREDIENTS

- 4 cups reduced-sodium chicken broth
- 1 cup water
- 1 large onion, chopped
- 1 large carrot, chopped
- 4 cloves garlic, minced
- 3 bay leaves
- 4 ounces skinless, boneless chicken breast halves
- 1 teaspoon olive oil or cooking oil

- 2 ounces small dried pasta (such as rotini, ditalini, fusilli, wagon wheel or shell macaroni, and/or broken spaghetti)
- 1 tablespoon snipped fresh sage

Soup with Mixed Pastas

Finally, the perfect use for all those leftover pastas that don't add up to a meal. And because your pantry stock is ever-changing, this soup is different every time.

Start to finish: 30 minutes

DIRECTIONS

1. In a large saucepan bring chicken broth and water to boiling. Add onion, carrot, garlic, and bay leaves; reduce heat. Simmer, uncovered, for 10 minutes.

2. Meanwhile, coarsely chop chicken. In a medium skillet heat oil over medium-high heat. Add chicken; cook and stir about 2 minutes or until browned.

3. Add chicken, pasta, and sage to broth mixture. Simmer, uncovered, for 8 to 10 minutes or until the larger pieces of pasta are tender but still firm. Remove bay leaves. Makes 3 servings.

NUTRITION FACTS PER SERVING:

220 calories
6 g total fat
1 g saturated fat
20 mg cholesterol
896 mg sodium
28 g carbohydrate
2 g fiber
14 g protein

Chicken Stew With Tortellini

This one-dish, healthful stew boasts an Italian flair. Just add a tossed green salad and Italian bread to complete the meal.

INGREDIENTS

1 14-ounce can reduced-sodium chicken broth

2 cups water

6 cups torn beet or turnip greens or torn spinach

1½ cups sliced carrots

1 medium zucchini or yellow summer squash, halved lengthwise and cut into ½-inch slices

1 cup packaged dried cheese-filled tortellini

1 red or green sweet pepper, coarsely chopped

1 medium onion, cut into bite-size wedges

1 teaspoon dried basil, crushed

½ teaspoon salt-free seasoning blend

½ teaspoon dried oregano, crushed

¼ teaspoon black pepper

2 cups chopped cooked chicken
   Coarsely ground black pepper (optional)

When a recipe calls

When a recipe calls for cooked chicken, you can use a package of frozen chopped cooked chicken. Or, purchase a deli-roasted chicken. A cooked whole chicken will yield 1½ to 2 cups chopped meat. If you have more time, you can poach chicken. For 2 cups chopped cooked chicken, poach 12 ounces skinless, boneless chicken breasts for 12 to 14 minutes.

Start to finish: 45 minutes

DIRECTIONS

1. In a large kettle or Dutch oven combine the chicken broth and water. Bring to boiling. Stir in the greens or spinach, carrots, zucchini or yellow squash, tortellini, sweet pepper, onion, basil, seasoning blend, oregano, and the ¼ teaspoon black pepper. Reduce heat. Simmer, covered, about 15 minutes or until tortellini and vegetables are nearly tender.

2. Stir in cooked chicken. Cook, covered, about 5 minutes more or until tortellini and vegetables are tender. If desired, sprinkle with coarsely ground black pepper. Makes 6 servings.

NUTRITION FACTS PER SERVING:

234 calories
6 g total fat
1 g saturated fat
45 mg cholesterol
530 mg sodium
22 g carbohydrate
3 g fiber
22 g protein

Asian Chicken Noodle Soup

INGREDIENTS

2 14-ounce cans chicken broth

1 cup water

¾ cup dried fine egg noodles

1 tablespoon soy sauce

1 teaspoon grated fresh ginger

⅛ teaspoon crushed red pepper

1 medium red sweet pepper, cut
   into ¾-inch pieces

1 medium carrot, chopped

⅓ cup thinly sliced green onions

1 cup chopped cooked chicken or
   turkey (5 ounces)

1 cup fresh pea pods, halved
   crosswise, or ½ of a 6-ounce
   package frozen pea pods,
   thawed and halved crosswise

Chicken soup is known universally as a comforting cure-all for the body and soul. Soy sauce, ginger, and pea pods add an Asian flair to this version of a classic favorite.

Start to finish: 20 minutes

DIRECTIONS

1. In a large saucepan combine chicken broth, water, noodles, soy sauce, ginger, and crushed red pepper. Bring to boiling. Stir in the sweet pepper, carrot, and green onions. Return to boiling; reduce heat. Simmer, covered, for 4 to 6 minutes or until vegetables are crisp-tender and noodles are tender.

2. Stir in chicken and pea pods. Simmer, uncovered, for 1 to 2 minutes more or until pea pods are crisp-tender. Makes 3 servings.

NUTRITION FACTS PER SERVING:

224 calories
6 g total fat
2 g saturated fat
58 mg cholesterol
1,280 mg sodium
17 g carbohydrate
2 g fiber
24 g protein

Chicken Noodle Soup Florentine

Look in the supermarket's spice section for fines herbes—an herb blend most commonly containing chervil, chives, parsley, and tarragon.

INGREDIENTS

1 49-ounce can chicken broth

8 ounces fresh mushrooms, sliced (about 3 cups)

8 green onions, sliced (1 cup)

1½ teaspoons dried fines herbes, crushed

¼ teaspoon pepper

2½ cups packaged dried medium noodles (5 ounces)

1 9-ounce package frozen diced cooked chicken (about 2 cups)

3 cups chopped fresh spinach or half of a 10-ounce package frozen chopped spinach

While the soup simmers, prepare and bake a brownie mix according to package directions. Immediately sprinkle the hot brownies with almond brickle pieces and semisweet chocolate pieces. Cool brownies completely.

Prep time: 15 minutes
Cooking time: 7 minutes

DIRECTIONS

1. In a 4½-quart kettle or Dutch oven combine chicken broth, mushrooms, green onions, fines herbes, and pepper. Bring to boiling; add noodles. Cook and stir until the mixture returns to boiling; reduce heat.

2. Cover and boil gently for 7 to 9 minutes or until noodles are tender (do not overcook). Add chicken and spinach to soup; heat through. Makes 6 servings.

Note: You can freeze half of the soup in a covered container for another meal. To reheat frozen soup, place in a medium saucepan over medium heat. Cover and heat through for 20 to 25 minutes, stirring occasionally.

NUTRITION FACTS PER SERVING:

222 calories
6 g total fat
1 g saturated fat
59 mg cholesterol
866 mg sodium
20 g carbohydrate
1 g fiber
22 g protein

INGREDIENTS

1½ cups small broccoli florets	1½ teaspoons instant chicken
1 cup sliced fresh mushrooms	bouillon granules
½ cup shredded carrot	1½ cups chopped cooked chicken
¼ cup chopped onion	or turkey
¼ cup margarine or butter	
¼ cup all-purpose flour	
1½ teaspoons snipped fresh basil	
or ½ teaspoon dried basil,	
crushed	
¼ teaspoon pepper	
3 cups milk	
1 cup half-and-half or light cream	
1 tablespoon white wine	
Worcestershire sauce	

Creamy Broccoli-Chicken Soup

This incredibly creamy soup is packed with vegetables, poultry, and just the right amount of seasoning.

Start to finish: 20 minutes

DIRECTIONS

1. In a medium saucepan cook and stir broccoli, mushrooms, carrot, and onion in hot margarine or butter for 6 to 8 minutes or until vegetables are tender.

2. Stir in flour, basil, and pepper. Add milk and half-and-half or light cream all at once; add Worcestershire sauce and bouillon granules. Cook and stir until thickened and bubbly. Stir in chicken or turkey; heat through. Makes 4 servings.

NUTRITION FACTS PER SERVING:

435 calories
26 g total fat
10 g saturated fat
86 mg cholesterol
675 mg sodium
23 g carbohydrate
2 g fiber
27 g protein

This hearty soup is an ideal way to use up leftover chicken or turkey. But if you don't have any on hand, purchase roasted chicken from your supermarket's deli section. Or, look in the freezer case for frozen chopped cooked chicken. If you prefer to cook your own, simmer skinless, boneless chicken breasts in water for 12 to 14 minutes or until tender and no longer pink. Plan that ¾ pound boneless breasts will give you about 1½ cups cooked chicken.

Fruit and Chicken Salad

Frozen juice concentrate is an ideal ingredient for making low-fat dressings. Because concentrate delivers a lot of punch in a small amount, you don't need to use much. Here, concentrate also lends body to the dressing.

½ cup fat-free dairy sour cream

½ cup fat-free mayonnaise dressing or salad dressing

1 tablespoon frozen orange juice concentrate, thawed

⅛ teaspoon ground ginger

Dash ground red pepper

3 green onions, sliced

2 cups thinly sliced celery

1½ cups seedless red or green grapes, halved

1½ cups chopped cooked chicken

½ cup dried apricots, cut into slivers

4 lettuce leaves

2 plum tomatoes, thinly sliced

1 cucumber, thinly sliced

Cut dried apricots easily

by using kitchen scissors or a sharp knife that has been coated with nonstick cooking spray. This keeps the fruit from sticking.

Prep time: 25 minutes

Chilling time: 2 hours

DIRECTIONS

1. For dressing, stir together the sour cream, mayonnaise dressing or salad dressing, orange juice concentrate, ginger, and red pepper. Stir in green onions.

2. In a large bowl toss together the celery, grapes, chicken, and apricots. Stir in the dressing. Cover and chill for 2 to 4 hours.

3. To serve, line 4 plates with lettuce leaves. Arrange the tomatoes and cucumber on top of lettuce. Top with the chicken mixture. Makes 4 servings.

NUTRITION FACTS PER SERVING:

264 calories
3 g total fat
1 g saturated fat
44 mg cholesterol
511 mg sodium
40 g carbohydrate
5 g fiber
21 g protein

INGREDIENTS

- 10 cups torn romaine
- 1 15-ounce can black beans, rinsed and drained
- 1½ cups chopped cooked chicken or turkey (about 8 ounces)
- 1½ cups red and/or yellow cherry tomatoes, halved
- ½ cup bottled reduced-calorie Caesar salad dressing
- 2 teaspoons chili powder
- ½ teaspoon ground cumin
- ½ cup broken tortilla chips
- 2 tablespoons snipped fresh cilantro or parsley
- Fresh cilantro sprigs (optional)

Southwestern Chicken and Black Bean Salad

Fusion cooking conquers two continents in this global collaboration of Caesar dressing and a Mexican ingredient list of black beans, tortilla chips, chili powder, and cilantro.

Start to finish: 25 minutes

DIRECTIONS

1. In a large bowl combine the romaine, black beans, chicken, and tomatoes.

2. For dressing, in a small bowl whisk together salad dressing, chili powder, and cumin. Pour dressing over salad; toss gently to coat. Sprinkle with tortilla chips and snipped cilantro. If desired, garnish with cilantro sprigs. Makes 4 servings.

NUTRITION FACTS PER SERVING:

295 calories
10 g total fat
1 g saturated fat
55 mg cholesterol
913 mg sodium
26 g carbohydrate
9 g fiber
27 g protein

Citrusy Chicken Salad

Brown-skinned jicama tastes like a cross between an apple and a water chestnut. Long used in Mexican cooking, it traverses the globe to add snap to a bright-colored, cumin-flavored salad with Mediterranean credentials.

INGREDIENTS

- ⅓ cup frozen orange juice concentrate, thawed
- ¼ cup olive oil
- 2 to 3 tablespoons white wine vinegar or white vinegar
- 1 teaspoon ground cumin
- ⅛ teaspoon ground red pepper
- 4 cups torn mixed salad greens
- 10 ounces cooked chicken or turkey, cut into bite-size pieces (2 cups)
- 2 medium oranges, peeled and sectioned
- 1 cup jicama cut into thin bite-size strips
- 1 medium red sweet pepper, cut into rings

Start to finish: 25 minutes

DIRECTIONS

1. For dressing, in a small bowl stir together the orange juice concentrate, olive oil, vinegar, cumin, and ground red pepper. Set aside.

2. In a large salad bowl toss together the salad greens, chicken, oranges, jicama, and sweet pepper. Pour dressing over salad; toss gently to coat. Makes 4 servings.

NUTRITION FACTS PER SERVING:

348 calories
20 g total fat
3 g saturated fat
68 mg cholesterol
73 mg sodium
20 g carbohydrate
2 g fiber
24 g protein

Dilled Chicken and Potato Salad

INGREDIENTS

- 1 pound whole tiny new potatoes, quartered
- 12 ounces skinless, boneless chicken breast halves
- 1 tablespoon olive oil or cooking oil
- 1 cup sliced celery
- 1 cup chopped green sweet pepper
- ½ cup fat-free Italian salad dressing
- 2 tablespoons snipped fresh dill
- 1 tablespoon Dijon-style mustard
- 2 large tomatoes, halved lengthwise and sliced
- 1 medium cucumber, thinly sliced
- Fresh dill (optional)

No time to cook the chicken? Use chopped roasted chicken from the deli instead.

Start to finish: 30 minutes

DIRECTIONS

1. In a covered saucepan cook potatoes in boiling lightly salted water for 6 to 8 minutes or until tender; drain.

2. Meanwhile, cut the chicken pieces into bite-size strips. In a large skillet cook the chicken strips in hot oil over medium-high heat for 2 to 3 minutes or until tender and no longer pink. Remove from skillet.

3. In a large bowl combine the potatoes, chicken, celery, and sweet pepper. Toss gently. In a small bowl stir together the salad dressing, snipped dill, and mustard. Drizzle over chicken mixture, tossing gently to coat.

4. Arrange sliced tomatoes and cucumber on 4 plates. Spoon the chicken mixture over tomatoes and cucumber. If desired, garnish with additional fresh dill. Makes 4 servings.

NUTRITION FACTS PER SERVING:

283 calories
7 g total fat
1 g saturated fat
45 mg cholesterol
597 mg sodium
36 g carbohydrate
4 g fiber
20 g protein

111

Stuffed Turkey Tenderloins

There's more than one way to stuff a turkey. Tender spinach and tangy goat cheese make a melt-in-your-mouth filling in these turkey tenderloins. When sliced, the rosy-red, spicy crust on the meat yields to a juicy, tender interior.

INGREDIENTS

- 2 8-ounce turkey breast tenderloins
- 2 cups chopped spinach leaves
- 3 ounces semisoft goat cheese (chèvre) or feta cheese, crumbled (about ¾ cup)
- ½ teaspoon black pepper
- 1 tablespoon olive oil
- 1 teaspoon paprika
- ½ teaspoon salt
- ⅛ to ¼ teaspoon ground red pepper

Prep time: 15 minutes
Grilling time: 16 minutes

DIRECTIONS

1. Make a pocket in each turkey tenderloin by cutting lengthwise from one side almost to, but not through, the opposite side; set aside. In a bowl combine the spinach, cheese, and black pepper. Spoon the spinach mixture into pockets. Tie 100% cotton kitchen string around each tenderloin in 3 or 4 places to hold in the stuffing.

2. In a small bowl combine the oil, paprika, salt, and ground red pepper; brush evenly over tenderloins.

3. Grill on the lightly greased rack of an uncovered grill directly over medium coals for 16 to 20 minutes or until turkey is tender and no longer pink in the center of the thickest part (170°), turning once halfway through cooking. Remove strings; slice tenderloins crosswise. Makes 4 servings.

NUTRITION FACTS PER SERVING:

220 calories
12 g total fat
4 g saturated fat
68 mg cholesterol
458 mg sodium
1 g carbohydrate
1 g fiber
26 g protein

INGREDIENTS

Nonstick cooking spray

4 turkey breast tenderloin steaks

(about 1 pound total)

2 cloves garlic, minced

½ cup reduced-sodium

chicken broth

¼ cup dry Marsala or dry sherry

1 tablespoon lemon juice

½ teaspoon salt-free

seasoning blend

⅛ teaspoon pepper

2 tablespoons snipped

fresh parsley

Steamed thinly sliced carrots

and zucchini (optional)

Turkey Marsala

For an alternative idea, try this dish with thinly sliced pork tenderloin or pounded boneless chicken breasts.

Start to finish: 20 minutes

DIRECTIONS

1. Coat an unheated large skillet with cooking spray. Preheat skillet over medium-high heat. Add the turkey steaks and garlic; cook for 8 to 10 minutes or until the turkey is tender and no longer pink (170°), turning once. Transfer turkey steaks to a serving platter; cover and keep warm.

2. For sauce, in the same skillet stir together the chicken broth, Marsala or sherry, lemon juice, seasoning blend, and pepper. Bring to boiling. Boil gently, uncovered, about 4 minutes or until reduced to ¼ cup liquid. Stir in parsley. Spoon sauce over turkey. If desired, serve over steamed carrots and zucchini. Makes 4 servings.

NUTRITION FACTS PER SERVING:

139 calories
3 g total fat
1 g saturated fat
50 mg cholesterol
56 mg sodium
2 g carbohydrate
0 g fiber
22 g protein

To accompany the turkey with thin ribbons of carrots and zucchini, use a vegetable peeler to make lengthwise slices down the vegetables. Steam the slices briefly just until crisp-tender.

Spinach-Stuffed Turkey Breast

A turkey breast allows you to enjoy the flavor of roast turkey without days of leftovers. This elegant recipe features a spinach and cheese stuffing.

INGREDIENTS

1   2½- to 3½-pound fresh or frozen turkey breast half with bone

1   10-ounce package frozen chopped spinach, thawed

½   of an 8-ounce package reduced-fat cream cheese (Neufchâtel), softened

3   tablespoons grated Parmesan cheese

2   tablespoons water

1   teaspoon dried basil, crushed

¼   teaspoon ground nutmeg

¼   teaspoon pepper

To carve the turkey, start at the outside of the breast half. Slice downward, keeping the slices thin. Continue slicing slightly higher up on the breast.

Prep time: 15 minutes
Roasting time: 2½ hours

DIRECTIONS

1. Thaw turkey, if frozen. Drain spinach thoroughly and squeeze out excess liquid. Place the spinach in a food processor bowl with cream cheese, Parmesan cheese, water, basil, nutmeg, and pepper. Cover and process until well combined.

2. With a small sharp knife, loosen the breast skin from turkey and pull skin back, leaving skin attached along one side. Spread the spinach mixture over exposed portion of meat; pull skin back over filling. Secure skin with wooden toothpicks along sides of breast. Place turkey, skin side up, on a rack in a shallow roasting pan. Insert a meat thermometer into center of breast, below stuffing and not touching bone. Cover turkey loosely with foil.

3. Roast in a 325° oven for 2½ to 3 hours or until the thermometer registers 170°. Remove foil for the last 30 minutes of roasting. Makes 8 servings.

NUTRITION FACTS PER SERVING:

170 calories
6 g total fat
3 g saturated fat
62 mg cholesterol
176 mg sodium
3 g carbohydrate
1 g fiber
25 g protein

INGREDIENTS

- 1 2½- to 3-pound fresh or frozen turkey breast half with bone
- 1½ cups cranberries
- ½ cup coarsely shredded carrot
- ½ teaspoon finely shredded orange peel
- ½ cup orange juice
- 2 tablespoons raisins
- 2 tablespoons sugar
  Dash ground cloves
- 1 tablespoon cold water
- 2 teaspoons cornstarch
  Fresh parsley (optional)

Turkey with Cranberry Sauce

Want to enjoy this classic combination any day of the week? Use turkey tenderloin steaks instead of the turkey breast half. Broil steaks 4 to 5 inches from the heat for 8 to 10 minutes, turning once.

Prep time: 10 minutes
Roasting time: 2½ hours

DIRECTIONS

1. Thaw turkey, if frozen. Remove skin and excess fat from turkey. Place turkey, bone side down, on a rack in a shallow roasting pan. Insert a meat thermometer into the thickest portion of the breast, not touching bone. Cover turkey loosely with foil.

2. Roast in a 325° oven for 2½ to 3 hours or until the thermometer registers 170°. Remove foil for the last 30 minutes of roasting.

3. Meanwhile, for sauce, in a small saucepan combine the cranberries, carrot, orange peel, orange juice, raisins, sugar, and cloves. Bring to boiling; reduce heat. Simmer, uncovered, for 3 to 4 minutes or until cranberry skins pop.

4. In a small bowl combine cold water and cornstarch. Stir into cranberry mixture in saucepan. Cook and stir until thickened and bubbly. Cook and stir for 2 minutes more.

5. Serve turkey with cranberry sauce. If desired, garnish with parsley. Makes 8 servings.

NUTRITION FACTS PER SERVING:

154 calories
2 g total fat
1 g saturated fat
50 mg cholesterol
49 mg sodium
11 g carbohydrate
1 g fiber
22 g protein

Turkey and Apple Stir-Fry

You can use regular button mushrooms (about 2 cups sliced) instead of dried mushrooms in this dish. The dried wild mushrooms give the dish a more earthy flavor.

INGREDIENTS

- 6 dried wild mushrooms (1 cup), such as shiitake or wood ear mushrooms
- 12 ounces turkey breast tenderloin
- ¾ cup cold water
- 3 tablespoons frozen orange, apple, or pineapple juice concentrate, thawed
- 2 tablespoons soy sauce
- 2 teaspoons cornstarch
- ¼ teaspoon ground ginger
- ¼ teaspoon ground cinnamon
- ⅛ to ¼ teaspoon ground red pepper
- ¼ cup sliced or slivered almonds
- 1 tablespoon cooking oil
- 2 medium green, red, orange, and/or yellow sweet peppers, cut into thin 2-inch strips (2 cups)
- 2 medium apples, cored and thinly sliced (2 cups)
- 2 cups hot cooked brown rice

Soaking time: 30 minutes
Prep time: 15 minutes
Cooking time: 9 minutes

DIRECTIONS

1. In a small bowl cover mushrooms with warm water. Soak for 30 minutes. Rinse and squeeze mushrooms to drain. Discard stems. Thinly slice mushroom caps. Set aside. Cut turkey into 1-inch pieces. Set aside.

2. For sauce, in a small bowl stir together cold water, juice concentrate, soy sauce, cornstarch, ginger, cinnamon, and red pepper. Set aside.

3. Preheat a wok or large skillet over medium-high heat. Add almonds; stir-fry for 2 to 3 minutes or until golden. Remove almonds from wok. Let wok cool. Pour oil into wok. (Add more oil as necessary during cooking.) Add drained mushrooms, sweet peppers, and apples; stir-fry for 1 to 2 minutes or until peppers and apples are crisp-tender. Remove from wok.

4. Add turkey to hot wok; stir-fry for 3 to 4 minutes or until no longer pink. Push turkey from center of wok. Stir sauce; add to center of wok. Cook and stir until thickened and bubbly. Return apple mixture to wok. Cook and stir for 1 to 2 minutes more or until heated through. Stir in the almonds. Serve immediately over hot brown rice. Makes 4 servings.

NUTRITION FACTS PER SERVING:

363 calories
10 g total fat
2 g saturated fat
38 mg cholesterol
557 mg sodium
48 g carbohydrate
4 g fiber
22 g protein

INGREDIENTS

- 2 quarts water
- 8 ounces packaged dried linguine or spaghetti, broken in half
- 3 cups small broccoli florets
- 1 8-ounce container soft-style cream cheese with garlic and herbs
- ⅔ cup milk
- ¼ teaspoon coarsely ground black pepper
- 6 ounces sliced smoked turkey breast, cut into bite-size strips

Start to finish: 30 minutes

DIRECTIONS

1. In a large pot or Dutch oven bring water to boiling. Add linguine or spaghetti a little at a time. Return to boiling. Reduce heat. Cook for 6 minutes. Add broccoli. Return to boiling. Cook for 2 to 3 minutes more or until pasta is tender and broccoli is crisp-tender. Drain.

2. In the same pot or Dutch oven combine cream cheese, milk, and pepper. Cook and stir over low heat until cream cheese is melted. Add pasta-broccoli mixture and turkey. Toss until coated with the cheese mixture. If necessary, stir in additional milk to make desired consistency. Makes 4 servings.

Herbed Turkey and Broccoli

Soft-style cream cheese makes an ultrarich sauce for this one-pan pasta dish.

NUTRITION FACTS PER SERVING:

516 calories
21 g total fat
11 g saturated fat
81 mg cholesterol
675 mg sodium
57 g carbohydrate
4 g fiber
25 g protein

117

Smoked Turkey Salad Sandwiches

On a hot summer day, this quick sandwich is light and refreshing. And, using fat-free mayonnaise dressing and fat-free yogurt keeps it low in fat.

INGREDIENTS

¼ cup fat-free mayonnaise dressing or regular mayonnaise or salad dressing

¼ cup plain fat-free yogurt

½ cup corn relish

2 cups chopped smoked turkey

1 stalk celery, thinly sliced

4 kaiser rolls, split

1 medium tomato, sliced

Simply pass a serve-yourself

relish tray filled with assorted pickles (try some pickled watermelon for a change), crisp cucumber slices, olives, and fresh berries to go with the turkey sandwiches.

Start to finish: 15 minutes

DIRECTIONS

1. For dressing, in a small mixing bowl stir together mayonnaise dressing and yogurt. Stir in corn relish.

2. In a large mixing bowl combine turkey and celery. Add dressing; toss gently to coat. Serve on rolls with tomato slices. Makes 4 servings.

NUTRITION FACTS PER SERVING:

292 calories
10 g total fat
1 g saturated fat
0 mg cholesterol
527 mg sodium
3 g carbohydrate
2 g fiber
18 g protein

Italian Turkey Sandwiches

A minty tomato spread elevates these submarine sandwiches from ordinary to super.

INGREDIENTS

- ⅓ cup chopped onion
- 2 oil-packed dried tomato halves, drained and thinly sliced (about 3 tablespoons)
- 1 teaspoon bottled minced garlic or 2 cloves garlic, minced
- 1 teaspoon dried Italian seasoning, crushed
- 1 tablespoon olive oil
- ¼ cup snipped fresh parsley
- ¼ cup snipped fresh mint
- 2 tablespoons lime juice
- 1 tablespoon Worcestershire sauce
- Dash pepper
- 4 6- to 7-inch French-style rolls, split horizontally
- 1 6-ounce package thinly sliced turkey ham, smoked turkey breast, or ham
- 2 medium tomatoes, thinly sliced
- ½ cup shredded mozzarella cheese (2 ounces)

Prep time: 20 minutes
Baking time: 7 minutes

DIRECTIONS

1. In a small saucepan cook and stir onion, dried tomatoes, garlic, and Italian seasoning in hot oil for 3 minutes. Add parsley, mint, lime juice, Worcestershire sauce, and pepper. Cook and stir for 1 minute more.

2. To assemble, spread parsley mixture onto bottom halves of rolls. Top with turkey or ham, tomato slices, and cheese; add top halves of rolls. Arrange sandwiches in a shallow baking pan. Bake, uncovered, in a 350° oven for 7 to 10 minutes or until heated through and cheese is melted. Makes 4 servings.

Fresh mint not available? You can substitute 1 teaspoon dried mint, crushed, and add an extra ¼ cup snipped fresh parsley.

NUTRITION FACTS PER SERVING:

385 calories
11 g total fat
3 g saturated fat
30 mg cholesterol
1,114 mg sodium
52 g carbohydrate
1 g fiber
21 g protein

119

Quick-to-Fix Turkey and Rice Soup

Turn your leftover Thanksgiving turkey into a meal your family will love.

INGREDIENTS

4 cups chicken broth

1 cup water

1 teaspoon snipped fresh rosemary or ¼ teaspoon dried rosemary, crushed

¼ teaspoon pepper

1 10-ounce package frozen mixed vegetables (2 cups)

1 cup quick-cooking rice

2 cups chopped cooked turkey or chicken

1 14½-ounce can tomatoes, cut up

Fresh herbs are highly perishable, so purchase them only as you need them. For short-term storage, immerse the freshly cut stems in water about 2 inches deep. Cover the leaves loosely with a plastic bag or plastic wrap. Store the herbs in the refrigerator for up to several days.

Prep time: 10 minutes
Cooking time: 10 minutes

DIRECTIONS

1. In a large saucepan or Dutch oven combine chicken broth, water, rosemary, and pepper. Bring to boiling.

2. Stir in mixed vegetables and rice. Return to boiling; reduce heat. Cover and simmer for 10 to 15 minutes or until vegetables and rice are tender. Stir in turkey or chicken and undrained tomatoes; heat through. Makes 6 servings.

NUTRITION FACTS PER SERVING:

231 calories
6 g total fat
2 g saturated fat
49 mg cholesterol
681 mg sodium
23 g carbohydrate
1 g fiber
21 g protein

Easy Cheesy Vegetable-Turkey Chowder

INGREDIENTS

1 cup small broccoli florets

1 cup frozen loose-pack whole
kernel corn

½ cup water

¼ cup chopped onion

1½ teaspoons snipped fresh thyme
or ½ teaspoon dried thyme,
crushed

2 cups milk

1½ cups chopped cooked turkey or
chicken

1 10¾-ounce can condensed
cream of potato soup

¾ cup shredded cheddar cheese
(3 ounces)

Dash pepper

¼ cup shredded cheddar cheese
(1 ounce)

This hearty chowder lives up to its name. It's easy—only takes about 20 minutes to cook—and with a cup of cheddar cheese, it's definitely cheesy!

Start to finish: 20 minutes

DIRECTIONS

1. In a large saucepan combine broccoli, corn, water, onion, and thyme. Bring to boiling; reduce heat. Cover and simmer for 8 to 10 minutes or until vegetables are tender. Do not drain.

2. Stir milk, turkey or chicken, potato soup, the ¾ cup cheddar cheese, and the pepper into vegetable mixture. Cook and stir over medium heat until cheese melts and mixture is heated through. Sprinkle the ¼ cup cheddar cheese over soup. Makes 4 servings.

NUTRITION FACTS PER SERVING:

368 calories
18 g total fat
9 g saturated fat
94 mg cholesterol
901 mg sodium
23 g carbohydrate
1 g fiber
30 g protein

Get a head start on meal preparation by stocking your shelves with products that are already shredded, chopped, or crumbled. They may cost a little more, but when you're racing the clock, every minute counts. For this recipe, buy precut broccoli florets and shredded cheese.

Curried Turkey Soup

This spiced chicken noodle soup can be ready in just 20 minutes. It's a good way to use leftover chicken. Or, if you don't have any, buy a roasted chicken from your supermarket's deli.

INGREDIENTS

- 5 cups water
- 1 3-ounce package chicken-flavored ramen noodles
- 2 to 3 teaspoons curry powder
- 1 cup sliced fresh mushrooms
- 2 cups cubed cooked turkey
- 1 medium apple, cored and coarsely chopped
- ½ cup sliced water chestnuts

Use an apple wedger to quickly core and cut the apple into wedges. Then chop the wedges. There's no need to peel the apple.

Prep time: 15 minutes
Cooking time: 5 minutes

DIRECTIONS

1. In a large saucepan combine the water, the flavoring packet from noodles, and curry powder. Bring to boiling. Break up noodles and add to mixture in saucepan along with the mushrooms. Return to boiling; reduce heat. Simmer, uncovered, for 3 minutes.

2. Stir in turkey, apple, and water chestnuts. Heat through. Makes 5 servings.

NUTRITION FACTS PER SERVING:

217 calories
8 g total fat
1 g saturated fat
54 mg cholesterol
449 mg sodium
17 g carbohydrate
1 g fiber
20 g protein

INGREDIENTS

1   6¼- or 6¾-ounce package quick-cooking long grain and wild rice mix

5   cups water

½   pound uncooked ground turkey or chicken

1   12-ounce can evaporated milk, chilled

2   tablespoons all-purpose flour Cracked black pepper (optional)

Turkey and Rice Soup

For a quick soup lunch or supper, cut up fresh vegetable sticks or purchase cleaned and ready-to-eat vegetables at your supermarket. Slice your favorite bread and dish up the soup!

Start to finish: 25 minutes

DIRECTIONS

1. In a 3-quart saucepan combine the rice mix with the seasoning packet and water. Bring to boiling.

2. Drop the ground turkey or chicken by small spoonfuls into the boiling mixture (about 36 pieces total). Reduce heat. Cover and simmer for 5 minutes.

3. Gradually stir chilled milk into flour until smooth; add to boiling mixture. Cook and stir until slightly thickened and bubbly. Cook and stir for 1 minute more. Ladle into soup bowls. If desired, sprinkle cracked black pepper over each serving. Makes 6 servings.

NUTRITION FACTS PER SERVING:

226 calories
6 g total fat
3 g saturated fat
35 mg cholesterol
728 mg sodium
30 g carbohydrate
0 g fiber
13 g protein

Ready-to-cook mixes, such as the rice mix used in this soup, offer a great deal of convenience. Keep several—including rice mixes, noodle mixes, and potato mixes—on hand for last-minute meals. Any of these will go well with a simple entrée such as broiled fish, poultry, or meat. If you're concerned about sodium, prepare the packaged mix using about half of the seasoning packet.

Curry Turkey and Fruit Salad

This light, bright salad makes a perfect entrée for a luncheon or summer supper. Select low-fat turkey or roast beef from the deli.

INGREDIENTS

2 cups strawberry halves

1 11-ounce can pineapple tidbits and mandarin orange sections, drained (juice pack), or one 11-ounce can mandarin oranges sections, drained (water pack)

¼ cup fat-free mayonnaise dressing or salad dressing

¼ cup fat-free dairy sour cream

2 tablespoons frozen orange juice concentrate

¾ to 1 teaspoon curry powder

4 to 5 tablespoons fat-free milk

6 cups torn mixed salad greens

8 ounces cubed cooked turkey, or cooked roast beef, thinly sliced and rolled up

Toasted coconut (optional)

Toast coconut by spreading it in a single layer in a shallow baking pan. Bake in a 350° oven for 5 to 10 minutes or until light golden brown. Stir the coconut once or twice during toasting so it doesn't burn.

Prep time: 20 minutes

DIRECTIONS

1. In a medium mixing bowl toss together the strawberries and drained canned fruit. Set aside.

2. For dressing, in a bowl stir together the mayonnaise or salad dressing, sour cream, orange juice concentrate, and curry powder. Stir in enough milk to make a dressing of drizzling consistency.

3. Divide mixed greens among 4 serving plates. Top with fruit mixture and turkey or beef. Drizzle each serving with dressing. If desired, garnish with coconut. Makes 4 servings.

NUTRITION FACTS PER SERVING:

229 calories
5 g total fat
1 g saturated fat
46 mg cholesterol
284 mg sodium
28 g carbohydrate
3 g fiber
20 g protein

Herbed Turkey and Bean Salad

You lower the sodium in this recipe by using cooked dried beans instead of canned ones. If you use the canned variety for convenience, be sure to rinse the beans well before adding them to the salad.

INGREDIENTS

- 2/3 cup herb vinegar, such as tarragon, basil, or dill
- 2 tablespoons sugar
- 2 cups cooked red kidney beans, cannellini beans, and/or other white beans*
- 1 cup chopped cooked turkey or chicken
- 1/2 cup thinly sliced celery
- 1/2 cup chopped red sweet pepper
- 2 tablespoons snipped fresh parsley
- Kale leaves (optional)

Prep time: 20 minutes
Chilling time: 4 hours

DIRECTIONS

1. In a small saucepan combine vinegar and sugar. Cook and stir over medium heat until sugar dissolves.

2. In a mixing bowl combine beans, turkey or chicken, celery, sweet pepper, and parsley. Add vinegar mixture; toss to coat.

3. Cover and chill for 4 to 24 hours. If desired, serve in kale-leaf-lined salad bowls. Makes 4 servings.

*Note: To cook dried beans, first soak about 3/4 cup of well-rinsed beans in cold water overnight. Drain and rinse. In a large saucepan cook the beans in boiling water for 1 to 1 1/2 hours or until tender, stirring occasionally. (To keep cooked beans on hand, prepare double or triple the amount you need. Place cooked beans in an airtight, freezer-safe container. Freeze for up to 6 months.)

NUTRITION FACTS PER SERVING:

216 calories
3 g total fat
1 g saturated fat
31 mg cholesterol
48 mg sodium
31 g carbohydrate
5 g fiber
19 g protein

Snapper Veracruz Recipe, page 142

Fish & Seafood

Salmon with Fresh Pineapple Salsa

You don't need to have a party—just a weeknight dinner will do—to enjoy the sweet-hot fruit salsa that's as pretty as a sprinkling of confetti on top of this grilled salmon fillet. Serve it with hot cooked rice.

INGREDIENTS

- 2   cups coarsely chopped fresh pineapple
- ½   cup chopped red sweet pepper
- ¼   cup finely chopped red onion
- 3   tablespoons lime juice
- 1   small fresh jalapeño pepper, seeded and finely chopped
- 1   tablespoon snipped fresh cilantro or chives
- 1   tablespoon honey
- 1   1-pound fresh skinless salmon fillet, about 1 inch thick
- ¼   teaspoon ground cumin

Start to finish: 30 minutes

DIRECTIONS

1. For salsa, in a medium bowl combine the pineapple, sweet pepper, onion, 2 tablespoons of the lime juice, the jalapeño pepper, cilantro, and honey. Set aside.

2. Rinse fish; pat dry. Brush both sides of fish with the remaining lime juice and sprinkle with cumin. Place fish in a well-greased wire grill basket, tucking under any thin edges. Grill fish on the rack of an uncovered grill directly over medium coals for 8 to 12 minutes or until fish flakes easily when tested with a fork, turning basket once halfway through cooking. Cut fish into 4 serving-size pieces. Serve with the salsa. Makes 4 servings.

NUTRITION FACTS PER SERVING:

170 calories
4 g total fat
1 g saturated fat
20 mg cholesterol
70 mg sodium
17 g carbohydrate
1 g fiber
17 g protein

Wasabi-Glazed Whitefish with Vegetable Slaw

Though its presence in this recipe is subtle, fans of fiery wasabi—the bright-green Japanese condiment—will notice its head-clearing heat. Wasabi is found in powdered or paste form in Japanese markets or in larger supermarkets.

INGREDIENTS

- 4 4-ounce fresh skinless white-fleshed fish fillets (such as whitefish, sea bass, or orange roughy), about 1 inch thick
- 2 tablespoons light soy sauce
- 1 teaspoon toasted sesame oil
- ½ teaspoon sugar
- ¼ teaspoon wasabi powder or 1 tablespoon prepared horseradish
- 1 medium zucchini, coarsely shredded (about 1⅓ cups)
- 1 cup sliced radishes
- 1 cup fresh pea pods
- 2 tablespoons snipped fresh chives
- 3 tablespoons rice vinegar

Prep time: 15 minutes
Grilling time: 8 minutes

DIRECTIONS

1. Rinse fish; pat dry. In a small bowl combine soy sauce, ½ teaspoon of the sesame oil, ¼ teaspoon of the sugar, and the wasabi powder. Brush soy mixture over fish.

2. Place fish in a well-greased wire grill basket, tucking under any thin edges. Grill fish on the rack of an uncovered grill directly over medium coals for 8 to 12 minutes or until fish flakes easily when tested with a fork, turning basket once halfway through cooking.

3. Meanwhile, for vegetable slaw, in a medium bowl combine zucchini, radishes, pea pods, and chives. Stir together vinegar, the remaining sesame oil, and remaining sugar. Drizzle over the zucchini mixture; toss gently to coat. Serve fish with slaw. Makes 4 servings.

NUTRITION FACTS PER SERVING:

141 calories
3 g total fat
1 g saturated fat
60 mg cholesterol
363 mg sodium
6 g carbohydrate
1 g fiber
24 g protein

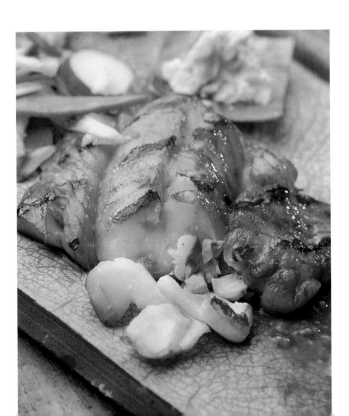

Grilled Tuna with Rosemary

Firm-fleshed fish, such as tuna, swordfish, halibut, shark, or salmon, grills nicely without falling apart.

INGREDIENTS

- 1 pound fresh or frozen tuna, swordfish, halibut, shark, or salmon steaks, cut 1 inch thick
- 2 teaspoons olive oil
- 2 teaspoons lemon juice
- ⅛ teaspoon salt
- ⅛ teaspoon pepper
- 2 cloves garlic, minced
- 2 teaspoons snipped fresh rosemary or tarragon or 1 teaspoon dried rosemary or tarragon, crushed
- 1 tablespoon capers, drained and slightly crushed
- Fresh rosemary (optional)

Prep time: 15 minutes
Grilling time: 8 minutes

DIRECTIONS

1. Thaw fish, if frozen. Rinse fish; pat dry with paper towels. Cut into 4 serving-size pieces. Brush both sides of fish with oil and lemon juice; sprinkle with salt and pepper. Rub garlic and snipped or dried rosemary or tarragon onto fish.

2. Grill fish on the rack of an uncovered grill directly over medium coals for 8 to 12 minutes or until fish flakes easily when tested with a fork, turning gently halfway through grilling. (Or, broil fish on the unheated rack of a broiler pan 4 inches from the heat for 8 to 12 minutes, turning gently halfway through broiling.)

3. To serve, top the fish with capers. If desired, garnish with additional fresh rosemary. Makes 4 servings.

NUTRITION FACTS PER SERVING:

164 calories
3 g total fat
0 g saturated fat
19 mg cholesterol
484 mg sodium
1 g carbohydrate
0 g fiber
32 g protein

Lake Trout with Corn Salsa

INGREDIENTS

1 **pound fresh or frozen lake trout or walleye fillets, ½ inch thick**

1 **cup frozen whole kernel corn, thawed and cooked**

¼ **cup water**

½ **cup small cherry tomatoes, quartered**

½ **cup finely chopped, peeled jicama**

¼ **cup snipped fresh cilantro or parsley**

2 **tablespoons lime juice**

1 **small fresh jalapeño pepper, seeded and finely chopped**

Dash salt

Nonstick cooking spray

3 **tablespoons fat-free Italian salad dressing**

1 **teaspoon chili powder**

Ask your butcher to skin the lake trout before you bring it home. If you opt to cook it with the skin on, then place the fish, skin side down, in the baking dish.

Prep time: 20 minutes
Baking time: 8 minutes

DIRECTIONS

1. Thaw fish, if frozen. Rinse fish; pat dry with paper towels. Cut into 4 serving-size pieces. In a small saucepan combine the corn and the water. Bring to boiling; reduce heat. Simmer, covered, for 5 minutes. Drain well.

2. For corn salsa, in a medium serving bowl combine the cooked corn, tomatoes, jicama, cilantro or parsley, lime juice, jalapeño pepper, and salt. Toss to combine. Set aside.

3. Coat a 2-quart rectangular baking dish with cooking spray. Stir together the Italian salad dressing and chili powder; brush over fish. Place fish in the prepared baking dish. Tuck under any thin edges.

4. Bake fish, uncovered, in a 450° oven for 8 to 12 minutes or until fish flakes easily when tested with a fork. Serve fish with corn salsa. Makes 4 servings.

NUTRITION FACTS PER SERVING:

157 calories
1 g total fat
0 g saturated fat
45 mg cholesterol
196 mg sodium
13 g carbohydrate
1 g fiber
24 g protein

Fennel and Fish Au Gratin

Bulb-shape with feathery, dill-like leaves, fennel emits a mild anise flavor. Try this tasty dish—and become a fennel fan.

INGREDIENTS

- 1 **pound fresh or frozen orange roughy, salmon, or other fish fillets, ½ to ¾ inch thick**
- 2 **fennel bulbs with leaves**
- 3 **carrots, cut into thin strips (1½ cups)**
- 1¼ **cups fat-free milk**
- 3 **tablespoons all-purpose flour**
- 2 **tablespoons dry white wine (optional)**
- ⅛ **teaspoon salt**
- ⅛ **teaspoon pepper**
- 2 **tablespoons grated Parmesan cheese**
- 1 **tablespoon fine dry bread crumbs**
- 2 **teaspoons margarine or butter, melted**

Prep time: 30 minutes
Baking time: 10 minutes

DIRECTIONS

1. Thaw fish, if frozen. Rinse fish; pat dry with paper towels. Cut into 4 serving-size pieces. Set aside.

2. Remove upper stalks from fennel, including feathery leaves; reserve leaves and discard stalks. Discard any wilted outer layers on fennel bulbs; cut off a thin slice from each base. Wash fennel and pat dry. Quarter each fennel bulb lengthwise and remove core; cut each quarter lengthwise into thin strips. Chop enough of the reserved fennel leaves to make ¼ cup.

3. In a large covered saucepan cook thinly sliced fennel and carrots in a small amount of boiling water for 8 to 10 minutes or until tender; drain. Transfer vegetables to a 2-quart square or rectangular baking dish. Rinse saucepan.

4. Meanwhile, in a large skillet cook the fish in a small amount of simmering water until fish flakes easily when tested with a fork (allow 4 to 6 minutes per ½-inch thickness of fish); drain. Arrange fish on top of vegetables in baking dish.

5. For sauce, in the large saucepan combine the milk and flour. Cook and stir over medium heat until thickened and bubbly. Stir in the ¼ cup chopped fennel leaves, the wine (if desired), salt, and pepper. Pour sauce over fish and vegetables. Combine Parmesan cheese, bread crumbs, and margarine or butter; sprinkle over the sauce. Bake, uncovered, in a 350° oven about 10 minutes or until heated through. Makes 4 servings.

NUTRITION FACTS PER SERVING:

199 calories
4 g total fat
1 g saturated fat
49 mg cholesterol
308 mg sodium
16 g carbohydrate
1 g fiber
24 g protein

INGREDIENTS

1¼ pounds fresh or frozen sole or
    other fish fillets, ½ to
    ¾ inch thick

1 14½-ounce can low-sodium
    tomatoes, undrained and
    cut up

8 green onions, thinly sliced

2 tablespoons lemon juice

1 teaspoon dried Italian seasoning,
    crushed

¼ teaspoon pepper

    Nonstick cooking spray

3 cups hot cooked spinach
    fettuccine

2 tablespoons crumbled feta
    cheese or 2 tablespoons
    sliced, pitted ripe olives

Sole with Feta and Tomatoes

A well-seasoned tomato sauce and sharp, salty feta cheese jazz up the delicate flavor of sole.

Prep time: 25 minutes
Baking time: 20 minutes

DIRECTIONS

1. Thaw fish, if frozen. Rinse fish; pat dry with paper towels. Cut into 4 serving-size pieces. Set aside.

2. For sauce, in a large skillet combine undrained tomatoes, green onions, lemon juice, Italian seasoning, and pepper. Bring to boiling; reduce heat. Simmer, uncovered, for 8 to 10 minutes or until nearly all the liquid has evaporated.

3. Coat a 2-quart square or rectangular baking dish with cooking spray. Arrange fish in prepared dish. Tuck under any thin edges. Spoon the sauce over fish.

4. Bake fish, covered, in a 350° oven for 20 to 25 minutes or until fish flakes easily when tested with a fork. Serve fish and sauce on top of fettuccine. Sprinkle with feta cheese or olives. Makes 4 servings.

When baking or broiling fish fillets, fold under the thin ends so the fish is an even thickness. This prevents the ends from cooking too quickly and drying out before the rest of the fish is done.

NUTRITION FACTS PER SERVING:

299 calories
4 g total fat
2 g saturated fat
74 mg cholesterol
220 mg sodium
34 g carbohydrate
2 g fiber
31 g protein

Grilled Rosemary Trout with Lemon Butter

Create the ambiance of campfire cooking by serving the fish and tomatoes in cast-iron skillets. Round out the meal with cottage-fried potatoes.

INGREDIENTS

- 4 teaspoons butter, softened
- 1 tablespoon finely chopped shallot or onion
- 1 teaspoon finely shredded lemon peel
- Salt
- Coarsely ground pepper
- 2 fresh rainbow trout, pan dressed and boned (8 to 10 ounces each)
- 1 tablespoon snipped fresh rosemary
- 1 tablespoon lemon juice
- 2 teaspoons olive oil
- 2 medium tomatoes, halved crosswise
- 1 tablespoon snipped fresh parsley

A pan-dressed fish has had the scales and internal organs removed. Often the head, fins, and tail also have been removed.

Prep time: 15 minutes
Grilling time: 6 minutes

DIRECTIONS

1. In a small bowl stir together the butter, half of the shallot or onion, and the lemon peel; sprinkle with salt and coarsely ground pepper. Set aside.

2. Rinse fish; pat dry with paper towels. Spread each fish open and place skin sides down. Rub the remaining shallot or onion and the rosemary onto fish. Sprinkle with additional salt and pepper and drizzle with lemon juice and olive oil.

3. Grill fish, skin sides down, on the greased rack of an uncovered grill directly over medium coals for 6 to 8 minutes or until fish flakes easily with a fork.

4. Meanwhile, place tomatoes, cut sides up, on grill rack; dot each with ¼ teaspoon of the butter mixture. Grill tomatoes about 5 minutes or until heated through. Remove fish and tomatoes from grill. Cut each fish in half lengthwise. In a small saucepan melt the remaining butter mixture; serve with fish and tomatoes. Sprinkle fish with parsley. Makes 4 servings.

NUTRITION FACTS PER SERVING:

206 calories
10 g total fat
3 g saturated fat
75 mg cholesterol
109 mg sodium
4 g carbohydrate
1 g fiber
24 g protein

Cod with Lemon Cream Sauce

Generally low in fat and calories, fish is great for dieters. Here, spinach noodles make both a colorful backdrop and a filling accompaniment (a ¾-cup serving has 158 calories).

INGREDIENTS

1 pound fresh or frozen cod or other fish fillets, ½ to ¾ inch thick

1½ cups water

1 tablespoon lemon juice

½ cup finely chopped carrot

½ cup finely chopped onion

½ cup fat-free milk

1 teaspoon cornstarch

1 teaspoon snipped fresh dill or ¼ teaspoon dried dillweed

½ teaspoon instant chicken bouillon granules

Hot cooked spinach noodles or other desired hot cooked noodles (optional)

Start to finish: 20 minutes

DIRECTIONS

1. Thaw fish fillets, if frozen. Rinse fish; pat dry with paper towels.

2. In a 12-inch skillet combine water and lemon juice. Bring to boiling. Add fish. Reduce heat. Simmer, covered, until fish flakes easily when tested with a fork (allow 4 to 6 minutes per ½-inch thickness of fish). Remove fish from skillet and keep warm.

3. In a small covered saucepan cook the carrot and onion in a small amount of boiling water about 3 minutes or until crisp-tender. Drain well. In a small bowl stir together the milk, cornstarch, dill, and bouillon granules. Stir into vegetables in saucepan. Cook and stir until thickened and bubbly. Cook and stir for 2 minutes more.

4. Serve the vegetable sauce over fish. If desired, serve with hot cooked noodles. Makes 4 servings.

NUTRITION FACTS PER SERVING:

114 calories
1 g total fat
0 g saturated fat
45 mg cholesterol
199 mg sodium
5 g carbohydrate
1 g fiber
20 g protein

Red Snapper with Ginger Sauce

Fresh ginger imparts a tantalizing zing to this distinctive Oriental-style sauce.

INGREDIENTS

- 1 pound fresh or frozen red snapper or other firm fish fillets, ¾ inch thick
- ¼ cup light soy sauce
- 3 tablespoons dry white or red wine or water
- 2 tablespoons sliced green onion
- 1 tablespoon grated ginger
- 1 clove garlic, quartered

  Nonstick cooking spray
- 2 cups red or green sweet pepper strips and/or sliced zucchini

  Thin, long green onion strips (optional)

Prep time: 20 minutes
Broiling time: 6 minutes

DIRECTIONS

1. Thaw fish, if frozen. Rinse fish; pat dry with paper towels. Cut into 4 serving-size pieces. Set aside.

2. For sauce, in a blender container or food processor bowl combine the soy sauce, wine or water, green onion, ginger, and garlic. Cover and blend or process until pureed. Set aside.

3. Coat the unheated rack of a broiler pan with cooking spray. Place fish and sweet pepper strips or zucchini slices on rack. Tuck under any thin edges of fish. Broil 4 inches from heat for 6 to 9 minutes or until fish flakes easily when tested with a fork and vegetables are tender, brushing fish and vegetables with the sauce halfway through broiling.

4. Place the remaining sauce in a small saucepan and bring to boiling. Boil gently, uncovered, for 1 minute. Transfer the fish and vegetables to a serving platter. Spoon the remaining sauce over fish. If desired, garnish with green onion strips. Makes 4 servings.

NUTRITION FACTS PER SERVING:

148 calories
2 g total fat
0 g saturated fat
42 mg cholesterol
607 mg sodium
4 g carbohydrate
0 g fiber
25 g protein

Sweet-Pepper-Stuffed Sole

Fines herbes transforms a simple wine sauce from ordinary to delicious. This herb mix usually contains chervil, parsley, chives, and tarragon. Look for it with the other dried herbs in your grocery store.

INGREDIENTS

- 4   4-ounce fresh or frozen sole or flounder fillets, ¼ to ½ inch thick
- 2   small red, yellow, and/or green sweet peppers, cut into thin bite-size strips
- 4   green onions, halved lengthwise and cut into 3-inch-long pieces
- 2   teaspoons margarine or butter
- ⅓   cup dry white wine or chicken broth
- ¼   teaspoon dried fines herbes, crushed
- ⅛   teaspoon salt (optional)
- ⅛   teaspoon black pepper
- 1   tablespoon cold water
- 2   teaspoons cornstarch
    Hot cooked wild rice and/or brown rice (optional)

Prep time: 30 minutes
Baking time: 25 minutes

DIRECTIONS

1. Thaw fish, if frozen. Rinse fish; pat dry with paper towels. Set aside. In a medium covered saucepan cook the sweet peppers and green onions in a small amount of boiling water for 3 minutes. Drain well.

2. Dot each fish fillet with ½ teaspoon of the margarine or butter. Place one-fourth of the pepper mixture across the center of each fillet. Starting from a short side, roll up the fish fillets. Secure with wooden toothpicks. Place fish, seam sides down, in a shallow baking dish. Stir together the wine or broth, fines herbes, salt (omit if using broth), and black pepper; drizzle over fish.

3. Bake, covered, in a 350° oven for 25 to 30 minutes or until fish flakes easily when tested with a fork. Transfer the fish to a serving platter. Keep warm.

4. For sauce, measure pan juices; add enough water to measure ¾ cup. In a small saucepan combine the 1 tablespoon cold water and the cornstarch; stir in pan juices. Cook and stir over medium heat until thickened and bubbly. Cook and stir for 2 minutes more. If desired, serve the fish on top of rice. Spoon the sauce over fish. Makes 4 servings.

NUTRITION FACTS PER SERVING:

148 calories
3 g total fat
1 g saturated fat
60 mg cholesterol
184 mg sodium
4 g carbohydrate
0 g fiber
22 g protein

Fish and Sweet Peppers

This simple recipe clamors for glistening fresh fish, for these ingredients won't mask its delicate flavor.

INGREDIENTS

- 1 pound fresh or frozen cod or other fish fillets, ½ to ¾ inch thick
- ¾ cup chicken broth
- 1 medium onion, sliced and separated into rings
- ½ teaspoon finely shredded lemon peel
- 1 tablespoon lemon juice
- 2¼ teaspoons snipped fresh oregano or marjoram or ¾ teaspoon dried oregano or marjoram, crushed
- 1 clove garlic, minced
- 2 small green and/or red sweet peppers, cut into bite-size strips (1½ cups)
- 1 tablespoon cold water
- 1½ teaspoons cornstarch
- 1 lemon, halved and sliced (optional)

Prep time: 25 minutes
Cooking time: 7 minutes

DIRECTIONS

1. Thaw fish, if frozen. Rinse fish; pat dry with paper towels. Cut into 4 serving-size pieces. Set aside.

2. In a large skillet combine the chicken broth, onion, lemon peel, lemon juice, oregano or marjoram, and garlic. Bring to boiling; reduce heat. Simmer, covered, about 3 minutes or until onion is tender.

3. Arrange the fish on top of onion mixture in skillet. Add sweet peppers. Cook, covered, over medium heat until fish flakes easily when tested with a fork (allow 4 to 6 minutes per ½-inch thickness of fish). Using a slotted spoon, transfer fish and vegetable mixture to a serving platter. Keep warm.

4. Combine cold water and cornstarch. Add to pan juices. Cook and stir until thickened and bubbly. Cook and stir for 2 minutes more. Spoon over the fish and vegetables. If desired, garnish with lemon slices. Makes 4 servings.

NUTRITION FACTS PER SERVING:

116 calories
1 g total fat
0 g saturated fat
45 mg cholesterol
211 mg sodium
6 g carbohydrate
1 g fiber
20 g protein

Cold Poached Salmon with Asparagus

Prepare this make-ahead dish as a spring or summer cold entrée, or use small servings for an elegant first course.

INGREDIENTS

- 1 pound fresh or frozen skinless salmon or other fish fillets, ½ to ¾ inch thick
- ½ teaspoon garlic-pepper seasoning or seasoned pepper
- 1½ cups water
- 1 pound asparagus spears
- 1 small onion, sliced
- ½ cup dry white wine or reduced-sodium chicken broth
- ¼ cup fat-free mayonnaise dressing or salad dressing
- 2 tablespoons fat-free milk or water
- 1 teaspoon finely shredded lime peel or lemon peel
- 1 tablespoon lime juice or lemon juice
- Fresh watercress and/or lettuce leaves (optional)

Prep time: 20 minutes
Cooking time: 8 minutes
Chilling time: 6 hours

DIRECTIONS

1. Thaw fish, if frozen. Rinse fish; pat dry with paper towels. Cut into 4 serving-size pieces. Rub fish fillets with garlic-pepper seasoning or seasoned pepper; set aside.

2. In a large skillet bring the water to boiling. Meanwhile, wash asparagus; snap off and discard woody bases. If desired, scrape off scales. Cook the asparagus in the boiling water, covered, for 4 to 8 minutes or until crisp-tender. Remove asparagus, reserving liquid in skillet. Rinse asparagus in cold water; drain and cool.

3. Add the onion and wine or broth to skillet; return to boiling. Add fish. Reduce heat. Simmer, covered, until fish flakes easily when tested with a fork (allow 4 to 6 minutes per ½-inch thickness of fish). Using a slotted spoon, remove fish from skillet; cool. Discard the cooking liquid, including onion. Transfer fish and asparagus to separate storage containers and chill for 6 to 24 hours.

4. For dressing, in a small bowl stir together the mayonnaise dressing or salad dressing, milk or water, lime or lemon peel, and lime or lemon juice. If desired, line 4 plates with watercress and/or lettuce. Arrange the fish and asparagus on top of greens. Spoon some of the dressing over fish. Pass the remaining dressing. Makes 4 servings.

NUTRITION FACTS PER SERVING:

162 calories
4 g total fat
1 g saturated fat
20 mg cholesterol
271 mg sodium
8 g carbohydrate
2 g fiber
18 g protein

Herb-Buttered Fish Steaks

If you can't find small fish steaks, buy two large ones and cut them in half before serving. As long as the steaks are 1 inch thick, the cooking time will be the same.

INGREDIENTS

4 small fresh or frozen halibut, salmon, shark, or swordfish steaks, cut 1 inch thick (about 1 pound total)

2 tablespoons butter or margarine, softened

1 teaspoon finely shredded lime peel or lemon peel

1 teaspoon lime juice or lemon juice

1 teaspoon snipped fresh tarragon or rosemary or ¼ teaspoon dried tarragon or rosemary, crushed

1 teaspoon butter or margarine, melted

To thaw fish,

place the unopened package in a container in the refrigerator, allowing a 1-pound package to thaw overnight. To thaw fish in the microwave oven, place 1 pound frozen steaks or fillets in a microwave-safe baking dish; cover with vented plastic wrap. Micro-cook on 30% power (medium-low) for 4 to 6 minutes, turning and separating fish after 3 minutes. Let steaks stand 15 minutes; fillets 10 minutes. Fish should be pliable and cold on the outside and slightly icy in the center of thick areas.

Prep time: 10 minutes
Broiling time: 8 minutes

DIRECTIONS

1. Thaw fish, if frozen. Rinse fish; pat dry. For the herb butter, in a small mixing bowl stir together the 2 tablespoons butter or margarine, the lime or lemon peel, lime or lemon juice, and tarragon or rosemary. Set aside.

2. Place the fish steaks on the lightly greased rack of a broiler pan. Brush with the 1 teaspoon melted butter or margarine. Broil 4 to 5 inches from the heat for 8 to 12 minutes or until fish flakes easily with a fork, turning once after half of the broiling time. To serve, top with herb butter. Makes 4 servings.

NUTRITION FACTS PER SERVING:

184 calories
9 g total fat
2 g saturated fat
36 mg cholesterol
140 mg sodium
0 g carbohydrate
0 g fiber
24 g protein

Vegetable-Topped Fish

INGREDIENTS

- 1 **pound fresh or frozen fish fillets**
- 2 **teaspoons margarine or butter, melted**
- ⅛ **teaspoon salt**
- ⅛ **teaspoon pepper**
- 1 **8-ounce jar (about 1 cup) salsa**
- 1 **small yellow summer squash or zucchini, halved lengthwise and cut into ¼-inch slices**

Salsa and summer squash make an easy sauce for baked fish fillets.

Start to finish: 15 minutes

DIRECTIONS

1. Thaw fish, if frozen. Rinse fish; pat dry. Measure thickness of fish. Place the fish in a greased shallow baking pan, tucking under any thin edges so fish cooks evenly. Brush fish with melted margarine or butter. Sprinkle with the salt and pepper. Bake, uncovered, in a 450° oven until fish flakes easily when tested with a fork. (Allow 4 to 6 minutes per ½-inch thickness of fish.)

2. Meanwhile, in a small saucepan stir together salsa and summer squash or zucchini. Bring to boiling; reduce heat. Cover and simmer for 5 to 6 minutes or until squash is crisp-tender. Serve squash mixture over baked fish fillets. Makes 4 servings.

Delicately flavored, skinless, and firm-textured fish fillets work best for this recipe. Orange roughy, cod, flounder, sea bass, and sole are excellent choices.

NUTRITION FACTS PER SERVING:

202 calories
10 g total fat
2 g saturated fat
44 mg cholesterol
638 mg sodium
13 g carbohydrate
1 g fiber
19 g protein

141

Snapper Veracruz

With its location on the Gulf of Mexico, it's no wonder Veracruz is famous for seafood. It was once the only East Coast port allowed to operate in New Spain. Snapper Veracruz, one of Mexico's best-known fish recipes, is a melding of flavors— Spanish green olives and capers with jalapeño peppers from nearby Jalapa, the capital of the state of Veracruz. To douse the fire caused by the peppers, this meal typically includes boiled potatoes.

INGREDIENTS

- 1½ pounds fresh or frozen skinless red snapper or other fish fillets
- ⅛ teaspoon salt
- ⅛ teaspoon ground black pepper
- 1 large onion, sliced and separated into rings
- 1 teaspoon bottled minced garlic or 2 cloves garlic, minced
- 1 tablespoon cooking oil
- 2 large tomatoes, chopped (2 cups)
- ¼ cup sliced pimiento-stuffed olives
- ¼ cup dry white wine
- 2 tablespoons capers, drained
- 1 to 2 fresh jalapeño or serrano peppers, seeded and chopped, or 1 to 2 canned jalapeño peppers, rinsed, drained, seeded, and chopped
- ½ teaspoon sugar
- 1 bay leaf

To prepare boiled potatoes,

peel and quarter 1½ pounds potatoes. In a covered medium saucepan cook potatoes in a small amount of boiling salted water for 20 to 25 minutes or until tender. Drain.

Start to finish: 30 minutes

DIRECTIONS

1. Thaw fish, if frozen. Rinse fish; pat dry. Cut fish into 6 serving-size pieces. Sprinkle fish fillets with the salt and black pepper.

2. For sauce, in a large skillet cook onion and garlic in hot oil until onion is tender. Stir in tomatoes, olives, wine, capers, jalapeño or serrano peppers, sugar, and bay leaf. Bring to boiling. Add fillets to skillet. Return to boiling; reduce heat. Cover and simmer for 6 to 10 minutes or until fish flakes easily when tested with a fork.

3. Use a slotted spatula to carefully transfer fish from skillet to a serving platter. Cover and keep warm.

4. Boil sauce in skillet for 5 to 6 minutes or until reduced to about 2 cups, stirring occasionally. Discard bay leaf. Spoon sauce over fish. Makes 6 servings.

NUTRITION FACTS PER SERVING:

174 calories
5 g total fat
1 g saturated fat
42 mg cholesterol
260 mg sodium
7 g carbohydrate
6 g fiber
24 g protein

Creole Cod And Rice

INGREDIENTS

1 pound fresh or frozen cod fillets, about ½ inch thick

1 4.3- to 4.7-ounce envelope quick-cooking rice and pasta mix with vegetables

1 8-ounce can tomatoes, cut up

¼ teaspoon ground black pepper

⅛ teaspoon ground red pepper (optional)

½ medium green sweet pepper, cut into strips or rings

When your family asks, "What can I do to help?" suggest they fix a tossed salad to cool the spicy entrée. If the greens weren't rinsed ahead, a salad spinner is a timesaver for busy, health-conscious families. Rinse, spin, and dry crisp greens in 5 minutes.

Start to finish: 25 minutes

DIRECTIONS

1. Thaw fish, if frozen. Rinse fish; pat dry. In 10-inch skillet prepare rice mix as directed on the envelope, except substitute undrained tomatoes for ½ cup of the liquid and add the black pepper and, if desired, red pepper to mixture. Cover and cook rice for half of the time directed on rice mix package.

2. Place fish fillets and green pepper on top of the rice mixture. Cover and cook over low heat about 10 minutes more or until fish flakes easily when tested with a fork. Makes 4 servings.

For the mix in this recipe, you'll find a variety of quick-cooking rice and pasta mixes with different vegetables (and some with cheese) at the grocery store. Any type in the range of 4.3 to 4.7 ounces will work. Just use what appeals to you.

NUTRITION FACTS PER SERVING:

263 calories
5 g total fat
1 g saturated fat
49 mg cholesterol
649 mg sodium
28 g carbohydrate
1 g fiber
25 g protein

Sweet-and-Sour Fish

Asian-style sweet-and-sour dishes are usually fried, but this version uses poached lean fish. Trimming calories and fat has not hurt the great flavor.

INGREDIENTS

1 pound fresh or frozen halibut, swordfish, tuna, or other fish steaks, cut 1 inch thick

2 tablespoons brown sugar

2 tablespoons vinegar

2 tablespoons reduced-sodium soy sauce

4 teaspoons cornstarch

⅔ cup reduced-sodium chicken broth

1 medium green or red sweet pepper, cut into 1-inch squares

1 medium carrot, thinly bias-sliced

½ cup seedless grapes, halved

2 cups hot cooked rice

Start to finish: 30 minutes

DIRECTIONS

1. Thaw fish, if frozen. Rinse fish; pat dry with paper towels. Cut into 1-inch cubes. In a covered large saucepan cook fish in boiling water about 5 minutes or until fish flakes easily when tested with a fork. Drain well. Cover and keep warm.

2. Meanwhile, in a small bowl combine the brown sugar, vinegar, soy sauce, and cornstarch. Set aside.

3. In a medium saucepan combine the chicken broth, sweet pepper, and carrot. Bring to boiling; reduce heat. Simmer, covered, about 3 minutes or until vegetables are crisp-tender.

4. Stir brown sugar mixture into vegetable mixture. Cook and stir until thickened and bubbly. Cook and stir for 2 minutes more. Gently stir in fish and grapes. Cook about 1 minute more or until heated through. Serve over hot cooked rice. Makes 4 servings.

NUTRITION FACTS PER SERVING:

294 calories
3 g total fat
1 g saturated fat
36 mg cholesterol
446 mg sodium
38 g carbohydrate
1 g fiber
27 g protein

Lime-Sauced Fish and Linguine

For fish stir-fries, such as this one, select a firm fish. Swordfish, shark, sea bass, cod, or orange roughy all work well.

INGREDIENTS

- 12 ounces fresh or frozen skinless, boneless fish
- ¼ cup dry white wine or chicken broth
- ¼ cup chicken broth
- 2 tablespoons lime juice
- 2 teaspoons cornstarch
- 1 teaspoon honey
- ¼ teaspoon ground ginger
- ¼ teaspoon ground coriander
- ⅛ teaspoon black pepper
- Nonstick cooking spray
- 1 medium cucumber, seeded and cut into 2×½-inch sticks
- 1 medium zucchini, cut into 2×½-inch sticks
- 1 medium red or green sweet pepper, cut into ¾-inch squares
- 1 teaspoon cooking oil
- 3 cups hot cooked linguine
- Lime wedges (optional)

Start to finish: 35 minutes

DIRECTIONS

1. Thaw fish, if frozen. Rinse fish; pat dry with paper towels. Cut into ¾-inch pieces. Set aside.

2. For sauce, in a small bowl stir together the wine, chicken broth, lime juice, cornstarch, honey, ginger, coriander, and black pepper. Set aside.

3. Coat an unheated wok or large skillet with cooking spray. Preheat over medium-high heat. Add the cucumber and zucchini; stir-fry for 1½ minutes. Add the sweet pepper; stir-fry about 1½ minutes more or until crisp-tender. Remove the vegetables from wok.

4. Add the oil to hot wok. Add fish; stir-fry for 2 to 3 minutes or until fish flakes easily when tested with a fork. Push the fish from center of wok. Stir sauce; add to center of wok. Cook and stir until thickened and bubbly. Return cooked vegetables to wok. Cook and stir about 2 minutes or until heated through. Serve immediately with linguine. If desired, garnish with lime wedges. Makes 4 servings.

NUTRITION FACTS PER SERVING:

312 calories
6 g total fat
1 g saturated fat
34 mg cholesterol
130 mg sodium
39 g carbohydrate
3 g fiber
23 g protein

Italian Fish Soup

In Italy, there are as many versions of *zuppa di pesce*, or fish soup, as there are coastal towns. Serve fish soup as the Italians do—with a slice of toasted Italian bread.

INGREDIENTS

- 8 ounces fresh or frozen haddock, bass, sole, or other fish fillets
- 6 ounces fresh or frozen, peeled and deveined shrimp
- 3 cups water
- 2 medium tomatoes, peeled and cut up
- 1 cup thinly sliced carrots (2 medium)
- ½ cup dry white wine or water
- ½ cup chopped celery (2 stalks)
- ⅓ cup chopped onion
- 2 teaspoons instant chicken bouillon granules
- 2 cloves garlic, minced
- 2 bay leaves
- ½ teaspoon dried marjoram, crushed
- ½ teaspoon finely shredded orange peel
- Dash bottled hot pepper sauce
- ¼ cup tomato paste
- 4 slices Italian bread, toasted

Adding wine to soup

Adding wine to soup often enhances its flavor. A dry white table wine adds zest to fish soup, crab or lobster bisque, or creamy chowder. A strongly flavored soup with beef benefits from a tablespoon of dry red table wine. And sherry or Madeira blends well with veal or chicken soup.

Prep time: 25 minutes
Cooking time: 18 minutes

DIRECTIONS

1. Thaw the fish fillets and shrimp, if frozen. Cut the fish into 1-inch pieces; halve the shrimp lengthwise. Rinse the fish and shrimp; pat dry with paper towels. Chill until needed.

2. In a large saucepan combine the 3 cups water, the tomatoes, carrots, wine or water, celery, onion, bouillon granules, garlic, bay leaves, marjoram, orange peel, and hot pepper sauce. Bring to boiling; reduce heat. Simmer, covered, for 15 to 20 minutes or until vegetables are nearly tender. Stir in tomato paste.

3. Stir the fish and shrimp into the tomato mixture. Bring mixture just to boiling; reduce heat. Simmer, covered, for 3 to 5 minutes more or until fish flakes easily when tested with a fork and shrimp turn opaque. Discard bay leaves.

4. To serve, place a slice of bread in each of 4 soup bowls. Ladle soup into bowls. Makes 4 servings.

NUTRITION FACTS PER SERVING:

252 calories
3 g total fat
0 g saturated fat
96 mg cholesterol
780 mg sodium
30 g carbohydrate
5 g fiber
24 g protein

Vegetable-Fish Soup

INGREDIENTS

- 8 ounces fresh or frozen fish fillets
- 2 cups water
- 2 cups frozen mixed vegetables
- 1 14½-ounce can tomatoes, undrained and cut up
- 1 cup thinly sliced celery
- ¾ cup chopped onion
- 4 teaspoons snipped fresh oregano or 1 teaspoon dried oregano, crushed (optional)
- 1½ teaspoons instant chicken bouillon granules
- 1 clove garlic, minced
- Several dashes bottled hot pepper sauce

Serve this flavorful vegetable-filled soup in just 30 minutes. Watch the soup carefully once you add the fish. Cook it just until the fish begins to flake easily when tested with a fork. Overcooked fish will be tough and chewy.

Start to finish: 30 minutes

DIRECTIONS

1. Thaw fish, if frozen. Rinse fish; pat dry with paper towels. Cut the fish into 1-inch pieces. Set aside.

2. In a large saucepan combine the water, frozen vegetables and drained tomatoes, celery, onion, dried oregano (if using), bouillon granules, garlic, and hot pepper sauce. Bring to boiling; reduce heat. Simmer, covered, about 10 minutes or until vegetables are tender.

3. Stir in the fish and fresh oregano (if using). Return just to boiling; reduce heat. Simmer gently, covered, for 3 to 5 minutes or until fish flakes easily with a fork. Makes 4 servings.

Check out your grocer's freezer case for vegetable combos. You'll find a huge selection of frozen mixtures in all types and colors. In addition, frozen vegetables are quick, easy to prepare, and packed with as much or more nutrition than fresh vegetables.

NUTRITION FACTS PER SERVING:

166 calories
2 g total fat
0 g saturated fat
27 mg cholesterol
623 mg sodium
23 g carbohydrate
4 g fiber
15 g protein

Fish Provençale

The sweet essence of fresh fennel blends nicely with fish, tomatoes, garlic, and onion. This orange-scented soup tastes as good as it smells.

INGREDIENTS

½ pound fresh or frozen skinless haddock, grouper, or halibut fillets

1 small fennel bulb

3 cups vegetable broth or chicken broth

1 large onion, finely chopped (1 cup)

1 small yellow summer squash, cubed (about 1 cup)

1 cup dry white wine

1 teaspoon finely shredded orange or lemon peel

1½ teaspoons bottled minced garlic or 3 cloves garlic, minced

2 cups chopped tomatoes or one 14½-ounce can diced tomatoes

2 tablespoons snipped fresh thyme
Snipped fresh thyme (optional)

Dry white wine adds zest to fish

soups, like this one, as well as to lobster bisque and creamy chowders. Be thrifty with salt in a soup to which wine is added; wine intensifies the saltiness.

Start to finish: 30 minutes

DIRECTIONS

1. Thaw fish, if frozen. Rinse fish; pat dry. Cut fish into 1-inch pieces; set aside.

2. Cut off and discard upper stalks of fennel. Remove any wilted outer layers; cut a thin slice from base. Wash fennel; cut in half lengthwise and thinly slice.

3. In a large saucepan combine fennel, broth, onion, squash, wine, orange peel, and garlic. Bring to boiling; reduce heat. Cover and simmer for 10 minutes. Stir in fish pieces, tomatoes, and the 2 tablespoons thyme. Cook about 3 minutes more or until fish flakes easily when tested with a fork. If desired, garnish with additional snipped thyme. Makes 4 servings.

NUTRITION FACTS PER SERVING:

156 calories
3 g total fat
0 g saturated fat
18 mg cholesterol
752 mg sodium
15 g carbohydrate
8 g fiber
14 g protein

INGREDIENTS

¾ pound fresh or frozen salmon
steaks, cut ¾ inch thick

3 cups sliced fresh shiitake or
other mushrooms

¾ cup thinly sliced leeks or ½ cup
thinly sliced green onion

2 tablespoons margarine or butter

2 cups chicken broth or vegetable
broth

1½ teaspoons snipped fresh dill or
½ teaspoon dried dillweed
Dash pepper

2 cups half-and-half or light cream

2 tablespoons cornstarch

2 tablespoons dry sherry

Sherried Salmon Bisque

Salmon, shiitake mushrooms, leeks, and dry sherry come
together to create this sophisticated soup.

Start to finish: 30 minutes

DIRECTIONS

1. Thaw salmon, if frozen.
Rinse salmon; pat dry. Cut
salmon into ¾-inch pieces.
Discard skin and bones. In
a large saucepan cook
mushrooms and leeks or
green onions in hot margarine
or butter until tender. Stir in
chicken broth or vegetable
broth, fresh dill or dried

dillweed, and pepper. Bring
to boiling.

2. Combine half-and-half
or light cream and cornstarch;
stir into mushroom mixture.
Cook and stir over medium
heat until thickened and
bubbly. Add salmon. Cover
and simmer about 4 minutes
or until fish flakes easily

when tested with a fork.
Gently stir in the dry sherry.
Makes 4 servings.

NUTRITION FACTS PER SERVING:

365 calories
24 g total fat
11 g saturated fat
60 mg cholesterol
563 mg sodium
18 g carbohydrate
3 g fiber
20 g protein

Choose mushrooms that are
firm, fresh, and plump with no
bruises. Store them, unwashed, in
the refrigerator for up to 2 days.
Store prepackaged mushrooms in
the package. Loose mushrooms or
those in an open package should
be stored in a paper bag or in a
damp cloth bag in the refrigerator.
This allows them to breathe so
they stay firmer longer. Don't store
mushrooms in plastic bags because
the mushrooms will deteriorate
more quickly.

Salmon Salad

This salad will remind you of a Caesar salad—without the raw eggs, anchovies, high fat, and calories. Plain yogurt adds the creamy texture to the garlic-and-lemon dressing.

INGREDIENTS

2 tablespoons olive oil

5 cloves garlic, thinly sliced

2 tablespoons lemon juice

1 tablespoon Worcestershire sauce

1 tablespoon Dijon-style mustard

1 tablespoon water

½ teaspoon pepper

⅓ cup plain fat-free yogurt

12 ounces fresh or frozen skinless, boneless salmon fillets, 1 inch thick

Nonstick cooking spray

10 cups torn romaine

½ cup thinly sliced red onion

¼ cup freshly grated Parmesan cheese

1 cup cherry tomatoes, halved

½ cup pitted ripe olives, halved (optional)

Prep time: 20 minutes
Marinating time: 30 minutes
Broiling time: 8 minutes

DIRECTIONS

1. For dressing, in a small saucepan heat olive oil over medium-low heat. Add the garlic. Cook and stir for 1 to 2 minutes or until garlic is light golden. Transfer garlic to a blender container. Add lemon juice, Worcestershire sauce, mustard, water, and pepper. Cover and blend until combined. Remove 2 tablespoons of the garlic mixture; set aside. Add the yogurt to the remaining garlic mixture in blender. Cover and blend until smooth. Chill until serving time.

2. Thaw fish, if frozen. Rinse fish; pat dry with paper towels. Brush the reserved garlic mixture evenly over fish. Cover and marinate in the refrigerator for 30 minutes.

3. Coat the unheated rack of a broiler pan with cooking spray. Place fish on rack; tuck under any thin edges. Broil 4 to 5 inches from the heat for 8 to 12 minutes or until fish flakes easily when tested with a fork, gently turning halfway through broiling.

4. Meanwhile, in a large bowl combine the romaine, red onion, and Parmesan cheese. Add the chilled yogurt dressing; toss to coat.

Divide the romaine mixture among 4 plates. Top with the fish, cherry tomatoes, and ripe olives (if desired). Makes 4 servings.

NUTRITION FACTS PER SERVING:

234 calories
13 g total fat
3 g saturated fat
21 mg cholesterol
331 mg sodium
12 g carbohydrate
4 g fiber
19 g protein

Tuna-Vegetable Salad

INGREDIENTS

1 cup chopped celery and/or chopped seeded cucumber

½ cup shredded carrot

2 tablespoons sliced green onion

⅓ cup fat-free mayonnaise dressing or salad dressing

1½ teaspoons snipped fresh dill or ½ teaspoon dried dillweed

½ teaspoon finely shredded lemon peel

⅛ teaspoon garlic powder

⅛ teaspoon pepper

1 6½-ounce can low-sodium chunk light or white tuna (water pack), drained and broken into chunks

4 medium tomatoes, sliced

Fresh dill (optional)

For a great sandwich, spread the tuna mixture between slices of whole wheat bread and top with tomato and lettuce.

Prep time: 15 minutes
Chilling time: 1 hour

DIRECTIONS

1. In a medium mixing bowl combine the celery or cucumber, carrot, and green onion. Stir in the mayonnaise dressing or salad dressing, snipped or dried dill, lemon peel, garlic powder, and pepper. Gently fold in tuna. Cover and chill mixture for 1 to 4 hours.

2. To serve, divide the sliced tomatoes among 4 plates. Spoon the tuna mixture over tomato slices.

If desired, garnish with additional fresh dill. Makes 4 servings.

NUTRITION FACTS PER SERVING:

109 calories
1 g total fat
0 g saturated fat
15 mg cholesterol
314 mg sodium
13 g carbohydrate
3 g fiber
13 g protein

151

Salmon Caesar Salad

Smoked salmon turns a classic side-dish salad into a hearty entrée for three.

INGREDIENTS

1   10-ounce package Caesar salad mix (includes greens, dressing, croutons, and Parmesan cheese)

1   small yellow, red, and/or green sweet pepper, cut into thin strips

¼   cup sliced pitted ripe olives

6   ounces smoked salmon, skinned, boned, and broken into chunks; or 3 to 4 ounces thinly sliced smoked salmon (lox-style), cut into bite-size strips

If you can't find packaged Caesar salad, substitute 5 cups torn mixed salad greens, ⅓ cup croutons, 3 tablespoons bottled Caesar or ranch salad dressing, and 2 tablespoons grated Parmesan cheese.

Start to finish: 10 minutes

DIRECTIONS

1. In a large salad bowl combine the lettuce and dressing from the salad mix, the sweet pepper strips, and olives. Toss mixture gently to coat. Add the croutons and cheese from the mix and the salmon. Toss gently. Makes 3 servings.

NUTRITION FACTS PER SERVING:

254 calories
18 g total fat
2 g saturated fat
19 mg cholesterol
971 mg sodium
10 g carbohydrate
1 g fiber
14 g protein

INGREDIENTS

¼ cup honey

¼ cup reduced-sodium soy sauce

1 teaspoon toasted sesame oil

½ teaspoon crushed red pepper

4 5-ounce fresh tuna steaks, cut ½ to 1 inch thick

12 cups mesclun or torn mixed bitter salad greens (about 8 ounces)

10 to 12 yellow or red pear-shaped tomatoes, halved

Honey-Glazed Tuna and Greens

Here's fusion cuisine—a hybrid of Asian and European cooking—made fast. As the tuna is quick-grilled to seal in the juices, a soy-honey sauce with a touch of heat from crushed red pepper caramelizes, creating a beautiful and delicious glaze.

Start to finish: 20 minutes

DIRECTIONS

1. In a small bowl combine the honey, soy sauce, sesame oil, and red pepper. Set aside 2 tablespoons of the mixture to brush on fish and reserve the remaining for dressing.

2. Rinse fish; pat dry. Brush both sides of fish with the 2 tablespoons soy mixture. Grill fish on the greased rack of an uncovered grill directly over medium coals until fish flakes easily when tested with a fork (allow 4 to 6 minutes per ½-inch thickness of fish). Gently turn fish steaks over halfway through cooking. (Or, broil on the greased unheated rack of a broiler pan about 4 inches from the heat (allow 4 to 6 minutes per ½-inch thickness of fish). Gently turn fish steaks over halfway through cooking.)

3. Toss together mesclun and tomatoes; arrange on 4 dinner plates. Cut fish across the grain into ½-inch-wide slices; arrange on greens. Drizzle with the reserved soy mixture. Makes 4 servings.

Toasted sesame oil is a flavoring oil, not a cooking oil, and is used sparingly in recipes because of its strong flavor. Once opened, it should be kept in the refrigerator to prevent it from becoming rancid. It can be stored for up to a year.

NUTRITION FACTS PER SERVING:

279 calories
2 g total fat
0 g saturated fat
24 mg cholesterol
1,015 mg sodium
22 g carbohydrate
1 g fiber
42 g protein

Shrimp and Roma Tomatoes With Pasta

Roma tomatoes and tarragon impart a garden-fresh flavor to this delightful combination.

INGREDIENTS

- 1 12-ounce package frozen, peeled, and deveined shrimp
- 1 9-ounce package refrigerated spinach or plain fettuccine
- 1 medium onion, chopped (½ cup)
- 1 teaspoon bottled minced garlic or 2 cloves garlic, minced
- 1 tablespoon olive oil or cooking oil
- 4 medium roma tomatoes, chopped (about 1⅔ cups)
- 2 teaspoons snipped fresh tarragon or ½ teaspoon dried tarragon, crushed
- ¼ teaspoon coarsely ground black pepper

Got a spare minute? Use it to chop an extra onion or green pepper by hand or with a food processor. Then store it by spreading the chopped onion or green pepper in a single layer in a shallow baking pan and freezing. Next, break up the frozen vegetables into pieces and put them into freezer bags or containers. Seal, label, and store them in the freezer for up to 1 month. To use, just add the amount you need to what you're cooking—no need to thaw!

Start to finish: 15 minutes

DIRECTIONS

1. In a large saucepan cook the shrimp with the fettuccine according to the package directions for the fettuccine. Drain. Return to the hot saucepan.

2. Meanwhile, in a medium saucepan cook onion and garlic in hot oil until onion is tender. Stir in tomatoes, tarragon, and pepper. Cook over low heat, stirring occasionally, for 2 to 3 minutes or until heated through.

3. Add tomato mixture to fettuccine mixture in saucepan. Toss to mix. Makes 4 servings.

NUTRITION FACTS PER SERVING:

277 calories
5 g total fat
1 g saturated fat
131 mg cholesterol
173 mg sodium
37 g carbohydrate
1 g fiber
20 g protein

INGREDIENTS

1½ cups water

¼ teaspoon salt

1½ cups quick-cooking rice

½ cup chicken broth

1½ teaspoons cornstarch

1 medium red sweet pepper, cut into thin strips

1 medium green sweet pepper, cut into thin strips

1 small onion, cut into thin wedges

2 teaspoons bottled minced garlic or 4 cloves garlic, minced

1 tablespoon margarine or butter

1 12-ounce package frozen, peeled and deveined shrimp, thawed

1 tablespoon margarine or butter

2 tablespoons snipped fresh parsley

Shrimp in Garlic Sauce

Stir-fry the shrimp just until they turn pink. Overcooking toughens them.

Start to finish: 20 minutes

DIRECTIONS

1. In a medium saucepan bring the water and salt to boiling. Stir in rice. Cover; remove from heat. Let stand until serving time. For sauce, stir together chicken broth and cornstarch. Set aside.

2. In a wok or large skillet cook red pepper, green pepper, onion, and garlic in 1 tablespoon hot margarine or butter over medium-high heat about 3 minutes or until pepper and onion are crisp-tender. Remove vegetables from the wok or skillet. Add shrimp and 1 tablespoon margarine or butter. Stir-fry over medium-high heat for 3 to 4 minutes or until shrimp turn opaque.

3. Push shrimp from the center of the wok or skillet. Stir sauce; add to the center of the wok. Cook and stir until thickened and bubbly. Return vegetables to the wok or skillet. Stir to coat with sauce. Cook and stir about 1 minute more or until heated through.

4. Stir parsley into rice. Immediately serve shrimp mixture over hot rice. Makes 4 servings.

NUTRITION FACTS PER SERVING:

285 calories

7 g total fat

1 g saturated fat

131 mg cholesterol

453 mg sodium

37 g carbohydrate

1 g fiber

18 g protein

155

Shrimp Salad

This salad has the makings of an elegant meal and deserves consideration for a special celebration menu. The flavors of asparagus and shrimp flourish with the addition of the balsamic vinaigrette.

INGREDIENTS

- 2 tablespoons dried tomato pieces (not oil-packed)
- ¼ cup balsamic vinegar
- 2 tablespoons olive oil
- 1 tablespoon snipped fresh basil
- 2 teaspoons Dijon-style mustard
- 2 cloves garlic, minced
- ¼ teaspoon sugar
- ⅛ teaspoon pepper
- 12 ounces fresh or frozen, peeled and deveined shrimp
- 4 cups water
- 1 clove garlic
- 8 ounces asparagus, cut into 2-inch pieces
- 6 cups torn mixed salad greens
- 2 medium pears, cored and thinly sliced

Cook shrimp quickly; overcooking toughens them. Cook shrimp just until they curl, the shells (if present) turn pink, and their flesh turns opaque.

Prep time: 20 minutes
Cooking time: 5 minutes
Chilling time: 4 hours

DIRECTIONS

1. In a small bowl pour enough boiling water over tomato pieces to cover. Soak for 2 minutes. Drain.

2. For dressing, in a screw-top jar combine the tomato pieces, vinegar, olive oil, basil, mustard, the 2 cloves garlic, the sugar, and pepper. Cover and shake well. If desired, cover and chill for up to 24 hours.

3. Thaw shrimp, if frozen. Rinse shrimp; pat dry with paper towels. In a large saucepan bring the water and the 1 clove garlic to boiling; add asparagus. Return to boiling; reduce heat. Simmer, uncovered, for 4 minutes.

4. Add shrimp to saucepan. Return to boiling; reduce heat. Simmer, uncovered, for 1 to 3 minutes more or until shrimp turn opaque. Drain, discarding garlic. Rinse under cold running water; drain well. Cover and chill for 4 to 24 hours.

5. To serve, divide greens and pears among 4 plates. Top with shrimp and asparagus. Shake dressing; drizzle over salads. Serves 4.

NUTRITION FACTS PER SERVING:

221 calories
8 g total fat
1 g saturated fat
131 mg cholesterol
260 mg sodium
21 g carbohydrate
4 g fiber
17 g protein

Shrimp with Tarragon Dressing

INGREDIENTS

- 1 pound fresh or frozen shrimp in shells
- 3 medium potatoes, sliced ¼ inch thick
- ¼ cup light mayonnaise dressing or salad dressing
- ¼ cup buttermilk or plain low-fat yogurt
- 2 green onions, sliced
- 2 tablespoons snipped fresh parsley
- 1 teaspoon snipped fresh tarragon or ¼ teaspoon dried tarragon, crushed

- 1 clove garlic, minced
- 4 cups water
- 2 tablespoons vinegar
- ½ teaspoon salt
- Lettuce leaves
- 8 cherry tomatoes (optional)

This flavorful salad is an easy make-ahead. Arrange the potatoes and shrimp on lettuce-lined plates. Make the dressing. Cover and chill salads and dressing until you're ready to serve. Just before serving, drizzle the dressing over the salads.

Start to finish: 40 minutes

DIRECTIONS

1. Thaw shrimp, if frozen. Peel and devein shrimp, leaving tails on if desired. Rinse shrimp; pat dry with paper towels. Cover and chill until needed.

2. In a covered saucepan cook the potatoes in a small amount of lightly salted boiling water for 8 to 12 minutes or until tender. Drain well. Set aside.

3. Meanwhile, for dressing, in a blender container combine the mayonnaise dressing or salad dressing,

buttermilk or yogurt, green onions, parsley, tarragon, and garlic. Cover and blend until smooth. Set aside.

4. In a large saucepan combine the water, vinegar, and salt. Bring to boiling. Add shrimp. Reduce heat. Simmer, uncovered, for 1 to 3 minutes or until shrimp turn opaque. Drain. Rinse with cold water; drain.

5. Arrange the potato slices and shrimp on 4 lettuce-lined plates. If necessary, stir some water into the dressing to make of drizzling consistency. Drizzle dressing over potatoes and shrimp. If desired, garnish with cherry tomatoes. Makes 4 servings.

To store fresh shrimp, first rinse them under cold running water, then drain well. Cover and store in the refrigerator for up to 2 days.

NUTRITION FACTS PER SERVING:

237 calories
6 g total fat
1 g saturated fat
131 mg cholesterol
553 mg sodium
28 g carbohydrate
1 g fiber
17 g protein

New Crab Cakes

This new take on a classic balances tender crab with the crunch of potato chips.

INGREDIENTS

- 1 recipe Herb Sauce (see recipe, below)
  Shredded lemon peel (optional)
- 1 beaten egg
- ½ cup finely crushed potato chips
- 2 tablespoons shredded coconut, toasted
- 1 green onion, finely chopped (2 tablespoons)
- 2 tablespoons mayonnaise or salad dressing
- 1 tablespoon snipped fresh parsley
- ½ teaspoon ground coriander
- 6 ounces cooked crabmeat, cut into bite-size pieces, or one 6-ounce can crabmeat, drained, flaked, and cartilage removed
- 2 tablespoons cooking oil

Toasting heightens the flavor of coconut and adds an appealing golden color. To toast, spread the coconut in a single layer in a shallow baking pan. Bake in a 350° oven for 5 to 10 minutes or until light golden brown, watching carefully and stirring once or twice so the coconut doesn't burn.

Start to finish: 25 minutes

DIRECTIONS

1. Prepare Herb Sauce. Cover and refrigerate at least 20 minutes to allow flavors to mellow. If desired, garnish with shredded lemon peel.

2. In a medium mixing bowl combine egg, ¼ cup of the crushed potato chips, the coconut, green onion, mayonnaise or salad dressing, parsley, and coriander. Stir in crabmeat; mix well. Shape crabmeat mixture into eight ½-inch-thick patties. Coat patties with remaining crushed potato chips.

3. In a large skillet heat oil. (Add additional oil if necessary during cooking.) Add crab cakes. Cook over medium heat 4 to 6 minutes or until golden and heated through, turning once. Serve immediately with Herb Sauce. Makes 4 servings.

Herb Sauce: In a small bowl combine ¼ cup mayonnaise or salad dressing, 1 tablespoon snipped fresh cilantro, and 1 teaspoon finely shredded lemon peel.

NUTRITION FACTS PER SERVING:

365 calories
32 g total fat
5 g saturated fat
108 mg cholesterol
351 mg sodium
10 g carbohydrate
1 g fiber
12 g protein

Crab and Fruit Salad

INGREDIENTS

- ½ cup mayonnaise or salad dressing
- 1 green onion, sliced (2 tablespoons)
- 1 tablespoon frozen orange juice concentrate, thawed
- ½ teaspoon ground ginger
  Dash ground red pepper
- ½ pound lump crabmeat or one 8-ounce package flake-style imitation crabmeat
- 6 cups torn mixed salad greens
- 2 cups fresh strawberries, halved
- 1 11-ounce can mandarin orange sections, drained
- ¼ cup pecan pieces (optional)

Store the can of mandarin orange sections in the refrigerator, and the oranges will be icy cold when you are ready to add them to the salad.

Start to finish: 20 minutes

DIRECTIONS

1. In a medium mixing bowl stir together the mayonnaise or salad dressing, green onion, orange juice concentrate, ginger, and red pepper. Gently stir in crabmeat or crab-flavored fish. Cover and chill in the freezer about 10 minutes or until cold.

2. Meanwhile, toss together salad greens, strawberries, and mandarin oranges. Arrange on 4 salad plates. Divide the crab mixture among the salad plates. If desired, sprinkle with pecans. Makes 4 servings.

NUTRITION FACTS PER SERVING:

334 calories
24 g total fat
3 g saturated fat
73 mg cholesterol
358 mg sodium
19 g carbohydrate
3 g fiber
14 g protein

Cut down on last-minute

work by tearing the salad greens ahead of time. When storing the torn greens, refrigerate them in a sealed plastic bag or a covered plastic container. Place a white paper towel in the bottom of the bag or container to absorb any excess water from the greens. For maximum freshness, prepare the greens only a day or two ahead.

159

Pan-Seared Scallops

This is a flash in the pan! Sweet scallops are given a Cajun-flavored crust, then tossed with balsamic vinegar-dressed spinach and crisp-cooked bacon. Serve with corn bread and cold beer and you have a meal that's both homey and elegant in no time flat.

INGREDIENTS

1 pound fresh sea scallops

2 tablespoons all-purpose flour

1 to 2 teaspoons blackened steak seasoning or Cajun seasoning

1 tablespoon cooking oil

1 10-ounce package prewashed spinach

1 tablespoon water

2 tablespoons balsamic vinegar

¼ cup cooked bacon pieces

Start to finish: 20 minutes

DIRECTIONS

1. Rinse scallops; pat dry. In a plastic bag combine flour and steak seasoning. Add scallops; toss gently to coat. In a large skillet cook the scallops in hot oil over medium heat for 3 to 5 minutes or until browned and opaque, turning once halfway through cooking. Remove scallops.

2. Add spinach to skillet; sprinkle with water. Cook, covered, over medium-high heat about 2 minutes or until spinach starts to wilt. Add vinegar; toss to coat evenly. Return scallops; heat through. Sprinkle with bacon. Makes 4 servings.

NUTRITION FACTS PER SERVING:

158 calories
6 g total fat
1 g saturated fat
37 mg cholesterol
323 mg sodium
9 g carbohydrate
2 g fiber
18 g protein

Scallops Scampi-Style

Shrimp scampi, listed on restaurant menus, is shrimp cooked in garlic, butter, white wine, and herbs. Our version of the popular dish features tender, sweet scallops.

INGREDIENTS

- 1 9-ounce package refrigerated spinach or plain fettuccine
- 12 ounces fresh or frozen bay or sea scallops
- ¾ cup reduced-sodium chicken broth
- ½ cup dry white wine
- 3 cloves garlic, minced
- ½ teaspoon dried oregano, crushed
- ½ teaspoon dried rosemary, crushed
- ¼ teaspoon cracked black pepper
- 4 teaspoons cornstarch
- 3 tablespoons snipped fresh parsley

Start to finish: 20 minutes

DIRECTIONS

1. Cook pasta according to package directions, omitting oil; drain. Keep warm.

2. Meanwhile, thaw scallops, if frozen. Halve or quarter any large scallops. Rinse scallops; pat dry with paper towels. In a large saucepan combine chicken broth, ¼ cup of the wine, the garlic, oregano, rosemary, and cracked pepper. Bring to boiling. Add scallops; return to boiling. Reduce heat. Simmer, covered, for 1 to 2 minutes or until scallops turn opaque. Drain, reserving the cooking liquid. Return liquid to saucepan.

3. In a small bowl combine the remaining wine and the cornstarch. Add to the cooking liquid. Cook and stir until thickened and bubbly. Cook and stir for 2 minutes more. Stir in scallops and parsley; heat through. Serve scallop mixture over cooked pasta. Makes 4 servings.

Sea scallops can be quite large.

For this recipe, halve or quarter them. The meat of either type of scallop can be creamy white, tan, or creamy pink.

NUTRITION FACTS PER SERVING:

272 calories
2 g total fat
0 g saturated fat
72 mg cholesterol
223 mg sodium
40 g carbohydrate
0 g fiber
19 g protein

Scallops and Artichoke Stir-Fry

Accent this light-and-lemony stir-fry by serving it over couscous, a quick-cooking grain commonly used in North African cuisine. Look for couscous near the rice or pasta in your grocery store.

INGREDIENTS

12	ounces fresh or frozen bay or sea scallops
¾	cup water
3	tablespoons lemon juice
1	tablespoon cornstarch
1	teaspoon sugar
1	teaspoon instant chicken bouillon granules
⅛	teaspoon black pepper
1	8- or 9-ounce package frozen artichoke hearts
	Nonstick cooking spray
2	medium green and/or red sweet peppers, cut into thin bite-size strips
2	cups sliced fresh shiitake, oyster, or brown mushrooms
1	tablespoon cooking oil
2	cups hot cooked couscous

NUTRITION FACTS PER SERVING:

208 calories
5 g total fat
1 g saturated fat
26 mg cholesterol
409 mg sodium
28 g carbohydrate
8 g fiber
17 g protein

Start to finish: 30 minutes

DIRECTIONS

1. Thaw scallops, if frozen. Halve any large scallops. Rinse scallops; pat dry with paper towels. Set aside.

2. For sauce, in a small bowl combine the water, lemon juice, cornstarch, sugar, bouillon granules, and black pepper. Set aside.

3. Place the artichokes in a colander. Run cold water over them until partially thawed. Halve any large pieces. Set artichokes aside.

4. Coat an unheated nonstick wok or large skillet with cooking spray. Preheat over medium-high heat. Add the artichokes; stir-fry for 2 minutes. Add the sweet peppers and mushrooms; stir-fry for 2 to 4 minutes or until peppers are crisp-tender. Remove vegetables from wok.

5. Add the oil to hot wok. Add the scallops; stir-fry about 2 minutes or until opaque. Push the scallops from center of wok.

6. Stir sauce; add to center of wok. Cook and stir until thickened and bubbly. Return the cooked vegetables to wok. Cook and stir about 2 minutes or until heated through. Serve immediately over hot cooked couscous. Makes 4 servings.

No-Chop Scallop Stir-Fry

Both bay and sea scallops are delicious in this easy stir-fry dish, but cut the larger sea scallops in half before cooking.

INGREDIENTS

- ¾ pound fresh or frozen bay or sea scallops
- 6 cups water
- 8 ounces Chinese egg noodles or vermicelli, broken into 3- to 4-inch-long pieces
- ¼ cup soy sauce
- 3 tablespoons dry sherry or apple juice
- ½ teaspoon ground ginger
- 1 tablespoon cooking oil
- 1½ teaspoons bottled minced garlic or 3 cloves garlic, minced
- 2 cups frozen loose-pack stir-fry vegetables

Start to finish: 15 minutes

DIRECTIONS

1. Thaw scallops, if frozen. Rinse scallops; pat dry and set aside. In a large saucepan bring water to boiling. Cook egg noodles or vermicelli in boiling water until al dente (tender, but still slightly firm when bitten. Allow 3 to 4 minutes for egg noodles or 5 to 7 minutes for vermicelli.) Drain. Rinse and drain again; set aside.

2. Meanwhile, for sauce, stir together soy sauce, sherry or apple juice, and ginger; set aside. Cut any large scallops in half; set aside.

3. Pour cooking oil into a wok or large skillet. (Add more oil as necessary during cooking.) Preheat over medium-high heat. Stir-fry garlic in hot oil for 15 seconds. Add frozen vegetables. Stir-fry for 2 to 3 minutes or until crisp-tender. Remove the vegetables from the wok.

4. Add the scallops to the hot wok. Stir-fry for 2 to 3 minutes or until opaque. Push scallops from the center of the wok. Stir sauce. Add sauce to the center of the wok. Return vegetables to the wok. Add noodles to the wok. Toss to coat with sauce. Serve immediately. Makes 4 servings.

NUTRITION FACTS PER SERVING:

285 calories
6 g total fat
1 g saturated fat
62 mg cholesterol
1,178 mg sodium
37 g carbohydrate
0 g fiber
18 g protein

163

Middle Eastern Bulgur-Spinach Salad Recipe, page 196

Meatless Entrées

Italian Three-Bean And Rice Skillet

Red beans, lima beans, and green beans are a tasty trio in this basil-accented skillet meal.

INGREDIENTS

1   15- to 15½-ounce can small red beans or red kidney beans, rinsed and drained

1   14½-ounce can Italian-style stewed tomatoes, undrained

1   cup vegetable broth or chicken broth

¾   cup quick-cooking brown rice

½   of a 10-ounce package frozen baby lima beans

½   of a 9-ounce package frozen cut green beans

½   teaspoon dried basil, crushed, or dried Italian seasoning, crushed

1   cup meatless spaghetti sauce

2   ounces thinly sliced mozzarella cheese or ¼ cup grated Parmesan cheese (optional)

Get meals on the table faster

by following these tips:

• Purchase food in the form called for (for example, shredded cheese or boned chicken breasts).

• Make turning on the oven or broiler (or starting the grill) your first cooking step.

• Overlap preparation steps. While waiting for water to boil, start chopping vegetables, opening cans, or mixing a filling.

• Measure liquids in an extra-large glass measuring cup. Then, rather than using a bowl, add the other ingredients to the cup and mix.

• Select a baking dish that doubles as a serving dish.

Prep time: 15 minutes
Cooking time: 15 minutes

DIRECTIONS

1. In a large skillet combine red beans or kidney beans, undrained tomatoes, broth, rice, lima beans, green beans, and basil or Italian seasoning. Bring to boiling; reduce heat. Cover and simmer about 15 minutes or until rice is tender.

2. Stir in spaghetti sauce. Heat through. If desired, top with mozzarella or Parmesan cheese. Makes 4 servings.

NUTRITION FACTS PER SERVING:

259 calories
4 g total fat
0 g saturated fat
0 mg cholesterol
1,103 mg sodium
50 g carbohydrate
10 g fiber
14 g protein

INGREDIENTS

- 1 medium spaghetti squash (2½ to 3 pounds), halved and seeded
- 1 10-ounce package frozen baby lima beans
- 1 15-ounce can red kidney beans, rinsed and drained
- ½ of a 7-ounce jar (½ cup) roasted red sweet peppers, rinsed, drained, and cut into short strips
- ½ teaspoon salt
- ¼ cup balsamic vinegar
- 3 tablespoons olive oil
- 1 tablespoon honey mustard
- 2 cloves garlic, minced

  Freshly ground black pepper

Spaghetti Squash With Balsamic Beans

It's not magic, just Mother Nature. When cooked, the golden flesh of spaghetti squash separates into strands that look like the ever-popular pasta. Top the squash strands with this sassy sauce of sweet-tart beans.

Start to finish: 30 minutes

DIRECTIONS

1. Place the squash halves in a large Dutch oven with about 1 inch of water. Bring to boiling. Cook, covered, for 15 to 20 minutes or until squash is tender.

2. Meanwhile, in a medium saucepan cook the lima beans according to package directions, adding kidney beans the last 3 minutes of cooking; drain. Return the beans to saucepan. Stir in roasted red peppers and salt; heat through.

3. Meanwhile, for the vinaigrette,* in a screw-top jar combine vinegar, oil, honey mustard, and garlic. Cover and shake well. Pour over warm bean mixture; toss to coat.

4. Use a fork to scrape the squash pulp from the shells in strands; return strands to each shell. Spoon warm bean mixture over squash strands in shells, drizzling any excess vinaigrette on top. Season to taste with freshly ground black pepper. To serve, cut each squash shell in half. Makes 4 servings.

*Note: The vinaigrette may be prepared ahead and refrigerated for up to 2 days. Allow it to sit at room temperature while preparing squash and beans.

NUTRITION FACTS PER SERVING:

421 calories
11 g total fat
2 g saturated fat
0 mg cholesterol
466 mg sodium
65 g carbohydrate
13 g fiber
21 g protein

Chickpea Pita Pockets

Packed in a pita, this grape, spinach, and garbanzo bean combo makes a satisfying meatless meal.

INGREDIENTS

1 15-ounce can garbanzo beans, rinsed and drained

1 cup shredded fresh spinach or lettuce

⅔ cup seedless grapes, halved

½ cup finely chopped red sweet pepper

⅓ cup thinly sliced celery

¼ cup finely chopped onion

¼ cup mayonnaise or salad dressing

2 tablespoons poppy seed salad dressing or desired creamy salad dressing

4 pita bread rounds, split in half crosswise

½ cup finely shredded Swiss cheese (2 ounces)

Garbanzo beans,

sometimes called chickpeas, are round, beige beans that stay slightly firm even when cooked. They have a mild, nutty flavor and often are used in Mediterranean and Mexican cooking. Look for them in the bean or Mexican food sections of your supermarket.

Start to finish: 20 minutes

DIRECTIONS

1. In a large bowl combine garbanzo beans, spinach or lettuce, grapes, sweet pepper, celery, and onion.

2. In a small bowl stir together mayonnaise or salad dressing and poppy seed dressing or desired dressing. Add to garbanzo bean mixture, stirring until combined. Spoon into pita bread halves. Top with cheese. Makes 4 servings.

NUTRITION FACTS PER SERVING:

476 calories
21 g total fat
5 g saturated fat
21 mg cholesterol
857 mg sodium
58 g carbohydrate
6 g fiber
15 g protein

Rice 'n' Bean Tostadas

INGREDIENTS

1½ cups water

1½ cups quick-cooking brown rice

1 medium onion, chopped (½ cup)

1 15-ounce can chili beans with
    chili gravy, undrained

1 8-ounce can whole kernel corn,
    drained

4 9- to 10-inch flour tortillas

3 cups torn mixed salad greens

½ cup shredded cheddar cheese
    (2 ounces)

¼ cup dairy sour cream

1 medium tomato, chopped
    (⅔ cup)

Quick-cooking brown rice, canned chili beans, shredded cheese, and a package of mixed salad greens make easy work of these tostadas.

Quick-cooking brown rice is fast because it has already been cooked, then dehydrated. When you prepare it at home, you're really just putting the water back.

Prep time: 20 minutes
Baking time: 10 minutes

DIRECTIONS

1. In a large saucepan bring water to boiling. Stir in rice and onion. Return to boiling; reduce heat. Cover and simmer for 5 minutes. Remove from heat. Stir. Cover and let stand for 5 minutes. Stir undrained chili beans and corn into rice mixture. Heat through.

2. Meanwhile, place tortillas on a large baking sheet, overlapping as necessary. Bake in a 400° oven about 10 minutes or until tortillas begin to brown around the edges.

3. Place each tortilla on a dinner plate. Top tortillas with salad greens and the rice-bean mixture. Sprinkle with cheddar cheese. Serve with sour cream and chopped tomato. Makes 4 servings.

NUTRITION FACTS PER SERVING:

512 calories
14 g total fat
6 g saturated fat
21 mg cholesterol
735 mg sodium
81 g carbohydrate
9 g fiber
19 g protein

Lentil and Veggie Tostadas

Sign up here for Dinner 101! This hearty, healthful entrée is ideal weeknight family fare and so easy that even rookie chefs can help prepare it.

INGREDIENTS

1¾ cups water

¾ cup red lentils, rinsed and drained

¼ cup chopped onion

1 to 2 tablespoons snipped fresh cilantro

1 clove garlic, minced

½ teaspoon salt

½ teaspoon ground cumin

4 tostada shells

2 cups chopped assorted fresh vegetables (such as broccoli, tomato, zucchini, and/or yellow summer squash)

¾ cup shredded Monterey Jack cheese (3 ounces)

Start to finish: 25 minutes

DIRECTIONS

1. In a medium saucepan stir together the water, lentils, onion, cilantro, garlic, salt, and cumin. Bring to boiling; reduce heat. Simmer, covered, for 12 to 15 minutes or until lentils are tender and most of the liquid is absorbed. Use a fork to mash the cooked lentils.

2. Spread the lentil mixture on tostada shells; top with vegetables and cheese. Place on a large baking sheet. Broil 3 to 4 inches from the heat about 2 minutes or until cheese is melted. Serve the tostadas immediately. Makes 4 servings.

NUTRITION FACTS PER SERVING:

288 calories
11 g total fat
5 g saturated fat
20 mg cholesterol
497 mg sodium
34 g carbohydrate
7 g fiber
16 g protein

INGREDIENTS

8 8-inch flavored or plain flour
    tortillas
1 cup vegetable broth or chicken
    broth
1 4-ounce can diced green chili
    peppers, drained
¼ teaspoon ground turmeric
    Dash black pepper
⅔ cup quick-cooking couscous
¼ cup sliced green onions
1 cup chopped tomatoes
¾ cup chopped green sweet pepper
½ cup finely shredded reduced-fat
    Mexican-blend cheese
    Salsa (optional)

Couscous Burritos

Moroccan pasta in a Mexican burrito? Why not! Let this speedy international wrap rocket your taste buds in an entirely new direction.

Start to finish: 20 minutes

DIRECTIONS

1. Wrap the tortillas in foil. Heat in a 350° oven for 10 minutes to soften. (Or, wrap tortillas in microwave-safe paper towels. Microwave on 100% power (high) for 30 seconds.)

2. Meanwhile, in a small saucepan combine the broth, green chili peppers, turmeric, and black pepper. Bring to boiling. Remove from heat and stir in couscous and green onions. Let stand, covered, for 5 minutes. Fluff couscous with a fork. Stir in tomatoes and sweet pepper.

3. To assemble each burrito, spoon about ⅓ cup of the couscous mixture onto a tortilla just below center. Top with 2 tablespoons of the cheese. Roll up the tortilla. If desired, serve with salsa. Makes 4 servings.

NUTRITION FACTS PER SERVING:

359 calories
8 g total fat
3 g saturated fat
5 mg cholesterol
661 mg sodium
60 g carbohydrate
7 g fiber
13 g protein

171

Cheesy Egg Wedges

This dish is perfect just about any time. On weeknights, dish it up as a quick supper along with a tossed salad. For a leisurely weekend brunch, team it with a coffee cake and mixed fruit. When you're planning a party, cut it into 16 wedges and serve it as an appetizer.

INGREDIENTS

- 4 beaten eggs
- ⅓ cup milk
- ¼ cup all-purpose flour
- ½ teaspoon baking powder
- ⅛ teaspoon garlic powder
- 2 cups shredded cheddar or mozzarella cheese (8 ounces)
- 1 cup cream-style cottage cheese with chives
- 1 cup meatless spaghetti sauce or salsa
- Fresh basil (optional)

If cottage cheese with chives isn't available, stir some snipped fresh or dried chives into regular cottage cheese.

Start to finish: 30 minutes

DIRECTIONS

1. In a medium bowl combine the eggs, milk, flour, baking powder, and garlic powder. Beat with a rotary beater until combined. Stir in cheddar or mozzarella cheese and cottage cheese.

2. Pour into a greased 9-inch pie plate. Bake, uncovered, in a 375° oven for 25 to 30 minutes or until golden brown and a knife inserted near the center comes out clean.

3. Meanwhile, in a small saucepan cook spaghetti sauce or salsa over medium-low heat about 5 minutes or until warm, stirring occasionally.

4. To serve, cut egg mixture into 6 wedges. Top with spaghetti sauce or salsa. If desired, garnish with fresh basil. Makes 6 servings.

NUTRITION FACTS PER SERVING:

273 calories
18 g total fat
10 g saturated fat
186 mg cholesterol
614 mg sodium
9 g carbohydrate
0 g fiber
20 g protein

Southwest Skillet

It's home on the range with a stove-top main course built on classic Southwestern flavors. Round up everything you need in the aisles of most supermarkets.

INGREDIENTS

- 2 tablespoons sliced almonds
- 1 yellow sweet pepper, coarsely chopped
- 1 fresh jalapeño pepper, seeded and chopped
- 1 tablespoon olive oil or cooking oil
- 4 medium tomatoes (about 1¼ pounds), peeled and coarsely chopped
- 1½ to 2 teaspoons Mexican seasoning or 1 to 1½ teaspoons chili powder and ½ teaspoon ground cumin
- ¼ teaspoon salt
- 4 eggs
- 1 medium ripe avocado, seeded, peeled, and sliced (optional)
- Fresh chili peppers (optional)

3 to 5 minutes or until the whites are completely set and the yolks begin to thicken but are not firm. To serve, using a slotted spoon, transfer eggs to 4 dinner plates. Stir mixture in skillet; spoon around eggs on plates. Sprinkle with toasted almonds. If desired, serve with avocado slices and garnish with fresh chili peppers. Makes 4 servings.

Start to finish: 25 minutes

DIRECTIONS

1. Spread the almonds in a large skillet. Cook over medium heat for 4 to 5 minutes or until lightly browned, stirring occasionally. Remove toasted almonds from skillet; set aside. In the same skillet cook the sweet pepper and chopped jalapeño pepper in hot oil about 2 minutes or until tender. Stir in the tomatoes, Mexican seasoning, and salt. Bring to boiling; reduce heat. Simmer, covered, for 5 minutes.

2. Break one of the eggs into a measuring cup. Carefully slide the egg into the simmering tomato mixture. Repeat with remaining eggs. Sprinkle the eggs lightly with salt and black pepper.

3. Cover and cook eggs over medium-low heat for

NUTRITION FACTS PER SERVING:

166 calories
11 g total fat
2 g saturated fat
213 mg cholesterol
216 mg sodium
10 g carbohydrate
2 g fiber
9 g protein

173

Olive-Potato Frittata

Toss a fresh green salad to serve with this
Spanish-style dinner omelet.

2 tablespoons olive oil or
   cooking oil

2 medium potatoes (such as long
   white, round white, round
   red, or yellow), thinly sliced
   (about 2 cups)

1 medium onion, cut into thin
   wedges

1 teaspoon bottled minced garlic
   or 2 cloves garlic, minced

¼ teaspoon salt

¼ teaspoon pepper

8 eggs

2 tablespoons snipped fresh
   oregano or 1 teaspoon dried
   oregano, crushed

¼ teaspoon salt

½ cup sliced pitted ripe olives

¼ cup finely shredded provolone or
   Parmesan cheese

Prep time: 15 minutes
Cooking time: 15 minutes

DIRECTIONS

1. Heat oil in a 10-inch broiler-proof or regular skillet. Add the potatoes, onion, garlic, ¼ teaspoon salt, and pepper. Cover and cook over medium heat for 5 minutes. Turn potato mixture with a spatula. Cover and cook for 5 to 6 minutes more or until potatoes are tender, turning mixture once more.

2. In a medium mixing bowl beat together the eggs, oregano, and ¼ teaspoon salt. Pour egg mixture over hot potato mixture. Sprinkle with olives. Cook over medium heat. As the mixture sets, run a spatula around the edge of the skillet, lifting egg mixture to allow the uncooked portion to flow underneath. Continue cooking and lifting edge until egg mixture is almost set (the surface will be moist).

3. Place the broiler-proof skillet under the broiler 4 to 5 inches from the heat. Broil for 1 to 2 minutes or until top is set. (Or, if using a regular skillet, remove skillet from heat; cover and let stand for 3 to 4 minutes or until the top is set.) Sprinkle with cheese. Cut frittata into wedges and serve immediately. Makes 4 servings.

NUTRITION FACTS PER SERVING:

340 calories
21 g total fat
6 g saturated fat
431 mg cholesterol
671 mg sodium
21 g carbohydrate
2 g fiber
17 g protein

INGREDIENTS

3 tablespoons snipped dried
  tomatoes (not oil-packed)

4 beaten eggs

1½ cups milk, half-and-half, or
  light cream

1 tablespoon snipped fresh basil
  or 1 teaspoon dried basil,
  crushed

4 cups torn English muffins or dry
  French bread

1½ cups fresh or frozen whole
  kernel corn

1 cup shredded reduced-fat
  cheddar cheese or hot pepper
  cheese (4 ounces)

1 tomato, cut into thin wedges
  (optional)

Corn and Tomato Bread Pudding

The proof of a delicious dinner is in this pudding, a classic baked custard dessert reinvented as a savory main course. Cut cubes from only firm, day-old (or older) bread, as fresh bread is too soft to soak up all the milk and eggs and hold its shape.

Prep time: 20 minutes
Baking time: 30 minutes

NUTRITION FACTS PER SERVING:

275 calories
9 g total fat
4 g saturated fat
160 mg cholesterol
486 mg sodium
32 g carbohydrate
3 g fiber
16 g protein

DIRECTIONS

1. Soak dried tomatoes in enough hot water to cover for 15 minutes; drain.

2. Meanwhile, in a medium bowl beat together the eggs, milk, and basil; set aside. In an ungreased 2-quart square baking dish toss together the torn English muffins or bread, corn, cheese, and dried tomatoes. Carefully pour egg mixture evenly over corn mixture in baking dish.

3. Bake in a 375° oven about 30 minutes or until a knife inserted near the center comes out clean. Cool slightly. To serve, if desired, spoon bread pudding on top of tomato wedges. Makes 6 servings.

To make this dish ahead, prepare the egg mixture and the corn mixture, but keep them separate. Cover and refrigerate each for up to 24 hours. Combine and bake as directed.

Angel Hair with Asparagus, Tomatoes, and Fresh Basil

This light and elegant dish goes from the grocery bag to the table in about 20 minutes.

INGREDIENTS

- 1 pound fresh asparagus spears
- 4 cloves garlic, thinly sliced
- ¼ teaspoon pepper
- 1 tablespoon olive oil
- 6 medium roma tomatoes, seeded and chopped (2¼ cups)
- ¼ cup dry white wine
- ¼ teaspoon salt
- 1 tablespoon butter
- 1 9-ounce package refrigerated angel hair pasta
- ¼ cup shredded fresh basil

Butter helps to bind the sauce in this dish. Because margarine does not have all the same properties as butter, it isn't an effective substitute here.

Start to finish: 20 minutes

DIRECTIONS

1. Snap off and discard woody bases from asparagus. Remove the tips; set aside. Bias slice the remaining portions of asparagus spears into 1- to 1½-inch-long pieces; set aside.

2. In a large skillet cook and stir garlic and pepper in hot oil over medium heat for 1 minute. Add the tomatoes; cook 2 minutes more, stirring often. Add the asparagus pieces, wine, and salt to the mixture in the skillet. Cook, uncovered, for 3 minutes. Add the asparagus tips; cook, uncovered, for 1 minute more. Add butter and stir until melted.

3. Meanwhile, cook the pasta according to package directions. Drain pasta; return to pan. Add asparagus mixture and basil to pasta, tossing to coat. Makes 3 servings.

NUTRITION FACTS PER SERVING:

484 calories
11 g total fat
3 g saturated fat
10 mg cholesterol
238 mg sodium
81 g carbohydrate
4 g fiber
15 g protein

Pasta and Peas au Gratin

Another time, try bite-size pieces of fresh asparagus instead of the peas. Simply add them to the pasta for the last 3 to 4 minutes of cooking time.

INGREDIENTS

- 1 9-ounce package refrigerated cheese-filled tortellini or cheese-filled ravioli
- 1 cup frozen peas
- 2 tablespoons all-purpose flour
- ⅛ teaspoon pepper
- 1 cup half-and-half, light cream, or milk
- 1 14-ounce can chunky tomatoes with garlic and spices, undrained
- 2 tablespoons shredded Parmesan cheese

Start to finish: 15 minutes

DIRECTIONS

1. In a large saucepan cook tortellini or ravioli according to package directions, except add peas for the last 1 minute of cooking. Drain. Return pasta mixture to the hot saucepan.

2. Meanwhile, in a medium saucepan stir together flour and pepper. Gradually stir in half-and-half, light cream, or milk. Cook and stir over medium heat until thickened and bubbly. Cook and stir for 1 minute more. Gradually stir in the undrained tomatoes. Pour over pasta. Toss to coat. Sprinkle with Parmesan cheese. Makes 4 servings.

This hearty main dish also makes a company-special side dish to serve with roasts, steaks, or chops. Simply dish up 8 servings instead of 4 and add an edible flower or a sprig of fresh herb for garnish.

NUTRITION FACTS PER SERVING:

433 calories
15 g total fat
5 g saturated fat
25 mg cholesterol
1,098 mg sodium
55 g carbohydrate
1 g fiber
18 g protein

Spaghetti with Vegetarian Sauce Bolognese

The cereal in the sauce creates a texture that is remarkably similar to ground meat. Serve it as you would regular spaghetti—with hot, crusty bread.

INGREDIENTS

8 ounces packaged dried spaghetti

1 tablespoon olive oil

½ cup finely chopped carrot

½ cup thinly sliced celery

1 medium onion, finely chopped (½ cup)

½ teaspoon dried oregano, crushed

¼ teaspoon pepper

1½ teaspoons bottled minced garlic or 3 cloves garlic, minced

¾ cup Grape Nuts cereal

1 14½-ounce can Italian-style stewed tomatoes, undrained

1 8-ounce can tomato sauce

¼ to ½ cup water

1 tablespoon olive oil

Grated Parmesan or Romano cheese (optional)

Fresh oregano (optional)

To make this sauce ahead,

prepare as directed, except cool completely. Transfer to a freezer container; seal, label, and freeze for up to 2 months. To serve, transfer the frozen sauce to a heavy saucepan. Add 1 to 2 tablespoons water. Cook, covered, over low heat 20 to 25 minutes or just until bubbly, stirring occasionally. Serve as directed.

Start to finish: 25 minutes

DIRECTIONS

1. Cook spaghetti according to package directions. Meanwhile, in a medium saucepan heat 1 tablespoon olive oil over medium-high heat. Add the carrot, celery, onion, dried oregano, and pepper; cook until onion is tender. Add garlic; cook for 1 minute more. Stir in the cereal. Add the undrained tomatoes, tomato sauce, and desired amount of the water. Bring to boiling; reduce heat. Cover and simmer for 5 to 10 minutes or until desired consistency.

2. Drain the cooked pasta. Toss pasta with 1 tablespoon olive oil. Divide the hot pasta among 4 dinner plates. Spoon sauce over. If desired, sprinkle with the Parmesan or Romano cheese and garnish with fresh oregano. Makes 4 servings.

NUTRITION FACTS PER SERVING:

416 calories
8 g total fat
1 g saturated fat
0 mg cholesterol
907 mg sodium
76 g carbohydrate
3 g fiber
12 g protein

Rotini and Sweet Pepper Primavera

Primavera means spring in Italian. This creamy pasta punctuated with tender asparagus, crisp sweet peppers, and tiny baby squash is the essence of that welcome season.

INGREDIENTS

- 14 ounces fresh asparagus spears
- 8 ounces packaged dried rotini or gemelli pasta (about 2½ cups)
- 1 cup mixed sweet pepper chunks from salad bar or 1 large red or yellow sweet pepper, cut into 1-inch pieces
- 1 cup halved baby pattypan squash or sliced yellow summer squash
- 1 10-ounce container refrigerated light alfredo sauce
- 2 tablespoons snipped fresh tarragon or thyme
- ¼ teaspoon crushed red pepper

Start to finish: 20 minutes

DIRECTIONS

1. Snap off and discard woody bases from asparagus. Bias-slice asparagus into 1-inch-long pieces (about 1½ cups).

2. Cook pasta according to package directions, adding asparagus, sweet pepper, and squash to pasta for the last 3 minutes of cooking; drain. Return pasta and vegetables to hot pan.

3. Meanwhile, in a small saucepan combine alfredo sauce, tarragon or thyme, and crushed red pepper. Cook and stir over medium heat about 5 minutes or until mixture is heated through. Pour over pasta and vegetables; toss gently to coat. Makes 4 servings.

NUTRITION FACTS PER SERVING:

421 calories
12 g total fat
6 g saturated fat
31 mg cholesterol
622 mg sodium
66 g carbohydrate
2 g fiber
15 g protein

Rotini and gemelli are two types of spiral pasta. Rotini or corkscrew macaroni are about 1½-inch-long spirals and come in plain, whole wheat, or tricolor versions. Gemelli or rope macaroni are 1½-inch pieces that look like two ropes of spaghetti twisted together.

179

Pasta with Three Cheeses

Cream cheese, Parmesan cheese, and your choice of Gouda, Edam, Havarti, fontina, cheddar, or Swiss cheese make up the flavor-rich sauce.

INGREDIENTS

10 ounces packaged dried medium shell macaroni or rotini

2 cups frozen loose-pack cauliflower, broccoli, and carrots or other vegetable combination

1 cup milk

1 3-ounce package cream cheese, cut up

¼ teaspoon coarsely ground black pepper

¾ cup shredded Gouda, Edam, Havarti, fontina, cheddar, or Swiss cheese (3 ounces)

¼ cup grated Parmesan cheese
Grated Parmesan cheese
(optional)

Spend a few extra minutes putting away groceries, and you'll save a great deal of time before dinner.

Chill cans of fruits, vegetables, or meats for salads so they're ready when you need them.

Divide rolls, muffins, and breads into meal-size portions before freezing. At mealtime, simply thaw out as many as you need.

Stack individual ground meat patties, steaks, or chops between two layers of waxed paper. Slip them into a freezer bag. Seal, label, and freeze. To use, remove the number of pieces you need.

Start to finish: 30 minutes

DIRECTIONS

1. In a large saucepan cook shell macaroni or rotini according to package directions, except add the frozen vegetables the last 5 minutes of cooking. Drain.

2. In the hot saucepan combine the milk, cream cheese, and pepper. Cook and stir over low heat until cheese is melted.

3. Return macaroni mixture to saucepan. Toss to coat with cream cheese mixture. Gently stir in the shredded cheese and the ¼ cup Parmesan cheese. Transfer to a serving bowl. If desired, sprinkle with additional Parmesan cheese. Makes 4 servings.

NUTRITION FACTS PER SERVING:

598 calories
25 g total fat
14 g saturated fat
86 mg cholesterol
596 mg sodium
66 g carbohydrate
3 g fiber
28 g protein

INGREDIENTS

- 1 9-ounce package refrigerated or frozen cheese-filled tortellini or meat-filled tortellini
- 1 12-ounce jar roasted red sweet peppers, drained
- 1 medium onion, chopped (½ cup)
- 1½ teaspoons bottled minced garlic or 3 cloves garlic, minced
- 1 tablespoon margarine or butter
- 2 teaspoons snipped fresh thyme or ½ teaspoon dried thyme, crushed
- 2 teaspoons snipped fresh oregano or ¼ teaspoon dried oregano, crushed
- 1 teaspoon sugar

  Fresh herb sprigs (optional)

Roasted Red Pepper Sauce over Tortellini

For leisurely dining, start in the fast lane by taking advantage of ready-to-use roasted peppers and tortellini. Then slow down and enjoy the delectable result.

Start to finish: 20 minutes

DIRECTIONS

1. Cook tortellini according to package directions; drain. Return to saucepan.

2. Meanwhile, place roasted sweet peppers in a food processor bowl. Cover and process until smooth. Set aside.

3. For sauce, in a medium saucepan cook the onion and garlic in hot margarine or butter until tender. Add pureed peppers, thyme, oregano, and sugar. Cook and stir until heated through. Pour sauce over pasta; toss to coat. Transfer to a warm serving dish. If desired, garnish with fresh herbs. Makes 3 servings.

This herb-accented sauce

is equally tasty spooned over grilled chicken or broiled fish. Sprinkle with a little crumbled farmer's or feta cheese for extra zing.

NUTRITION FACTS PER SERVING:

343 calories
15 g total fat
4 g saturated fat
75 mg cholesterol
298 mg sodium
40 g carbohydrate
2 g fiber
14 g protein

181

Polenta with Mushrooms and Asparagus

Something green always beats the winter blues. This rustic polenta, starring spring's first asparagus, may bring just the lift you need. A little chocolate for dessert will prolong the good mood.

INGREDIENTS

- 1 cup quick-cooking polenta mix
- 1 small onion, chopped
- 1 tablespoon olive oil
- 3 cups sliced fresh mushrooms (such as crimini, shiitake, or oyster) (8 ounces)
- 1 pound asparagus spears, trimmed and cut into 1-inch pieces (2¼ cups)
- 3 cloves garlic, minced
- ⅓ cup dry white wine, Marsala wine, vegetable broth, or chicken broth
- ¼ teaspoon salt
- ⅓ cup chopped walnuts or pecans, or pine nuts, toasted
- ¼ cup finely shredded Parmesan cheese

Start to finish: 30 minutes

DIRECTIONS

1. Prepare the polenta according to package directions. Cover and keep polenta warm.

2. Meanwhile, in a large skillet cook onion in hot oil over medium heat until tender. Stir in the mushrooms, asparagus, and garlic. Cook, uncovered, about 4 minutes or until almost tender. Stir in wine or broth and salt. Cook, uncovered, over medium-high heat for 1 minute.

3. To serve, divide polenta among 4 bowls. Spoon the mushroom mixture over polenta. Sprinkle each serving with nuts and Parmesan cheese. Makes 4 servings.

NUTRITION FACTS PER SERVING:

426 calories
12 g total fat
1 g saturated fat
5 mg cholesterol
220 mg sodium
64 g carbohydrate
10 g fiber
14 g protein

Polenta with Fresh Tomato Sauce

Making polenta the traditional way takes a strong stirring hand and time for cooking, chilling, and slicing. This expeditious version serves up medallions of polenta that are crisp on the outside and creamy on the inside, on top of a rosemary-olive tomato sauce.

INGREDIENTS

- ½ teaspoon bottled minced garlic
- 4 teaspoons olive oil
- 6 roma tomatoes, coarsely chopped (about 2 cups)
- ¼ cup pitted halved kalamata olives or sliced pitted ripe olives
- 2 teaspoons snipped fresh rosemary or 2 tablespoons snipped fresh thyme
- Salt
- Pepper
- 1 16-ounce package prepared polenta
- ½ cup shredded smoked Gouda or Swiss cheese (2 ounces)

Start to finish: 18 minutes

DIRECTIONS

1. For sauce, in a medium saucepan cook garlic in 2 teaspoons of the hot oil over medium heat for 30 seconds. Add tomatoes; cook for 2 minutes. Stir in olives and rosemary or thyme. Bring to boiling; reduce heat. Simmer, uncovered, for 8 minutes, stirring occasionally. Season to taste with salt and pepper.

2. Meanwhile, cut polenta into 8 slices. In a large nonstick skillet or on a griddle heat the remaining 2 teaspoons oil over medium heat. Add polenta; cook about 6 minutes or until golden brown, turning once halfway through cooking. Sprinkle with cheese. Serve polenta on top of tomato sauce. Makes 4 servings.

NUTRITION FACTS PER SERVING:

226 calories
10 g total fat
3 g saturated fat
16 mg cholesterol
608 mg sodium
27 g carbohydrate
5 g fiber
8 g protein

Fresh herbs turn ordinary dishes

into extraordinary ones. Some herbs—typically those with a sturdier constitution such as rosemary, bay leaf, and sage—are good for long-simmering or roasting. More delicate fresh herbs—such as basil, coriander, dill, and oregano—are best added right at the end of cooking. To substitute dry herbs for fresh, generally use one-third the amount of fresh herb called for in a recipe. (If a recipe uses 1 tablespoon fresh herb, add 1 teaspoon dry.)

Veggie Skillet

For a zestier flavor, use 1 cup tomato sauce and 1 cup salsa in place of the spaghetti sauce.

INGREDIENTS

3   cups frozen loose-pack diced hash brown potatoes with onions and peppers

2   tablespoons cooking oil

2   cups meatless spaghetti sauce with mushrooms or Italian cooking sauce

1   cup frozen loose-pack peas and carrots

1   cup frozen loose-pack whole kernel corn

½   cup shredded cheddar cheese or mozzarella cheese (2 ounces)

Make kitchen chores a breeze with these timesaving utensils:

• Kitchen shears—to cut dried fruit, fresh herbs, canned tomatoes, and pizza.

• Vegetable peeler—to easily peel potatoes, apples, and cucumbers. It is also handy for cutting chocolate curls or strips of citrus peel for garnish.

• Egg slicer—to slice hard-cooked eggs, mushrooms, and small cooked potatoes.

• Melon baller—to hollow out vegetables and fruits for stuffing, to pit peaches or plums, as well as to make melon balls.

Start to finish: 20 minutes

DIRECTIONS

1. In a large skillet cook potatoes in hot oil over medium heat for 6 to 8 minutes or until nearly tender, stirring occasionally.

2. Stir spaghetti sauce or Italian cooking sauce, peas and carrots, and corn into the potatoes in the skillet. Bring to boiling; reduce heat. Cover and simmer for 5 to 7 minutes or until vegetables are tender. Sprinkle with cheese. Let stand, covered, about 1 minute or until cheese starts to melt. Makes 4 servings.

NUTRITION FACTS PER SERVING:

406 calories
21 g total fat
6 g saturated fat
20 mg cholesterol
742 mg sodium
49 g carbohydrate
5 g fiber
10 g protein

Vegetable Quesadillas

The next time the occasion calls for a celebration, throw a Mexican fiesta. Serve these colorful tortilla fold-overs as appetizers instead of as a main dish. Simply cut quesadillas into wedges to make 6 servings.

INGREDIENTS

- ¾ cup finely chopped broccoli
- ¼ cup shredded carrot
- 2 green onions, sliced (¼ cup)
- 2 tablespoons water
- 6 6-inch flour tortillas
- 1 teaspoon cooking oil
- 1 8-ounce package shredded cheddar or Monterey Jack cheese with jalapeño peppers
- Dairy sour cream (optional)
- Sliced green onion (optional)
- Sliced pitted ripe olives (optional)
- Salsa (optional)

Prep time: 20 minutes
Baking time: 6 minutes

DIRECTIONS

1. In a 1-quart microwave-safe casserole combine the broccoli, carrot, the 2 green onions, and water. Micro-cook, covered, on 100% power (high) for 2 to 4 minutes or until vegetables are crisp-tender. Drain.

2. Brush one side of 3 tortillas with some of the oil. Place tortillas, oiled side down, on a baking sheet. Top with the cheese, vegetable mixture, and remaining tortillas. Brush tops with remaining oil. Bake in a 450° oven about 6 minutes or until light brown.

3. To serve, cut each tortilla into wedges. If desired, serve with sour cream, additional green onion, olives, and salsa. Makes 3 servings.

NUTRITION FACTS PER SERVING:

499 calories
30 g total fat
17 g saturated fat
80 mg cholesterol
728 mg sodium
32 g carbohydrate
1 g fiber
24 g protein

Mix together a

Mock Tequila Sunrise to go along with the Southwest flavors of the quesadilla. In a small pitcher combine 2 cups orange juice, 1 cup apricot nectar, and 3 tablespoons lemon juice. Pour over ice in glasses. Slowly add 1 to 2 teaspoons grenadine syrup to each glass, then stir. Garnish with lime wedges.

Succotash Soup And Dumplings

To cut fresh corn from the cob, hold each ear of corn so an end rests on a cutting board. Then, with a sharp knife, cut down the ear from top to bottom, cutting through the base of each kernel.

INGREDIENTS

INGREDIENTS

- 3 cups water
- 2 cups cut fresh corn or one 10-ounce package frozen whole kernel corn
- 1 cup frozen lima beans
- ½ cup chopped celery
- ½ cup sliced carrot
- ½ cup chopped onion
- 1 tablespoon snipped fresh dill or ½ teaspoon dried dillweed
- 2 teaspoons instant vegetable bouillon granules
- 1 recipe Cornmeal Dumplings
- ⅓ cup packaged instant mashed potato flakes

Start to finish: 45 minutes

DIRECTIONS

1. In a large saucepan combine the 3 cups water, the corn, lima beans, celery, carrot, onion, dill, and bouillon granules. Bring to boiling; reduce heat. Simmer, covered, for 8 to 10 minutes or until the vegetables are almost tender.

2. Meanwhile, prepare Cornmeal Dumplings. Set aside. Stir potato flakes into the soup. Cook and stir until slightly thickened and bubbly.

3. Drop the dumpling mixture from a tablespoon into 8 mounds directly on top of the bubbling soup. Cover tightly and simmer for 10 to 12 minutes (do not lift cover) or until a wooden toothpick inserted in a dumpling comes out clean. To serve, ladle soup and dumplings into bowls. Makes 4 servings.

Cornmeal Dumplings: In a medium saucepan combine 1 cup water, ⅓ cup yellow cornmeal, ¼ teaspoon salt, and dash pepper. Cook and stir until thickened and bubbly. Remove from heat; cool slightly. Add 1 beaten egg, beating until smooth. In a small bowl stir together ⅔ cup all-purpose flour, 1 tablespoon grated Parmesan cheese, 1 tablespoon snipped fresh parsley, and 1 teaspoon baking powder. Stir into the cornmeal mixture with a fork just until moistened.

NUTRITION FACTS PER SERVING:

279 calories
3 g total fat
1 g saturated fat
55 mg cholesterol
765 mg sodium
55 g carbohydrate
4 g fiber
11 g protein

INGREDIENTS

- 2 stalks celery, finely chopped
- 1 large onion, finely chopped
- 2 cloves garlic, minced
- 1 tablespoon olive oil
- 5 cups beef broth
- 1 cup water
- ½ cup uncooked Arborio rice or short grain rice
- 6 cups torn spinach
- 1 15-ounce can Great Northern beans, rinsed and drained
- 3 medium tomatoes, chopped (about 2 cups)
- 1 medium zucchini, coarsely chopped (about 1½ cups)
- ¼ cup snipped fresh thyme
- ¼ teaspoon cracked pepper
- ½ cup crumbled feta cheese (2 ounces)
- Spinach leaves (optional)

Greek Minestrone

Arborio rice is an Italian-grown grain that is shorter and plumper than any other short-grain rice. Traditionally used to make creamy risotto, it adds a similar texture to this bean and vegetable soup.

Start to finish: 40 minutes

DIRECTIONS

1. In a Dutch oven cook the celery, onion, and garlic in hot oil until tender. Add the beef broth, water, and rice. Bring to boiling; reduce heat. Simmer, covered, for 15 minutes.

2. Add the torn spinach, beans, tomatoes, zucchini, thyme, and pepper. Cook and stir until heated through. Ladle into soup bowls. Top each serving with cheese. If desired, garnish with spinach leaves. Makes 6 servings.

NUTRITION FACTS PER SERVING:

252 calories
6 g total fat
2 g saturated fat
8 mg cholesterol
834 mg sodium
39 g carbohydrate
8 g fiber
13 g protein

187

Cheesy Vegetable Chowder

Gruyère cheese is known for its rich, sweet, nutty flavor. We recommend aged Gruyère, which is usually produced in France. Processed Gruyère just can't compare in flavor with the aged variety.

INGREDIENTS

2 cups vegetable broth

2 cups cubed potatoes

¾ cup chopped onion

½ cup chopped celery

1 tablespoon snipped fresh thyme
  or ½ teaspoon dried thyme,
  crushed

⅛ teaspoon black pepper

2 cups cut fresh corn or frozen
  whole kernel corn

2 cups chopped cabbage

¼ cup chopped green sweet pepper

2 cups fat-free milk

2 tablespoons all-purpose flour

1 cup shredded Gruyère or Swiss
  cheese (4 ounces)

Fresh thyme (optional)

When a recipe calls
for vegetable broth, you can use canned broth, bouillon cubes, or prepare a homemade stock. An easy way to make your own stock is to keep saving the water in which vegetables are boiled. Freeze the liquid in a covered container, and in time you'll have a basic stock that's ready to use.

Start to finish: 40 minutes

DIRECTIONS

1. In a large saucepan combine the vegetable broth, potatoes, onion, celery, snipped or dried thyme, and black pepper. Bring to boiling; reduce heat. Simmer, covered, for 10 minutes. Stir in the corn, cabbage, and sweet pepper. Cook, covered, about 5 minutes more or until the potatoes and corn are just tender, stirring occasionally.

2. Meanwhile, in a screw-top jar combine ½ cup of the milk and the flour. Shake well. Add to the potato mixture in the saucepan along with the remaining milk. Cook and stir until thickened and bubbly. Cook and stir for 1 minute more. Remove from heat.

3. Add the Gruyère or Swiss cheese to the potato mixture, stirring until melted. To serve, ladle soup into bowls. If desired, garnish with additional fresh thyme. Makes 5 servings.

NUTRITION FACTS PER SERVING:

288 calories
9 g total fat
5 g saturated fat
26 mg cholesterol
512 mg sodium
41 g carbohydrate
6 g fiber
15 g protein

Mixed Bean Soup

INGREDIENTS

- ½ cup dry baby lima beans or garbanzo beans
- ½ cup dry pinto beans or kidney beans
- ½ cup dry navy beans or Great Northern beans
- 4 cups cold water
- 1 cup chopped celery
- 1 cup chopped onion
- 1 cup chopped carrot
- 3 cloves garlic, minced
- 1 tablespoon olive oil or cooking oil
- 3 cups water
- 1 14-ounce can vegetable broth
- 1 teaspoon dried thyme, crushed
- ½ teaspoon dried marjoram, crushed
- ¼ teaspoon pepper
- 1 14½-ounce can diced tomatoes, undrained
- 1½ cups low-sodium vegetable juice
- Fresh marjoram (optional)

If you don't want to store extra beans, buy a package of mixed dried beans instead of the three different kinds. Prepare the recipe as directed using 1½ cups of the bean mix.

Prep time: 40 minutes
Standing time: 1 hour
Cooking time: 1¼ hours

DIRECTIONS

1. Rinse beans; transfer to a 4-quart Dutch oven. Add the 4 cups water. Bring to boiling; reduce heat. Simmer, uncovered, for 2 minutes; remove from heat. Cover and let stand for 1 hour. (Or, omit simmering; in a covered Dutch oven soak beans in cold water overnight.) Drain and rinse beans in a colander.

2. In the same Dutch oven cook the celery, onion, carrot, and garlic in the hot oil until tender, stirring once or twice. Add the beans. Stir in the 3 cups water, the vegetable broth, thyme, dried marjoram, and pepper.

3. Bring to boiling; reduce heat. Simmer, covered, for 1¼ to 1½ hours or until beans are tender. Stir in the undrained tomatoes and the vegetable juice. Heat through. To serve, ladle the soup into bowls. If desired, garnish with fresh marjoram. Makes 5 servings.

Fat-smart cooks

know to look for recipes that are full of beans. Unlike other high-protein sources, such as meat and cheese, beans contain almost no saturated fat and no cholesterol. In addition, they're high in fiber.

NUTRITION FACTS PER SERVING:

267 calories
4 g total fat
1 g saturated fat
0 mg cholesterol
594 mg sodium
49 g carbohydrate
5 g fiber
14 g protein

189

Spring Vegetable Soup

This Italian-style soup plays up asparagus, fava beans, peas, and young artichokes, with a hint of flavor from fresh fennel and pancetta.

INGREDIENTS

- 12 baby artichokes
- 6 cups chicken broth or reduced-sodium chicken broth
- 1 cup small boiling onions, peeled and halved, or pearl onions
- 4 ounces pancetta (Italian bacon) or 5 slices bacon, crisp-cooked, drained, and cut into small pieces
- 1 teaspoon fennel seed, crushed
- ¼ teaspoon pepper
- 2 cups cooked or canned fava or lima beans, rinsed and drained
- 12 ounces asparagus spears, trimmed and cut into 1-inch pieces
- 1 medium fennel bulb, chopped Fresh fennel leaves

To cook fresh or frozen fava or lima beans,

simmer, covered, in a small amount of boiling water for 15 to 25 minutes or until tender. Drain and cool slightly. When cool, remove skins from fava beans. For 2 cups of cooked fava beans, purchase 2 pounds of fava beans in the pod.

Prep time: 30 minutes
Cooking time: 20 minutes

DIRECTIONS

1. Remove the tough outer green leaves from the artichokes (inside leaves will be more tender and greenish yellow). Snip off about 1 inch from the leaf tops, cutting where the green meets the yellow. Trim the stems. Quarter artichokes lengthwise; set aside.

2. In a 4-quart Dutch oven combine the chicken broth, onions, pancetta or bacon, fennel seed, and pepper. Bring to boiling; reduce heat. Simmer, covered, for 10 minutes. Stir in the artichokes and beans. Cook for 5 minutes. Stir in the asparagus and chopped fennel. Cook about 5 minutes more or until the vegetables are tender.

3. To serve, ladle the soup into bowls. Garnish each serving with fennel leaves. Makes 4 servings.

NUTRITION FACTS PER SERVING:

152 calories
3 g total fat
1 g saturated fat
4 mg cholesterol
695 mg sodium
21 g carbohydrate
6 g fiber
11 g protein

INGREDIENTS

  1 **cup dry lentils**

  ½ **cup chopped onion**

1½ **to 2 teaspoons curry powder**

  2 **teaspoons cooking oil**

2½ **cups water**

  2 **cups cubed peeled rutabagas**
        or turnips

  1 **cup sliced carrots**

  ¼ **teaspoon salt**

  ⅛ **teaspoon pepper**

  1 **9-ounce package frozen cut**
        green beans

  3 **cups vegetable juice**

Curried Lentil Stew

High in protein and fiber, lentils give an enticing, earthy vegetable flavor to all types of soups and stews. Look for lentils near the dried beans in your supermarket.

Start to finish: 45 minutes

DIRECTIONS

1. Rinse and drain lentils; set aside. In a large saucepan cook onion and curry powder in hot oil for 3 minutes, stirring occasionally. Add the lentils, water, rutabagas or turnips, carrots, salt, and pepper. Bring to boiling; reduce heat. Simmer, covered, for 15 to 20 minutes or until vegetables and lentils are almost tender.

2. Stir the frozen green beans into the lentil mixture. Return to boiling; reduce heat. Simmer, covered, for 6 to 8 minutes more or until the vegetables and lentils are tender. Stir in the vegetable juice. Heat through. Makes 6 servings.

NUTRITION FACTS PER SERVING:

106 calories
2 g total fat
0 g saturated fat
0 mg cholesterol
566 mg sodium
24 g carbohydrate
4 g fiber
5 g protein

191

Mexican Fiesta Salad

Prepare this creamy salad in the morning and look forward all day to a hearty, corn-and-bean-studded treat. Lime and cilantro infuse the sour cream dressing.

INGREDIENTS

- 2 cups dried penne or rotini pasta
- ½ cup frozen whole kernel corn
- ½ cup light dairy sour cream
- ⅓ cup mild or medium chunky salsa
- 1 tablespoon snipped fresh cilantro
- 1 tablespoon lime juice
- 1 15-ounce can black beans, rinsed and drained
- 3 medium roma tomatoes, chopped (1 cup)
- 1 medium zucchini, chopped (1 cup)
- ½ cup shredded sharp cheddar cheese (2 ounces)

Start to finish: 30 minutes

DIRECTIONS

1. Cook pasta according to package directions, adding corn to the water with pasta the last 5 minutes of cooking; drain in colander. Rinse with cold water; drain again.

2. Meanwhile, for dressing, in a small bowl stir together sour cream, salsa, cilantro, and lime juice. Set aside.

3. In a large bowl combine the pasta mixture, black beans, tomatoes, zucchini, and cheese. Pour dressing over pasta mixture; toss gently to coat. Serve immediately. (Or, if desired, cover and refrigerate up to 24 hours. Before serving, if necessary, stir in enough milk to make of desired consistency.) Makes 4 servings.

NUTRITION FACTS PER SERVING:

373 calories
9 g total fat
4 g saturated fat
19 mg cholesterol
470 mg sodium
61 g carbohydrate
7 g fiber
20 g protein

Grilled Vegetable Salad with Garlic Dressing

Vegetables, sweet and smoky from the grill, give pasta and cheese a jolt of flavor and color. By doing the grilling ahead, and storing the savory dressing in the refrigerator, this maximum-impact dish is done in the time it takes to simmer pasta.

INGREDIENTS

- 2 red and/or yellow sweet peppers
- 2 Japanese eggplants, halved lengthwise
- 2 medium zucchini or yellow summer squash, halved lengthwise, or 8 to 10 yellow sunburst or pattypan squash*
- 1 tablespoon olive oil
- 2 cups dried rigatoni pasta
- 1 recipe Roasted Garlic Dressing
- ¾ cup cubed fontina cheese (3 ounces)
- 1 to 2 tablespoons snipped fresh Italian flat-leaf parsley or regular parsley

Fresh Italian flat-leaf parsley or regular parsley sprigs (optional)

Start to finish: 25 minutes

DIRECTIONS

1. Halve the sweet peppers lengthwise; remove and discard the stems, seeds, and membranes. Brush the sweet peppers, eggplants, and zucchini with oil. Grill the vegetables on the rack of an uncovered grill directly over medium-hot coals for 8 to 12 minutes or until tender, turning occasionally. Remove vegetables from the grill; cool slightly. Cut vegetables into 1-inch pieces.

2. Meanwhile, cook pasta according to package directions; drain in colander. Rinse with cold water; drain again. In a large bowl combine pasta and grilled vegetables. Pour Roasted Garlic Dressing over pasta mixture; toss gently to coat. Stir in cheese; sprinkle with snipped parsley. If desired, garnish with parsley sprigs.

Makes 4 servings.

Roasted Garlic Dressing: In a screw-top jar combine 3 tablespoons balsamic vinegar or red wine vinegar, 2 tablespoons olive oil, 1 tablespoon water, 1 teaspoon bottled roasted minced garlic, ¼ teaspoon salt, and ¼ teaspoon black pepper. Cover and shake well.

***Note:** If using sunburst or pattypan squash, precook in a small amount of boiling water for 3 minutes before grilling.

NUTRITION FACTS PER SERVING:

369 calories
19 g total fat
6 g saturated fat
61 mg cholesterol
317 mg sodium
40 g carbohydrate
5 g fiber
12 g protein

193

Penne Salad with Italian Beans and Gorgonzola

Assertive blue-veined Gorgonzola, tart sorrel, and bitter radicchio lose some attitude, but not their tasty sass, paired with meaty green beans, pasta, and a mellow herb dressing.

INGREDIENTS

- 6 ounces dried penne or cut ziti pasta, or elbow macaroni
- 8 ounces Italian green beans, bias-sliced into 2-inch pieces
- ⅓ cup bottled fat-free Italian salad dressing
- 1 tablespoon snipped fresh tarragon or ½ teaspoon dried tarragon, crushed
- ½ teaspoon freshly ground pepper
- 2 cups torn radicchio or 1 cup finely shredded red cabbage
- 4 cups sorrel or spinach leaves
- ½ cup crumbled Gorgonzola or other blue cheese (2 ounces)

If you can't find fresh Italian green beans, substitute one 9-ounce package frozen Italian green beans, thawed. Add the thawed frozen beans to the water with pasta the last 3 to 4 minutes of cooking.

Start to finish: 25 minutes

DIRECTIONS

1. Cook pasta according to package directions, adding green beans to the water with pasta the last 5 to 7 minutes of cooking; drain pasta mixture in colander. Rinse with cold water; drain again.

2. In a large bowl combine the Italian salad dressing, tarragon, and pepper. Add pasta mixture and radicchio; toss gently to coat.

3. To serve, divide sorrel or spinach leaves among 4 dinner plates. Top with pasta mixture. Sprinkle each serving with Gorgonzola cheese. Makes 4 servings.

NUTRITION FACTS PER SERVING:

269 calories
6 g total fat
3 g saturated fat
13 mg cholesterol
566 mg sodium
42 g carbohydrate
3 g fiber
12 g protein

Fontina and Melon Salad

Put the "lazy" back in Sundays. Organize brunch around a new take on the fruit-and-cheese course, made in a flash with bottled poppy seed dressing. Accompany with mimosas, the Sunday paper, and a cushiony chair.

INGREDIENTS

- 1½ cups dried large bow-tie pasta (about 6 ounces)
- 2 cups cantaloupe and/or honeydew melon chunks
- 1 cup cubed fontina or Swiss cheese (4 ounces)
- ⅓ cup bottled fat-free poppy seed salad dressing
- 1 to 2 tablespoons snipped fresh mint
- 2 cups watercress, stems removed Cantaloupe and/or honeydew melon shells (optional)

Start to finish: 25 minutes

DIRECTIONS

1. Cook pasta according to package directions; drain in colander. Rinse with cold water; drain again.

2. In a large bowl toss together the pasta, cantaloupe or honeydew melon chunks, and cheese. Combine salad dressing and mint. Pour over pasta mixture; toss gently to coat. Serve salad immediately or cover and refrigerate up to 24 hours.

3. To serve, stir watercress into pasta mixture. If desired, serve the salad in melon shells. Makes 4 servings.

NUTRITION FACTS PER SERVING:

319 calories
11 g total fat
6 g saturated fat
73 mg cholesterol
309 mg sodium
41 g carbohydrate
1 g fiber
14 g protein

Middle Eastern Bulgur-Spinach Salad

Bulgur or cracked wheat is a Middle Eastern staple. It's often cooked with lamb, but this vegetarian mélange of grain, fruits, and vegetables is equally satisfying and boasts a preparation that's simplicity itself.

INGREDIENTS

- 1 cup bulgur
- 1 cup boiling water
- ½ cup plain yogurt
- ¼ cup bottled red wine vinaigrette salad dressing
- 2 tablespoons snipped fresh parsley
- ½ teaspoon ground cumin
- 6 cups torn spinach
- 1 15-ounce can garbanzo beans, rinsed and drained
- 1 cup coarsely chopped apple
- ½ of a medium red onion, thinly sliced and separated into rings
- 3 tablespoons raisins (optional)

Start to finish: 30 minutes

DIRECTIONS

1. In a medium bowl combine bulgur and boiling water. Let stand about 10 minutes or until bulgur has absorbed all of the water. Cool for 15 minutes.

2. Meanwhile, for dressing, in a small bowl stir together the yogurt, vinaigrette salad dressing, parsley, and cumin.

3. In a large bowl combine the bulgur, spinach, beans, apple, onion, and, if desired, raisins. Pour dressing over salad; toss gently to coat. Makes 4 servings.

NUTRITION FACTS PER SERVING:

340 calories
11 g total fat
2 g saturated fat
2 mg cholesterol
673 mg sodium
53 g carbohydrate
16 g fiber
13 g protein

INGREDIENTS

1 pound green beans

1 16-ounce can sliced beets, drained

2 tablespoons orange juice

2 tablespoons olive oil

1 tablespoon balsamic vinegar

2 teaspoons bottled roasted minced garlic

⅛ teaspoon salt

¼ cup soft-style herbed cream cheese or ¼ cup spreadable Brie cheese

8 slices French bread, lightly toasted

Mixed salad greens

Coarsely ground pepper

Warm Beet Salad With Roasted Garlic Dressing

Garlic groupies, this stellar salad has your name on it, spelled out in a garlic-spiked dressing for succulent beets and crunchy green beans. Serve the vegetables warm so they absorb the sauce to the fullest.

Start to finish: 30 minutes

DIRECTIONS

1. In a covered large saucepan cook green beans in a small amount of boiling, lightly salted water about 15 minutes or until almost tender. Add beets and cook, covered, for 2 to 3 minutes more or until the beets are heated through. Drain and keep warm.

2. Meanwhile, for dressing, in a screw-top jar combine the orange juice, oil, vinegar, garlic, and salt. Cover and shake well. Pour dressing over warm beans and beets. Spread cream cheese over French bread slices.

3. To serve, divide salad greens among 4 salad bowls or dinner plates. Top with the warm or room temperature beet mixture. If desired, sprinkle salads with coarsely ground pepper. Serve with French bread slices. Makes 4 servings.

In place of the homemade dressing, you can substitute a bottled garlic salad dressing or stir the bottled roasted minced garlic into a bottled Italian salad dressing.

NUTRITION FACTS PER SERVING:

320 calories
13 g total fat
4 g saturated fat
12 mg cholesterol
632 mg sodium
43 g carbohydrate
4 g fiber
8 g protein

197

Roasted Sweet Pepper Salad Recipe, page 226

Side Dishes

Zucchini Alla Romana

For best results, select zucchini that are small, firm, and free of cuts and soft spots. Pass over large zucchini. They tend to have tough skins and lots of seeds. If you're lucky enough to find baby squash, use them instead.

INGREDIENTS

2   cloves garlic

2   teaspoons olive oil

4   cups sliced zucchini
    (4 to 5 small)

1   teaspoon dried mint or basil,
    crushed, or 1 tablespoon
    snipped fresh mint or basil

¼   teaspoon salt

    Dash pepper

2   tablespoons finely shredded
    Parmesan or Romano cheese

When storing herbs by the bunch, place them in a loose-fitting bag in the crisper drawer of your refrigerator. Or trim the stem ends and place them in a tall container of water, immersing the stems about 2 inches. Cover the leaves loosely with a plastic bag and refrigerate.

Prep time: 8 minutes

Cooking time: 5 minutes

DIRECTIONS

1. In a large skillet cook the whole garlic cloves in hot oil until lightly browned; discard garlic. Add the zucchini, dried mint or basil (if using), salt, and pepper to the oil in the skillet.

2. Cook, uncovered, over medium heat about 5 minutes or until the zucchini is crisp-tender, stirring occasionally. To serve, sprinkle with the Parmesan cheese and fresh mint or basil (if using). Makes 6 servings.

NUTRITION FACTS PER SERVING:

35 calories

2 g total fat

1 g saturated fat

2 mg cholesterol

130 mg sodium

3 g carbohydrate

1 g fiber

2 g protein

Broccoli and Peppers

INGREDIENTS

- 1 **pound broccoli, cut into florets**
- 1 **red or yellow sweet pepper, cut into 1-inch pieces**
- 2 **tablespoons reduced-calorie margarine**
- 1 **teaspoon finely shredded lemon peel**
- 1 **tablespoon lemon juice**
- ⅛ **teaspoon black pepper**

If you don't have a steamer basket, improvise with a metal colander to prepare this dish.

Prep time: 10 minutes
Cooking time: 8 minutes

DIRECTIONS

1. Place broccoli and sweet pepper in a steamer basket over simmering water. Steam, covered, for 8 to 12 minutes or until vegetables are crisp-tender. Arrange vegetables on a serving platter.

2. Meanwhile, in a small saucepan melt the margarine. Stir in the lemon peel, lemon juice, and black pepper. Drizzle over the vegetables. Makes 6 servings.

NUTRITION FACTS PER SERVING:

42 calories
2 g total fat
0 g saturated fat
0 mg cholesterol
63 mg sodium
5 g carbohydrate
3 g fiber
2 g protein

201

Lemony Asparagus And New Potatoes

With spring comes fresh asparagus and new potatoes. This recipe showcases both in a healthful side dish with a snippet of lemon and thyme.

INGREDIENTS

- 12 ounces asparagus spears
- 8 whole tiny new potatoes, cut into quarters (about 10 ounces)
- 2 teaspoons olive oil or cooking oil
- ½ teaspoon finely shredded lemon peel
- ¼ teaspoon salt
- ¼ teaspoon dried thyme, crushed
- Fresh thyme (optional)

Prep time: 10 minutes
Cooking time: 18 minutes

DIRECTIONS

1. Snap off and discard the woody bases from the asparagus. If desired, scrape off the scales. Cut into 2-inch pieces. Set aside.

2. In a 2-quart covered saucepan cook the potatoes in a small amount of boiling water for 10 minutes. Add the asparagus. Cook, covered, about 8 minutes more or until the asparagus is crisp-tender and the potatoes are tender. Drain. Transfer the vegetables to a serving bowl.

3. Meanwhile, in a small bowl combine the oil, lemon peel, salt, and dried thyme. Pour over the vegetables, tossing gently to coat. If desired, garnish with fresh thyme. Makes 4 servings.

NUTRITION FACTS PER SERVING:

- 105 calories
- 3 g total fat
- 0 g saturated fat
- 0 mg cholesterol
- 141 mg sodium
- 19 g carbohydrate
- 2 g fiber
- 3 g protein

INGREDIENTS

- 2 **fennel bulbs with leaves**
- ½ **cup apple juice or apple cider**
- ¼ **cup cider vinegar**
- 1 **teaspoon instant chicken bouillon granules**
- 3 **cloves garlic, minced**
- 1 **tablespoon cooking oil**
- 1 **10-ounce package shredded red cabbage (about 4 cups)**
- 2 **tablespoons brown sugar**
- ¼ **teaspoon fennel seed, crushed**

Red Cabbage With Fennel

Fennel's feathery green leaves look like fresh dill but have a delicate anise flavor.

Start to finish: 30 minutes

DIRECTIONS

1. Remove upper stalks from fennel, including feathery leaves; reserve leaves and discard stalks. Discard any wilted outer layers on fennel bulbs; cut off a thin slice from each base. Wash fennel and pat dry. Quarter each fennel bulb lengthwise. Chop enough of the reserved fennel leaves to make 2 teaspoons; set aside along with a few sprigs of the feathery leaves.

2. In a small bowl combine the apple juice or cider and vinegar. In a medium saucepan combine the fennel wedges, ½ cup of the apple juice mixture, the bouillon granules, and garlic. Bring to boiling; reduce heat. Simmer, covered, for 14 to 16 minutes or until the fennel is tender.

3. Meanwhile, pour oil into a large skillet or wok. Preheat over medium-high heat. Add the cabbage; stir-fry for 3 to 5 minutes or until cabbage is crisp-tender. Combine the remaining apple juice mixture and the brown sugar; stir into cabbage along with the fennel seed. Cook and stir about 1 minute more or until heated through.

4. Transfer the cabbage to a serving platter. Remove the fennel wedges from the liquid with a slotted spoon. Place on top of cabbage. Garnish with the reserved chopped fennel leaves and the reserved sprigs. Makes 4 to 6 servings.

NUTRITION FACTS PER SERVING:

107 calories
4 g total fat
1 g saturated fat
0 mg cholesterol
258 mg sodium
19 g carbohydrate
13 g fiber
2 g protein

203

Caramelized Sweet Potatoes

Just like other potatoes, sweet potatoes can be baked, mashed, or hashed, but are sweetly sublime when sautéed with onions and brown sugar, as in this side dish.

INGREDIENTS

- 2 large red or white onions, cut into ¾-inch chunks
- 4 teaspoons margarine or butter
- 2 large sweet potatoes or yams, peeled and sliced ½ inch thick (about 1 pound)
- ¼ cup water
- 2 tablespoons brown sugar
- ¾ teaspoon snipped fresh rosemary or ¼ teaspoon dried rosemary, crushed
- Fresh rosemary sprigs (optional)

Sweet potatoes and yams can be used interchangeably in most recipes. Yams are a tropically grown tuber with brownish skin and yellow to white starchy flesh. They are not widely available in the United States and many times, the vegetables labeled yams in supermarkets are a type of sweet potato.

Start to finish: 30 minutes

DIRECTIONS

1. In a large skillet cook onions in hot margarine or butter over medium-high heat for 3 to 4 minutes or until onions are nearly tender; stir frequently. Stir in sweet potatoes and water. Cover and cook over medium heat for 10 to 12 minutes or until sweet potatoes are nearly tender, stirring occasionally.

2. Uncover skillet; add brown sugar and the snipped fresh or dried rosemary. Cook, stirring gently, over medium-low heat for 4 to 5 minutes or until onions and sweet potatoes are glazed. If desired, garnish with fresh rosemary sprigs. Makes 4 servings.

NUTRITION FACTS PER SERVING:

173 calories
4 g total fat
1 g saturated fat
0 mg cholesterol
57 mg sodium
33 g carbohydrate
4 g fiber
2 g protein

Sweet-and-Sour Onions

These onions, in a piquant sauce of vinegar and brown sugar, provide a perfect accompaniment to roasted beef, pork, or chicken.

INGREDIENTS

- 3 cups pearl white and/or red onions or one 16-ounce package frozen small whole onions
- 2 teaspoons margarine or butter
- ¼ cup white wine vinegar or balsamic vinegar
- 2 tablespoons brown sugar
- ⅛ teaspoon pepper
- 1 ounce prosciutto or thinly sliced cooked ham, cut into short, thin strips

Start to finish: 35 minutes

NUTRITION FACTS PER SERVING:

94 calories
2 g total fat
0 g saturated fat
3 mg cholesterol
372 mg sodium
16 g carbohydrate
2 g fiber
3 g protein

DIRECTIONS

1. In a medium covered saucepan cook the unpeeled pearl onions (if using) in a small amount of boiling water about 10 minutes or until onions are just tender. Drain. Cool onions slightly; trim ends and remove skins. (Or cook the frozen onions in a medium saucepan according to package directions; drain.)

2. In the same saucepan melt the margarine or butter over medium heat. Stir in the vinegar, brown sugar, and pepper. Cook and stir about 30 seconds or until combined. Stir in the onions and the prosciutto or ham.

3. Cook, uncovered, for 7 to 8 minutes more or until the onions are golden brown and slightly glazed, stirring occasionally. Makes 4 servings.

Everyone knows vegetables are good for them, but do they know why? Vegetables provide our bodies with vitamins A and C, folic acid, iron, magnesium, and other important nutrients. In addition, they're low in fat and high in fiber. Vegetables are so important to our diets, that health experts recommend 3 to 5 servings a day.

Vegetable Kabobs

These crisp-tender vegetable kabobs are the essence of simplicity—a swath of rosemary-scented oil-and-vinegar dressing is their only embellishment. Threaded onto rosemary stalks, the colorful components look like jewels on a string.

INGREDIENTS

8 tiny new potatoes, quartered

2 tablespoons water

8 baby sunburst squash

4 miniature sweet peppers and/or
   1 medium red sweet pepper,
   cut into 1-inch pieces

2 small red onions, each cut into
   8 wedges, or 8 tiny red
   onions, halved

8 baby zucchini or 1 small zucchini,
   halved lengthwise and sliced

¼ cup bottled oil-and-vinegar salad
   dressing

2 teaspoons snipped fresh
   rosemary or ½ teaspoon dried
   rosemary, crushed

Prep time: 20 minutes
Grilling time: 10 minutes

DIRECTIONS

1. In a 2-quart microwave-safe casserole combine the potatoes and water. Microwave, covered, on 100% power (high) for 5 minutes. Gently stir in the sunburst squash, sweet peppers, and onions. Microwave, covered, on high for 4 to 6 minutes or until almost tender. Drain and cool slightly.

2. On eight 10-inch skewers alternately thread the potatoes, sunburst squash, sweet peppers, onions, and zucchini. In a small bowl combine the salad dressing and rosemary; brush over the vegetables.

3. Grill kabobs on the rack of an uncovered grill directly over medium coals for 10 to 12 minutes or until the vegetables are crisp-tender and browned, turning and brushing occasionally with dressing mixture. Makes 4 servings.

NUTRITION FACTS PER SERVING:

161 calories
8 g total fat
1 g saturated fat
0 mg cholesterol
217 mg sodium
22 g carbohydrate
2 g fiber
3 g protein

Grilled Tomatoes With Pesto

INGREDIENTS

3 to 5 small to medium red,
   orange, and/or yellow
   tomatoes, cored and halved
   crosswise

2 tablespoons pesto

6 very thin onion slices

½ cup shredded Monterey Jack
   cheese (2 ounces)

⅓ cup smoky-flavored whole
   almonds, chopped

2 tablespoons snipped fresh
   parsley

Salt

Pepper

They say there are two things money can't buy: love and homegrown tomatoes. If you don't have the latter, search out a farmer's market for the makings of this summer dish. It will garner you love from all who are lucky enough to taste it.

Prep time: 15 minutes
Grilling time: 15 minutes

DIRECTIONS

1. Using a spoon, hollow out the top ¼ inch of tomato halves. Top with pesto, then onion slices. Place tomatoes in a disposable foil pie plate.

2. In a charcoal grill with a cover arrange medium-hot coals around edge of grill. Test for medium heat in the center of the grill. Place the tomatoes in center of grill rack. Cover and grill for 10 to 15 minutes or until tomatoes are heated through. (For a gas grill, adjust for indirect cooking; grill as directed.)

3. Meanwhile, in a small bowl stir together the cheese, almonds, and parsley. Sprinkle over the tomatoes. Cover and grill about 5 minutes more or until the cheese is melted. Season to taste with salt and pepper. Makes 6 servings.

NUTRITION FACTS PER SERVING:

132 calories
10 g total fat
2 g saturated fat
9 mg cholesterol
119 mg sodium
6 g carbohydrate
2 g fiber
5 g protein

Mexicali Stuffed Zucchini

These savory stuffed zucchini "wheels" can be made a day ahead: Prepare them up to the baking step; then cover the dish with plastic wrap and refrigerate. About 25 minutes before serving, simply remove the wrap and bake.

INGREDIENTS

3 medium zucchini, ends trimmed (about 1¾ pounds total)

2 cloves garlic, minced

2 teaspoons cooking oil

1 medium red sweet pepper, chopped

3 green onions, thinly sliced

2 tablespoons snipped fresh cilantro

1 fresh or canned jalapeño pepper, seeded and finely chopped

½ cup shredded Monterey Jack cheese (2 ounces)

1 recipe Cucumber Raita

Prep time: 25 minutes
Baking time: 21 minutes

DIRECTIONS

1. Cut the zucchini into 1½-inch rounds. Scoop out pulp, leaving ¼- to ½-inch-thick shells. Chop enough of the pulp to make ⅓ cup. In a medium skillet cook garlic in hot oil over medium-high heat for 1 minute. Add the reserved zucchini pulp, the sweet red pepper, green onions, 1 tablespoon of the cilantro, and the jalapeño pepper. Cook and stir about 2 minutes or until vegetables are crisp-tender.

2. Place zucchini shells in a lightly greased 2-quart rectangular baking dish. Fill each shell with pepper mixture. Bake, uncovered, in a 350° oven for 20 to 25 minutes or until zucchini is tender. Sprinkle with cheese and bake for 1 to 2 minutes more or until cheese is melted.

3. Sprinkle zucchini with the remaining 1 tablespoon cilantro. Serve with the Cucumber Raita. Makes 5 or 6 servings.

Cucumber Raita: In a small bowl combine ½ cup plain low-fat yogurt, ¼ cup peeled and finely chopped cucumber, 1 tablespoon snipped fresh cilantro, and ⅛ teaspoon salt.

NUTRITION FACTS PER SERVING:

101 calories
6 g total fat
3 g saturated fat
11 mg cholesterol
135 mg sodium
9 g carbohydrate
2 g fiber
5 g protein

Roasted Vegetables with Balsamic Vinegar

Roasting brings out the natural sweetness of vegetables. These earthy and elegant roasted green beans and summer squash balance just about any entrée—steaks, chicken, pork chops, or salmon.

INGREDIENTS

- 8 ounces green beans
- 1 small onion, cut into thin wedges
- 1 clove garlic, minced
- 1 tablespoon olive oil
  Dash salt
  Dash pepper
- 2 medium yellow summer squash, halved lengthwise and sliced ¼ inch thick
- ⅓ cup balsamic vinegar

Start to finish: 25 minutes

DIRECTIONS

1. If desired, remove the tips from green beans. In a shallow roasting pan combine the beans, onion, and garlic. Drizzle with olive oil and sprinkle with salt and pepper. Toss mixture until beans are evenly coated. Spread into a single layer.

2. Roast in a 450° oven for 8 minutes. Stir in squash and roast for 5 to 7 minutes more or until vegetables are tender and slightly browned.

3. Meanwhile, in a small saucepan bring the balsamic vinegar to boiling over medium-high heat; reduce heat. Boil gently, uncovered, about 5 minutes or until reduced by half (vinegar will thicken slightly).

4. Drizzle the vinegar over roasted vegetables; toss to coat. Makes 4 to 6 servings.

Balsamic vinegar develops its intense, sweet-tart flavor through years of pampered rest in casks of differing woods. The most prized elixirs are concocted in the Italian city of Modena following ancient secret formulas. More a condiment than a cooking liquid, the best quality balsamic vinegar should be savored in small amounts.

NUTRITION FACTS PER SERVING:

81 calories
4 g total fat
1 g saturated fat
0 mg cholesterol
45 mg sodium
12 g carbohydrate
1 g fiber
1 g protein

209

Grilled Herbed Vegetables

For easy cleanup and fuss-free cooking, grill or bake mixed veggies of your choice in a foil packet.

INGREDIENTS

1 tablespoon olive oil

2 teaspoons snipped fresh rosemary or 1/2 teaspoon dried rosemary, crushed; or 2 tablespoons snipped fresh basil or 1 teaspoon dried basil, crushed

1 clove garlic, minced

1/4 teaspoon salt

4 cups mixed vegetables, such as eggplant chunks; halved small yellow summer squash, zucchini, or pattypan squash; green beans; red onion wedges; and/or sliced yellow, red, or green sweet pepper

Black pepper

Prep time: 5 minutes
Standing time: 2 hours
Grilling time: 20 minutes

DIRECTIONS

1. In a medium mixing bowl combine the olive oil, rosemary or basil, garlic, and salt. Let the mixture stand for 2 hours.

2. Add the vegetables to the oil mixture, tossing to coat. Spoon the vegetable mixture onto a 24×12-inch piece of heavy foil. Bring the opposite edges of the foil together; seal tightly with a double fold. Fold in the remaining ends to completely enclose the vegetables, leaving a little space for steam to build.

3. Grill the vegetable packet on the rack of an uncovered grill directly over medium-hot coals about 20 minutes or until vegetables are tender, turning the packet over halfway through grilling. (Or bake the vegetable packet in a 350° oven about 25 minutes or until tender.) Season the vegetables to taste with black pepper. Makes 4 servings.

NUTRITION FACTS PER SERVING:

63 calories
4 g total fat
0 g saturated fat
0 mg cholesterol
136 mg sodium
8 g carbohydrate
3 g fiber
1 g protein

INGREDIENTS

- 3½ cups broccoli florets
- ½ cup pitted ripe olives
- ½ of a 2-ounce can anchovy fillets, drained and finely chopped (optional)
- 2 tablespoons snipped fresh oregano or Italian flat-leaf parsley
- 2 tablespoons red wine vinegar
- 2 tablespoons olive oil
- 5 cloves garlic, minced
- ½ teaspoon crushed red pepper
- Dash salt

Piquant Grilled Broccoli And Olives

Broccoli on the grill? You bet! The grilled florets take on a pleasing smokiness and still stay crisp-tender. This intensely flavored side dish goes great with any grilled meat or poultry— or toss it with hot cooked pasta for a vegetarian entrée.

Prep time: 15 minutes
Marinating time: 10 minutes
Grilling time: 6 minutes

DIRECTIONS

1. In a covered large saucepan cook broccoli in a small amount of boiling water for 2 minutes. Drain well. In a medium bowl combine broccoli and olives. For marinade, in a small bowl whisk together anchovies (if desired), oregano or parsley, vinegar, oil, garlic, red pepper, and salt. Pour the marinade over the broccoli and olives. Marinate at room temperature for 10 minutes, stirring occasionally. Drain broccoli and olives; discard marinade.

2. On long skewers alternately thread broccoli florets and olives. Grill on the rack of an uncovered grill directly over medium coals for 6 to 8 minutes or until broccoli is lightly browned and crisp-tender, turning occasionally. Remove the broccoli and olives from skewers. Makes 4 servings.

NUTRITION FACTS PER SERVING:

91 calories
8 g total fat
1 g saturated fat
0 mg cholesterol
125 mg sodium
6 g carbohydrate
3 g fiber
3 g protein

211

Brown Rice Pilaf

Shredded carrot adds a slight sweetness and a splash of color to this pilaf. Use wild mushrooms, such as shiitake, chanterelle, or porcini, for a more exotic dish.

INGREDIENTS

- 1 cup water
- 1 teaspoon instant chicken bouillon granules
- 1 cup sliced fresh mushrooms
- ¾ cup quick-cooking brown rice
- ½ cup shredded carrot
- ¾ teaspoon snipped fresh marjoram or ¼ teaspoon dried marjoram, crushed
- Dash pepper
- ¼ cup thinly sliced green onions
- 1 tablespoon snipped fresh parsley
- Fresh marjoram (optional)

Prep time: 10 minutes
Cooking time: 12 minutes
Standing time: 5 minutes

DIRECTIONS

1. In a medium saucepan stir together the water and bouillon granules. Bring to boiling. Stir in the mushrooms, uncooked rice, carrot, snipped or dried marjoram, and pepper. Return to boiling; reduce heat. Simmer, covered, for 12 minutes.

2. Remove from heat. Let stand, covered, for 5 minutes. Add the green onions and parsley; toss lightly with a fork. If desired, garnish with additional fresh marjoram. Makes 4 servings.

NUTRITION FACTS PER SERVING:

60 calories
1 g total fat
0 g saturated fat
0 mg cholesterol
230 mg sodium
13 g carbohydrate
2 g fiber
2 g protein

INGREDIENTS

- ¼ cup thinly sliced celery
- ¼ cup thinly sliced shallots or green onions
- 2 cloves garlic, minced
- ⅛ teaspoon pepper
- 1 tablespoon margarine or butter
- 1 cup Arborio or long grain rice
- 1 14-ounce can reduced-sodium chicken broth
- 1¾ cups water
- ½ cup fresh or frozen peas, thawed
- ½ cup coarsely chopped yellow summer squash and/or zucchini
- ½ teaspoon finely shredded lemon peel
- Fresh herbs (optional)

Risotto Primavera

Risotto usually takes an inordinate amount of patience to prepare, due to all the stirring, stirring, stirring at the stove. This modified recipe is easy to make.

For cooks who want a more classic risotto, the traditional method of adding a little broth at a time while stirring constantly is included.

Prep time: 15 minutes
Cooking time: 25 minutes
Standing time: 5 minutes

DIRECTIONS

1. In a 3-quart saucepan cook the celery, shallots or green onions, garlic, and pepper in hot margarine or butter until tender. Add the uncooked rice. Cook and stir for 2 minutes.

2. Carefully stir in the chicken broth and water. Bring to boiling; reduce heat. Simmer, covered, for 25 minutes. (Do not lift cover.) Remove from heat.

3. Stir in the peas, yellow squash or zucchini, and lemon peel. Let stand, covered, for 5 minutes. Serve immediately. If desired, garnish with fresh herbs. Makes 6 servings.

Traditional Method: Cook celery mixture as directed; add the uncooked rice. Cook and stir for 2 minutes. In another saucepan bring the broth and water to boiling; reduce heat and simmer. Slowly add ¾ cup of the broth to the rice mixture, stirring constantly. Cook and stir over medium heat until the liquid is absorbed. Continue to add broth, ¾ cup at a time, and continue to cook and stir until the rice is slightly creamy and just tender. (This should take about 20 minutes.) During cooking, adjust the heat as necessary to keep the broth at a gentle simmer. Stir in the peas, yellow squash or zucchini, and lemon peel. Let stand, covered, for 5 minutes. Serve immediately.

NUTRITION FACTS PER SERVING:

156 calories
3 g total fat
0 g saturated fat
0 mg cholesterol
227 mg sodium
29 g carbohydrate
1 g fiber
4 g protein

213

Spring Herb Rice

This recipe brings out the best in short grain rice by cooking it quickly, keeping ingredients simple, and pairing the rice with the freshest of the season's herbs.

INGREDIENTS

1¾   cups water

1   cup short grain rice

1   cup chopped onion

1   tablespoon olive oil

1   tablespoon margarine or butter

1   cup sliced celery

1   cup sliced fresh mushrooms

½   teaspoon salt

¼   teaspoon pepper

2   tablespoons snipped fresh herbs
      (such as basil, oregano,
      parsley, thyme, verbena,
      and/or lemon thyme)

1   teaspoon snipped fresh rosemary

Keep olive oil at its peak by storing

it in a cool, dark place—it will stay fresh for up to a year. When you use it in a salad dressing that is chilled, the olive oil may solidify and the dressing may be too thick to pour immediately. This won't affect the flavor. Simply let the dressing stand at room temperature for 10 to 15 minutes, shake or mix it, and serve.

Start to finish: 30 minutes

DIRECTIONS

1. In a saucepan bring the water to boiling; stir in uncooked rice. Return to boiling; reduce heat. Cover and simmer about 15 minutes or until liquid is absorbed. Remove saucepan from heat; let rice stand, covered, for 5 minutes.

2. Meanwhile, in a large skillet cook and stir onion in hot oil and margarine or butter over medium heat for 3 minutes. Add celery, mushrooms, salt, and pepper. Cook and stir for 1 minute more or until vegetables are tender. Remove skillet from heat. Stir in cooked rice, desired fresh herbs, and rosemary just until combined. Makes 6 servings.

NUTRITION FACTS PER SERVING:

173 calories
4 g total fat
1 g saturated fat
0 mg cholesterol
224 mg sodium
30 g carbohydrate
1 g fiber
3 g protein

INGREDIENTS

- 1 cup Arborio rice or other short grain rice
- 2 tablespoons olive oil or cooking oil
- 1 teaspoon bottled minced garlic or 2 cloves garlic, minced
- 3¼ to 3½ cups reduced-sodium chicken broth or vegetable broth
- 1 cup shredded carrot
- ¼ cup thinly sliced green onions
- ¼ to ½ cup shredded Parmesan or Romano cheese

- 2 tablespoons snipped fresh basil
- Long, thin carrot curls (optional)
- Basil leaves (optional)

Garden Risotto

Slow cooking is the key to producing the creamy results in this classic Italian dish.

Start to finish: 30 minutes

DIRECTIONS

1. In a large saucepan cook and stir uncooked rice in hot oil over medium heat for 5 minutes. Add garlic; cook and stir 1 minute more.

2. Meanwhile, in a medium saucepan bring broth to boiling; reduce heat so broth is simmering. Slowly add 1 cup of the broth to the rice mixture (be careful of spattering); stir constantly. Cook and stir over medium heat until broth is absorbed (about 5 minutes).

3. Add 2 more cups of the broth, ½ cup at a time, stirring constantly until broth is absorbed. Stir in remaining broth, shredded carrot, and green onions. Cook and stir until rice is creamy and just tender. Stir in Parmesan or Romano cheese and snipped basil.

4. If desired, garnish with carrot curls and basil leaves. Makes 4 servings.

NUTRITION FACTS PER SERVING:

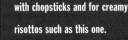

289 calories
10 g total fat
1 g saturated fat
5 mg cholesterol
611 mg sodium
42 g carbohydrate
1 g fiber
8 g protein

Short grain rices, such as Arborio rice, have almost round grains and a high starch content that causes the rice to stick together. This quality makes short grain rice ideal for Oriental dishes that are eaten with chopsticks and for creamy risottos such as this one.

Garlic Asparagus And Pasta with Lemon Cream

Delicate asparagus requires tender, loving care to show off its simple perfection. Providing just the coddling it needs are succulent baby squash, curly pasta ribbons, and a low-fuss, lemon-infused cream sauce.

INGREDIENTS

- 6 ounces dried mafalda or rotini pasta
- 1 tablespoon margarine or butter
- 2 cups asparagus cut into 2-inch pieces
- 8 baby sunburst squash and/or pattypan squash, halved (4 ounces)*
- 2 cloves garlic, minced
- 1 12-ounce can (1⅓ cups) evaporated fat-free milk
- 1 tablespoon all-purpose flour
- ¼ cup Parmesan cheese
- 2 teaspoons finely shredded lemon peel

Keep cooked pasta hot by draining it quickly. Don't let it stand in the colander longer than necessary. Then return the pasta to the hot cooking pan immediately. The heat of the pan will help keep the pasta warm.

Start to finish: 25 minutes

DIRECTIONS

1. Cook pasta according to package directions; drain and keep warm.

2. Meanwhile, in a large skillet melt margarine or butter; add asparagus, squash, and garlic. Cook, stirring frequently, for 2 to 3 minutes or until vegetables are crisp-tender. Remove with a slotted spoon and add to pasta.

3. In a medium saucepan stir the evaporated milk into the flour. Cook and stir over medium heat until mixture is thickened and bubbly. Cook and stir for 1 minute more. Add the ¼ cup Parmesan cheese and the lemon peel. Heat through.

4. To serve, pour sauce over pasta and vegetables. Toss to coat. If desired, serve with additional Parmesan cheese. Makes 6 side-dish or 4 main-dish servings.

*Note: One medium yellow squash or zucchini cut into 16 pieces can be substituted for the baby sunburst squash and/or pattypan squash.

NUTRITION FACTS PER SERVING:

213 calories
4 g total fat
1 g saturated fat
5 mg cholesterol
144 mg sodium
33 g carbohydrate
2 g fiber
11 g protein

Pasta and Fresh Tomato Sauce

INGREDIENTS

4 ounces packaged dried rotini (corkscrew) or fusilli pasta

2 cups coarsely chopped roma tomatoes

2 teaspoons olive oil

¼ teaspoon salt

3 tablespoons shredded fresh basil

¼ cup shaved or grated Parmesan or Romano cheese

¼ teaspoon pepper

This pasta sauce, the essence of simplicity, contains chopped roma tomatoes lightly sautéed in a little olive oil and seasoned with basil. Served on the side, it's the ideal accompaniment to beef, chicken, or seafood.

Start to finish: 20 minutes

DIRECTIONS

1. Cook the pasta according to package directions; drain well.

2. Meanwhile, in a medium saucepan combine the tomatoes, olive oil, and salt. Cook over medium-low heat until heated through and tomatoes start to juice out slightly. Stir in the basil.

3. Divide the pasta among 4 plates. Top with the tomato mixture. Sprinkle with the Parmesan or Romano cheese and the pepper. Makes 4 servings.

Here's a slick trick for shredding fresh basil. Layer the basil leaves on top of each other, then roll up the leaves into a tight spiral. Using a sharp knife, cut the basil into fine strips.

NUTRITION FACTS PER SERVING:

184 calories
5 g total fat
2 g saturated fat
5 mg cholesterol
260 mg sodium
28 g carbohydrate
2 g fiber
7 g protein

Farfalle With Spinach and Mushrooms

If you're using spinach that hasn't been washed, be sure to rinse it well because very often it is sandy.

INGREDIENTS

- 6 ounces packaged dried farfalle pasta (bow ties) (3 cups)
- ¾ cup chopped onion
- 1 cup sliced fresh mushrooms (such as portobello, chanterelle, shiitake, and/or crimini)
- 1 teaspoon bottled minced garlic or 2 cloves garlic, minced
- 1 tablespoon margarine or butter
- 4 cups thinly sliced fresh spinach, or 2 cups thinly sliced fresh sorrel and 2 cups thinly sliced fresh spinach
- 1 teaspoon snipped fresh thyme
- ⅛ teaspoon pepper
- 1 tablespoon licorice liqueur (optional)
- 2 tablespoons finely shredded Parmesan cheese

How much pasta is enough?

When preparing pasta, plan on 1 to 1½ ounces of dried pasta per serving for a side-dish portion. As a main-dish serving, 2 to 3 ounces dried pasta (or about 4 ounces fresh) served with a hearty sauce provides a satisfying serving. A 4-ounce bundle of dried spaghetti is about the same diameter as a quarter.

Start to finish: 25 minutes

DIRECTIONS

1. Cook pasta according to package directions. Drain.

2. Meanwhile, in a large skillet cook and stir onion, mushrooms, and garlic in hot margarine or butter over medium heat for 2 to 3 minutes or until mushrooms are nearly tender. Stir in spinach or sorrel and spinach, thyme, and pepper; cook about 1 minute or until heated through and spinach is slightly wilted.

3. Stir in cooked pasta and, if desired, liqueur; toss gently to mix. Sprinkle with Parmesan cheese. Makes 4 servings.

NUTRITION FACTS PER SERVING:

214 calories
6 g total fat
1 g saturated fat
39 mg cholesterol
127 mg sodium
33 g carbohydrate
2 g fiber
9 g protein

Mixed Pastas With Fresh Herbs

INGREDIENTS

8   ounces assorted packaged
    dried pastas

2   tablespoons walnut oil or
    olive oil

2   tablespoons coarsely snipped
    mixed fresh herbs (such as
    sage, rosemary, and basil)

¼   teaspoon salt

¼   teaspoon coarsely ground
    black pepper

Use interesting pasta shapes in this simple recipe. Try shapes that have similar cooking times so you can cook them together. The pastas shown in the photo are trenne *(tren-NAY)* and red-pepper quadrelle *(kwah-DRELL-e)*.

Start to finish: 20 minutes

DIRECTIONS

1. Cook pasta according to package directions. Drain. Toss the hot pasta with the oil, herbs, salt, and pepper. Makes 8 servings.

NUTRITION FACTS PER SERVING:

170 calories
7 g total fat
1 g saturated fat
0 mg cholesterol
67 mg sodium
22 g carbohydrate
0 g fiber
4 g protein

The distinctively nutty flavor of walnut oil is delicious in this simple pasta side dish, as well as in oil-and-vinegar salad dressings. Look for walnut oil in large supermarkets or specialty food shops.

219

Linguine with Mixed Nuts and Gorgonzola

When cooks say nuts are as good as gold, they aren't kidding. Early American settlers considered them to be such a valuable delicacy that they exchanged nuts for tools. Today nuts still add delicious crunch and flavor to everything from soups to desserts to pasta dishes like this one.

INGREDIENTS

- 1 9-ounce package refrigerated linguine or fettuccine
- ¾ cup chopped hazelnuts (filberts), pecans, and/or pine nuts
- 1 tablespoon butter
- 1 tablespoon olive oil
- ½ cup crumbled Gorgonzola or blue cheese (2 ounces)
- ¼ cup shredded Parmesan cheese (1 ounce)
- 2 tablespoons snipped fresh basil
   Fresh basil (optional)

Refrigerated fresh pastas

are increasingly available in supermarket deli cases. Fresh pastas go better with lighter sauces (such as wine- or broth-based sauces) that don't overpower their subtle flavors. Use dried pastas for heavier sauces, such as cream-, meat-, or tomato-based sauces.

Start to finish: 15 minutes

DIRECTIONS

1. Cook pasta according to package directions. Drain. Return to pan; keep warm.

2. Meanwhile, in a medium skillet cook the hazelnuts, pecans, or pine nuts in hot butter and oil until toasted and butter begins to brown, stirring frequently. Add nut mixture to pasta. Add the Gorgonzola or blue cheese, Parmesan cheese, and the snipped basil; toss gently to coat. If desired, garnish with fresh basil leaves. Makes 6 servings.

NUTRITION FACTS PER SERVING:

298 calories
19 g total fat
4 g saturated fat
23 mg cholesterol
212 mg sodium
25 g carbohydrate
1 g fiber
9 g protein

Mexicana Couscous

Quick couscous helps put this dish, reminiscent of Spanish rice, on the table in no time.

INGREDIENTS

¾ cup chopped onion

1 teaspoon bottled minced garlic or 2 cloves garlic, minced

1 tablespoon cooking oil

½ teaspoon ground cumin

1 cup reduced-sodium chicken broth

¾ cup frozen loose-pack peas

¾ cup coarsely chopped tomato or ¾ cup canned diced tomatoes

2 tablespoons snipped fresh cilantro or 2 teaspoons dried cilantro, crushed

¾ cup quick-cooking couscous

Fresh cilantro sprigs (optional)

Start to finish: 15 minutes

DIRECTIONS

1. In a medium saucepan cook and stir onion and garlic in hot oil over medium heat until tender. Stir in cumin; cook for 30 seconds.

2. Carefully add the broth, peas, tomato, and snipped fresh or dried cilantro. Bring mixture to boiling. Stir in couscous; remove from heat. Cover and let stand for 5 minutes. Fluff with a fork. If desired, garnish with cilantro sprigs. Makes 6 servings.

NUTRITION FACTS PER SERVING:

134 calories
3 g total fat
0 g saturated fat
0 mg cholesterol
124 mg sodium
23 g carbohydrate
6 g fiber
4 g protein

Couscous is a commercially produced grain product that's shaped in tiny beads. It's a staple of North African cooking and can be used in recipes or served as a side dish in place of rice. You'll find it in the rice or pasta section of the supermarket or at specialty food stores.

Grilled Corn Relish

Terrific as a side dish for grilled chicken or pork, this colorful corn relish also makes a light meal stirred with some cooked black beans, rolled up with some shredded Monterey Jack cheese in a flour tortilla, then warmed on the grill.

INGREDIENTS

- 3 tablespoons lime juice
- 1 tablespoon cooking oil
- 2 cloves garlic, minced
- 2 fresh ears of corn, husked and cleaned
- 1 teaspoon chili powder
- 1 small avocado, seeded, peeled, and cut up
- ½ cup chopped red sweet pepper
- ¼ cup snipped fresh cilantro
- ¼ teaspoon salt

Before buying avocados, think about how you'll be using them. Firm-ripe avocados are ideal for slicing and chopping; very ripe fruit is perfect for guacamole and mashing in recipes. Avocados peel most easily when they're firm-ripe. Simply cut them in half (moving the knife around the seed), remove the seed, then peel the halves. For a very ripe avocado being used for mashing, just halve the avocado and scoop the pulp away from the skin.

Prep time: 15 minutes
Grilling time: 25 minutes

DIRECTIONS

1. In a medium bowl combine the lime juice, oil, and garlic. Brush corn lightly with juice mixture. Sprinkle with chili powder. Grill corn on the rack of an uncovered grill directly over medium coals for 25 to 30 minutes or until tender, turning corn occasionally.

2. Meanwhile, add the avocado, sweet pepper, cilantro, and salt to remaining lime juice mixture; toss gently to coat. Cut the corn kernels from cobs; stir into avocado mixture. Makes 4 servings.

NUTRITION FACTS PER SERVING:

159 calories
12 g total fat
2 g saturated fat
0 mg cholesterol
152 mg sodium
15 g carbohydrate
3 g fiber
3 g protein

Sweet and Spicy Pepper-Pineapple Salsa

INGREDIENTS

- 12 ounces peeled and cored fresh pineapple, sliced ½ inch thick
- 2 large red and/or green sweet peppers, quartered
- 1 ½-inch-thick slice sweet onion (such as Vidalia or Walla Walla)
- ¼ cup apricot jam
- 2 tablespoons rice vinegar
- ¼ teaspoon salt
- ¼ teaspoon ground cinnamon
- ¼ teaspoon ground allspice
- ¼ teaspoon bottled hot pepper sauce

To make this colorful salsa quickly, buy the peeled fresh pineapple that's available now in most grocery stores. The zippy condiment perks up grilled beef and pork particularly well.

Prep time: 15 minutes
Grilling time: 13 minutes

DIRECTIONS

1. Grill the pineapple, sweet peppers, and onion on the rack of an uncovered grill directly over medium coals for 10 to 12 minutes or until sweet peppers are slightly charred, turning once halfway through cooking. Transfer pineapple and vegetables to a cutting board; cool slightly and coarsely chop.

2. Meanwhile, in a heavy medium saucepan* combine the jam, vinegar, salt, cinnamon, allspice, and hot pepper sauce. Place saucepan on grill rack near edge of grill. Cook and stir for 3 to 5 minutes or until jam is melted. Stir the chopped pineapple, sweet peppers, and onion into the mixture in saucepan. Serve salsa warm or at room temperature over grilled meats or poultry. Makes 6 servings.

*Note: The heat from the grill will blacken the outside of the saucepan, so use an old one or a small cast-iron skillet.

NUTRITION FACTS PER SERVING:

76 calories
0 g total fat
0 g saturated fat
0 mg cholesterol
93 mg sodium
20 g carbohydrate
1 g fiber
1 g protein

Marinated Tomato Platter

When "keep it simple" is your mealtime motto, reach for this easy, fresh salad recipe. Ripe tomatoes and garden zucchini star, with a drizzle of an oil-and-vinegar dressing.

INGREDIENTS

- 3 tablespoons olive oil
- 3 tablespoons white wine vinegar
- 1 tablespoon thinly sliced green onion or snipped chives
- 2 teaspoons honey mustard
- ⅛ teaspoon pepper
- 2 medium zucchini or cucumbers
  Leaf lettuce (optional)
- 3 large red and/or yellow tomatoes, sliced
- ¼ cup crumbled feta cheese with tomato and basil or plain feta cheese (1 ounce)

Cheeses once considered exotic are now widely available, and because they are so flavorful, a little goes a long way. Consider flavored fetas, any of the blue cheeses (such as Gorgonzola, Maytag blue, or Roquefort), goat cheese (chèvre), Parmesan or Pecorino Romano.

Prep time: 15 minutes
Chilling time: 30 minutes

DIRECTIONS

1. For dressing, in a screw-top jar combine the olive oil, vinegar, green onion or chives, mustard, and pepper. Cover and shake well. Chill until needed.

2. Cut the zucchini or cucumbers in half lengthwise. Seed cucumbers, if using. Using a vegetable peeler, cut zucchini or cucumber halves into thin, lengthwise strips (½ to 1 inch wide).

3. Line a serving platter with leaf lettuce (if desired) and top with the sliced tomatoes. Arrange the zucchini or cucumber strips among the tomatoes, tucking and folding the strips as desired.

4. Shake dressing; drizzle over vegetables. Cover and chill for at least 30 minutes. Before serving, sprinkle the vegetables with feta cheese. Makes 6 servings.

NUTRITION FACTS PER SERVING:

117 calories
9 g total fat
3 g saturated fat
9 mg cholesterol
138 mg sodium
7 g carbohydrate
2 g fiber
3 g protein

INGREDIENTS

¾ **cup packaged dried rotini (corkscrew) pasta or elbow macaroni**

1 **cup broccoli florets**

1 **cup cauliflower florets**

1 **9-ounce package frozen artichoke hearts**

½ **cup thinly sliced carrot**

¼ **cup sliced green onions**

½ **cup reduced-calorie Italian salad dressing**

Leaf lettuce (optional)

Vegetable and Pasta Toss

Double all of the ingredients and tote this simple pasta salad to your next potluck. No one will guess it's low in calories. Use any flavor of fat-free or reduced-calorie dressing you like.

Prep time: 25 minutes
Chilling time: 2 hours

DIRECTIONS

1. Cook the pasta according to package directions, except omit any oil; add the broccoli and cauliflower to boiling pasta for the last 1 minute of cooking. Drain. Rinse with cold water; drain well.

2. Meanwhile, cook the artichoke hearts according to package directions. Drain. Rinse with cold water; drain well. Halve any large pieces.

3. In a large mixing bowl combine the pasta mixture, artichoke hearts, carrot, and green onions. Add the Italian dressing; toss to coat.

4. Cover and chill for 2 to 24 hours. If desired, serve on lettuce-lined salad plates. Makes 6 servings.

NUTRITION FACTS PER SERVING:

91 calories
2 g total fat
0 g saturated fat
1 mg cholesterol
208 mg sodium
16 g carbohydrate
4 g fiber
4 g protein

Roasted Sweet Pepper Salad

Use any leftovers of this flavorful salad for an extra-special sandwich topping. It's especially tasty on a grilled chicken sandwich.

INGREDIENTS

6 medium red, yellow, and/or green sweet peppers

3 tablespoons balsamic vinegar

2 tablespoons capers, drained

2 tablespoons snipped fresh basil or 1 teaspoon dried basil, crushed

1 tablespoon snipped fresh oregano or 1 teaspoon dried oregano, crushed

1 tablespoon olive oil

2 cloves garlic, minced

¼ teaspoon black pepper

Lettuce leaves

What are capers?
They're the unopened flower buds on a bush that's grown primarily in Europe. The buds are packed in a vinegar brine and usually are drained, and sometimes rinsed, before using. Tangy and pungent, they have a flavor that can't easily be substituted.

Start to finish: 55 minutes

DIRECTIONS

1. Halve sweet peppers; remove stems, seeds, and membranes. Place pepper halves, cut sides down, on a foil-lined baking sheet. Bake in a 450° oven for 15 to 20 minutes or until skins are blistered and dark. Fold up foil on baking sheet around peppers to form a packet, sealing edges. Let stand about 20 minutes to loosen skins. With a small sharp knife, peel skin from peppers. Discard skin. Cut the peppers into strips.

2. In a medium bowl combine the sweet pepper strips, vinegar, capers, basil, oregano, oil, garlic, and black pepper; toss to coat. Serve immediately or cover and chill for up to 24 hours. Serve on lettuce-lined salad plates. Makes 6 to 8 servings.

NUTRITION FACTS PER SERVING:

58 calories
3 g total fat
0 g saturated fat
0 mg cholesterol
55 mg sodium
9 g carbohydrate
3 g fiber
1 g protein

INGREDIENTS

- 1 16-ounce package frozen white whole kernel corn (shoe peg), thawed
- 1 16-ounce package frozen baby peas, thawed
- 1 cup chopped, peeled jicama
- ⅔ cup chopped celery
- ½ cup thinly sliced green onions
- ¼ cup chopped red and/or orange sweet pepper
- ½ cup seasoned rice vinegar
- 2 tablespoons brown sugar
- 1 tablespoon snipped fresh parsley

- ½ teaspoon salt
- ¼ teaspoon ground white pepper
- 1 tablespoon snipped fresh mint

White Corn and Baby Pea Salad

A tangy vinaigrette-style dressing perks up a crunchy combo of white shoe peg corn, baby peas, jicama, and fresh mint.

Prep time: 15 minutes

Chilling time: 1 hour

DIRECTIONS

1. In a large mixing bowl combine the corn, peas, jicama, celery, green onions, and sweet pepper.

2. For dressing, in a screw-top jar combine the vinegar, brown sugar, parsley, salt, and white pepper. Cover and shake well. Pour over the corn mixture; toss gently to coat. Stir in mint. Cover and chill for 1 to 2 hours. Makes 10 to 12 servings.

NUTRITION FACTS PER SERVING:

90 calories
0 g total fat
0 g saturated fat
0 mg cholesterol
151 mg sodium
21 g carbohydrate
2 g fiber
4 g protein

Caribbean Slaw

As the temperature heats up, cool down with this refreshing fruit-and-vegetable slaw and one of your grilled poultry or fish favorites.

2   tablespoons snipped fresh basil or 1 teaspoon dried basil, crushed

2   tablespoons snipped fresh mint or 1 teaspoon dried mint, crushed

2   tablespoons olive oil

2   tablespoons rice vinegar or white wine vinegar

2   teaspoons soy sauce

4   cups thinly sliced Napa cabbage (about ½ of a small head)

1   mango, peeled, pitted, and sliced; or 2 peaches or nectarines, pitted and sliced

1   large cucumber, peeled, seeded, and cut into pieces

1   small red sweet pepper, cut into thin bite-size strips

½   of a small red onion, quartered and thinly sliced

When ripe, mangoes should be fully colored (yellow or green with a tinge of red), smell fruity, and feel fairly firm when pressed. Since the meat holds tightly to the seed, remove the meat by cutting through the mango and sliding a sharp knife next to the seed along one side of the mango. Repeat on the other side of the seed, resulting in two large pieces. Then cut away any meat that remains around the seed. Remove the peel and slice.

Start to finish: 30 minutes

DIRECTIONS

1. For dressing, in a screw-top jar combine the basil, mint, oil, vinegar, and soy sauce. Cover and shake well. Set aside.

2. In a large bowl combine the cabbage; mango, peaches, or nectarines; cucumber; sweet pepper; and red onion. Add the dressing; toss gently to combine. Serve immediately. Makes 5 servings.

NUTRITION FACTS PER SERVING:

98 calories
6 g total fat
1 g saturated fat
0 mg cholesterol
145 mg sodium
12 g carbohydrate
2 g fiber
2 g protein

Greek Salad

INGREDIENTS

- 3 medium tomatoes, cut into wedges
- 1 medium cucumber, halved lengthwise and thinly sliced
- 1 small red onion, cut into thin wedges
- 2 tablespoons olive oil or salad oil
- 2 tablespoons lemon juice
- 2 teaspoons snipped fresh oregano or ½ teaspoon dried oregano, crushed
- ⅛ teaspoon salt
- ⅛ teaspoon pepper
- 8 to 10 Greek black olives
- ½ cup crumbled feta cheese (2 ounces)

Feta cheese—a key ingredient in Greek cooking—gets its sharp, salty flavor from the brine in which it is cured.

Start to finish: 15 minutes

DIRECTIONS

1. In a salad bowl combine the tomatoes, cucumber, and red onion. Set aside.

2. For dressing, in a screw-top jar combine the olive or salad oil, lemon juice, oregano, salt, and pepper. Cover and shake well.

3. Pour dressing over tomato mixture; toss gently to combine. Sprinkle with Greek olives and feta cheese. Makes 4 servings.

Greek olives

are ripe Kalamata olives that are imported from Greece. They have a saltier, more intense flavor than the more commonly available black or Mission olive.

NUTRITION FACTS PER SERVING:

143 calories
12 g total fat
3 g saturated fat
12 mg cholesterol
273 mg sodium
9 g carbohydrate
2 g fiber
4 g protein

New Potato-Green Bean Salad

This salad offers a wonderful choice for potlucks and summertime picnics and parties.

INGREDIENTS

2   pounds whole tiny new potatoes, halved or quartered, or 6 medium red potatoes, cubed

1   9-ounce package frozen French-style green beans or cut green beans, cooked and drained

    Shredded lettuce

4   roma tomatoes, cut into wedges

1   recipe Yogurt-French Dressing

Prep time: 30 minutes
Cooling time: 20 minutes
Chilling time: 2 hours

DIRECTIONS

1. In a large covered saucepan cook the potatoes in boiling water for 15 to 20 minutes or just until tender. Drain; cool for 20 minutes. Cover and chill potatoes and beans for 2 to 24 hours.

2. To serve, line a serving platter with lettuce. Arrange the potatoes, green beans, and tomato wedges on lettuce. Drizzle the Yogurt-French Dressing over the vegetables. Serve immediately. Makes 6 servings.

Yogurt-French Dressing:
In a small bowl stir together ¼ cup bottled fat-free French salad dressing; 3 tablespoons plain fat-free yogurt; 1 tablespoon fat-free mayonnaise dressing or salad dressing; and 1 green onion, sliced.

NUTRITION FACTS PER SERVING:

110 calories
1 g total fat
0 g saturated fat
1 mg cholesterol
134 mg sodium
24 g carbohydrate
2 g fiber
3 g protein

INGREDIENTS

¼ cup olive oil

3 tablespoons red wine vinegar

3 tablespoons snipped fresh
   oregano

½ teaspoon sugar

¼ teaspoon salt

¼ teaspoon ground black pepper

4 ounces whole wheat sourdough
   or other country-style bread,
   cut into 1½-inch cubes

½ of a 10-ounce package
   (about 5 cups) purchased
   torn Italian-style mixed
   salad greens

1 medium tomato, cut into thin
   wedges

¼ cup halved yellow cherry
   tomatoes or yellow sweet
   pepper, cut into ½-inch
   pieces

½ cup Greek black olives or
   other olives

Quick Bread Salad

In Italy, day-old bread is put to good use as a replacement for croutons. The large cubes of sourdough bread hold the dressing as croutons only wish they could.

Start to finish: 20 minutes

DIRECTIONS

1. In a screw-top jar combine the olive oil, wine vinegar, oregano, sugar, salt, and black pepper. Cover tightly and shake well.

2. In a large salad bowl combine the bread cubes, mixed greens, tomato wedges, yellow cherry tomatoes or sweet pepper, and olives. Add dressing; toss gently to combine. Serve immediately. Makes 6 servings.

Although Italian-style mixed greens may vary by brand, they usually are a combination of romaine lettuce and radicchio.

NUTRITION FACTS PER SERVING:

151 calories
11 g total fat
1 g saturated fat
0 mg cholesterol
238 mg sodium
13 g carbohydrate
1 g fiber
2 g protein

Fresh Pear Custard Tart Recipe, page 264

Desserts

Apple Crumble

Sliced, peeled pears make an equally delicious stand-in for the cooking apples.

INGREDIENTS

Nonstick cooking spray

8 cups sliced, peeled
    cooking apples

1 tablespoon lemon juice

½ cup rolled oats

¼ cup all-purpose flour

¼ cup packed brown sugar

1 teaspoon ground cinnamon

¼ teaspoon ground nutmeg

3 tablespoons butter, chilled

    Vanilla low-fat yogurt (optional)

    Honey (optional)

There's no better low-fat

choice for dessert than fresh fruit. Choose the best quality you can find for the most after-dinner satisfaction. Fruits should be plump, brightly colored, and heavy for their size (this indicates moistness). Avoid fruits with mold, mildew, bruises, cuts, or other blemishes.

Prep time: 20 minutes
Baking time: 40 minutes

DIRECTIONS

1. Coat a 2-quart square baking dish with cooking spray. Place the apples in the prepared dish. Sprinkle with the lemon juice.

2. In a medium bowl stir together the rolled oats, flour, brown sugar, cinnamon, and nutmeg. Using a pastry blender, cut in the butter until the mixture resembles coarse crumbs. Sprinkle oat mixture evenly over apples.

3. Bake in a 350° oven for 40 to 45 minutes or until the apples are tender. Serve warm. If desired, top with yogurt sweetened with a little honey. Makes 6 servings.

NUTRITION FACTS PER SERVING:

211 calories
7 g total fat
3 g saturated fat
15 mg cholesterol
70 mg sodium
38 g carbohydrate
4 g fiber
2 g protein

INGREDIENTS

- 1 **16-ounce can peach slices (juice-pack), drained and cut up**
- 1 **16-ounce can pear halves (juice-pack), drained and cut up**
- 1 **teaspoon grated fresh ginger**
- ½ **cup finely crushed gingersnaps**
- ½ **cup quick-cooking rolled oats**
- 2 **tablespoons brown sugar**

Gingered Peach And Pear Crisp

You get a double dose of ginger with each bite of this luscious dessert. Fresh grated ginger flavors the fruit filling, and gingersnaps—combined with rolled oats—form the crumb topping.

Prep time: 15 minutes
Baking time: 15 minutes

DIRECTIONS

1. In an 8-inch quiche dish or 8×1½-inch round baking pan place the peaches, pears, and fresh ginger. Toss to mix.

2. In a small bowl stir together the gingersnaps, oats, and brown sugar. Sprinkle evenly over fruit. Bake in a 425° oven for 15 to 20 minutes or until heated through. Makes 6 servings.

NUTRITION FACTS PER SERVING:

138 calories
1 g total fat
1 g saturated fat
0 mg cholesterol
48 mg sodium
32 g carbohydrate
2 g fiber
2 g protein

Crunch-Topped Peach Pizza

Starting with an Italian bread shell takes most of the work out of this peachy dessert-style pizza.

INGREDIENTS

1 16-ounce (12-inch) Italian bread shell (Boboli)

1 21-ounce can peach or apple pie filling

⅓ cup quick-cooking rolled oats

¼ cup packed brown sugar

3 tablespoons all-purpose flour

3 tablespoons butter or margarine, melted

Supermarkets often stock summer fruits in the dead of winter. That's because on the other side of the equator (especially in Chile), these fruits are picked and shipped north during our winter. Because these fruits are harvested when mature but still unripe, they need ripening at room temperature in a paper bag. Save these imported gems for fresh fruit bowls or lunch-box treats. For baked desserts that require cupfuls of fruit, use frozen fruits or canned pie filling as in this recipe.

Prep time: 15 minutes

Baking time: 12 minutes

DIRECTIONS

1. Place the Italian bread shell on a pizza pan or large baking sheet. Top with the peach or apple pie filling, spreading evenly.

2. In a small bowl stir together the rolled oats, brown sugar, and flour. Stir in the melted butter or margarine until well mixed. Sprinkle over pie filling. Bake in a 400° oven for 12 to 15 minutes or until heated through. Makes 8 servings.

NUTRITION FACTS PER SERVING:

334 calories

8 g total fat

1 g saturated fat

8 mg cholesterol

389 mg sodium

61 g carbohydrate

1 g fiber

8 g protein

Cherry-Peach Cobbler

INGREDIENTS

- 1 cup all-purpose flour
- 2 tablespoons sugar
- 1½ teaspoons baking powder
- ¼ teaspoon ground nutmeg
- 2 tablespoons margarine or butter
- ½ cup sugar
- 4 teaspoons cornstarch
- ⅓ cup water
- 3 cups fresh or frozen unsweetened sliced, peeled peaches
- 2 cups fresh or frozen unsweetened pitted tart red cherries
- ⅓ cup plain fat-free yogurt
- ¼ cup refrigerated or frozen egg product, thawed
- Ground nutmeg (optional)

We cut the calories and fat by using fat-free yogurt to tenderize the biscuit-like topping on this traditional homespun cobbler.

Prep time: 15 minutes
Baking time: 20 minutes

DIRECTIONS

1. For topping, in a mixing bowl stir together the flour, the 2 tablespoons sugar, the baking powder, and the ¼ teaspoon nutmeg. Using a pastry blender, cut in the margarine or butter until the mixture resembles coarse crumbs. Set aside.

2. For filling, in a large saucepan stir together the ½ cup sugar and the cornstarch. Stir in water. Add the peach slices and cherries. Cook and stir until thickened and bubbly. Keep the filling hot while finishing topping.

3. To finish topping, stir together the yogurt and egg product. Add the yogurt mixture to the flour mixture, stirring just until moistened.

4. Transfer the filling to a 2-quart square baking dish. Drop the topping from a spoon into 8 mounds directly on top of the hot filling.

5. Bake cobbler in a 400° oven about 20 minutes or until a wooden toothpick inserted into the topping comes out clean. Serve warm. If desired, sprinkle with additional ground nutmeg. Makes 8 servings.

NUTRITION FACTS PER SERVING:

202 calories
3 g total fat
1 g saturated fat
0 mg cholesterol
120 mg sodium
41 g carbohydrate
2 g fiber
4 g protein

Chocolate Ricotta-Filled Pears

Discover all the wonderful flavors of the classic Sicilian ricotta-chocolate-fruit-filled cake called cassata—without turning on your oven or chopping a thing. Be sure the pears are ripe. Serve them with an Italian dessert wine, such as Vin Santo.

INGREDIENTS

1   cup ricotta cheese

⅓   cup sifted powdered sugar

1   tablespoon unsweetened cocoa powder

¼   teaspoon vanilla

2   tablespoons miniature semisweet chocolate pieces

1   teaspoon finely shredded orange peel

3   large ripe Bosc, Anjou, or Bartlett pears

2   tablespoons orange juice

2   tablespoons slivered or sliced almonds, toasted

Fresh mint leaves (optional)

Orange peel curls (optional)

Start to finish: 20 minutes

DIRECTIONS

1. In a medium bowl beat the ricotta cheese, powdered sugar, cocoa powder, and vanilla with an electric mixer on medium speed until combined. Stir in chocolate pieces and the 1 teaspoon orange peel. Set aside.

2. Peel the pears; cut in half lengthwise and remove the cores. Remove a thin slice from the rounded sides so the pear halves will sit flat. Brush the pears all over with the orange juice. Place the pears on 6 dessert plates. Spoon the ricotta mixture on top of the pears and sprinkle with almonds. If desired, garnish with mint leaves and orange curls. Makes 6 servings.

NUTRITION FACTS PER SERVING:

166 calories
6 g total fat
2 g saturated fat
13 mg cholesterol
52 mg sodium
24 g carbohydrate
3 g fiber
6 g protein

Strawberry Shortcake

Another time, use a combination of summer berries, such as raspberries, blackberries, and blueberries.

INGREDIENTS

- 3 cups sliced strawberries
- 2 tablespoons sugar
- 1⅔ cups all-purpose flour
- 1 tablespoon sugar
- 2 teaspoons baking powder
- ¼ teaspoon baking soda
- 3 tablespoons margarine or butter
- 1 beaten egg
- ½ cup buttermilk or sour fat-free milk

- 2 cups frozen light whipped dessert topping, thawed, or one 1.3-ounce envelope whipped dessert topping mix
- Strawberry fans (optional)

Prep time: 25 minutes
Chilling time: 1 hour
Baking time: 7 minutes

DIRECTIONS

1. In a medium bowl combine sliced strawberries and the 2 tablespoons sugar. Cover; chill for at least 1 hour.

2. In a medium mixing bowl stir together the flour, the 1 tablespoon sugar, the baking powder, and baking soda. Using a pastry blender, cut in the margarine or butter until the mixture resembles coarse crumbs. Combine the egg and buttermilk or sour milk; add to flour mixture all at once, stirring just until moistened.

3. Drop the dough from a tablespoon into 8 mounds on an ungreased baking sheet. Bake in a 450° oven for 7 to 8 minutes or until golden brown. Transfer the shortcakes to a wire rack and cool about 10 minutes. Meanwhile, if using topping mix, prepare according to package directions using fat-free milk.

4. To serve, cut shortcakes in half horizontally. Spoon the strawberries and half of the whipped topping over bottom layers. Replace tops. Spoon the remaining topping onto shortcakes. If desired, garnish with strawberry fans. Makes 8 servings.

To make a strawberry fan,

place the strawberry on a cutting board with the pointed end facing you. Using a paring knife, make 4 or 5 lengthwise cuts from the pointed end not quite to the stem end. Fan the slices apart slightly, being careful to keep all slices attached to the cap.

NUTRITION FACTS PER SERVING:

- 206 calories
- 6 g total fat
- 1 g saturated fat
- 27 mg cholesterol
- 215 mg sodium
- 34 g carbohydrate
- 2 g fiber
- 4 g protein

Berry-Lemon Trifle

This heavenly dessert starts with angel food cake—
either a homemade or a bakery cake will do.

INGREDIENTS

2   cups cubed angel food cake

1   8-ounce carton lemon
    fat-free yogurt

¼   of an 8-ounce container frozen
    light whipped dessert
    topping, thawed

1   cup mixed fresh berries, such as
    raspberries, blueberries, or
    sliced strawberries

    Fresh mint (optional)

How did angel food cake earn such a heavenly name?

Maybe it's because a slice (¹⁄₁₂ of a cake) has about 130 calories and less than 1 gram of fat. A similar serving of homemade chocolate cake has over 300 calories and 13 grams of fat. When you want to splurge, angel food cake is definitely more saintly.

Prep time: 12 minutes

DIRECTIONS

1. Divide angel food cake cubes among 4 individual dessert dishes. In a small mixing bowl fold together the yogurt and whipped topping.

2. Spoon the yogurt mixture on top of the cake cubes. Sprinkle with berries. If desired, garnish with fresh mint. Makes 4 servings.

NUTRITION FACTS PER SERVING:

104 calories
2 g total fat
0 g saturated fat
1 mg cholesterol
152 mg sodium
19 g carbohydrate
1 g fiber
3 g protein

Gingered Shortcake with Spiced Fruit

INGREDIENTS

- 1 recipe Gingered Shortcake
- 1 cup whipping cream
- 2 tablespoons granulated sugar
- ½ teaspoon vanilla
- 3 tablespoons butter
- 3 medium cooking apples, Fuyu persimmons, and/or pears, cored (if necessary) and thinly sliced
- 3 tablespoons brown sugar
- ¼ teaspoon ground nutmeg
- 1 cup blueberries

Shortcake isn't just for summer berries anymore! Enjoy this warming dessert with fall fruits such as apples, persimmons, or pears. The shortcake can be made ahead and refrigerated, then warmed—wrapped in foil—in a 350° oven about 25 minutes.

Prep time: 25 minutes
Baking time: 18 minutes
Cooling time: 40 minutes

DIRECTIONS

1. Prepare Gingered Shortcake. In a chilled bowl combine cream, granulated sugar, and vanilla. Beat with chilled beaters of an electric mixer until soft peaks form. Cover and refrigerate. In a large skillet melt butter over medium heat. Add apples; cook for 2 to 5 minutes or until almost tender. Stir in brown sugar and nutmeg. Cook for 1 to 3 minutes more or until apples are tender. Stir in blueberries.

2. Place bottom cake layer on a serving plate. Spoon about two-thirds of the fruit mixture and half of the whipped cream over cake. Top with second cake layer and remaining fruit mixture. Pass remaining whipped cream. Makes 8 servings.

Gingered Shortcake: Combine 2 cups all-purpose flour, ¼ cup granulated sugar, and 2 teaspoons baking powder. Cut in ½ cup butter until mixture resembles coarse crumbs. Combine 1 beaten egg, ⅔ cup milk, and 1 tablespoon grated fresh ginger; add to dry mixture. Stir just until moistened. Spread batter in a greased 8×1½-inch round baking pan. Bake in a 450° oven for 18 to 20 minutes or until a wooden toothpick inserted near center comes out clean. Cool in pan for 10 minutes. Remove from pan; cool on a wire rack for 30 minutes. Split into 2 layers.

NUTRITION FACTS PER SERVING:

457 calories
28 g total fat
17 g saturated fat
111 mg cholesterol
280 mg sodium
47 g carbohydrate
2 g fiber
5 g protein

241

Fresh Fruit with Minted Yogurt

With summer produce at its peak, you'll have no trouble finding your favorite fruits to mix and match in this "plum good" dessert.

1 16-ounce carton plain
low-fat yogurt

3 tablespoons honey

2 tablespoons snipped fresh mint

4 medium plums, pitted and thinly
sliced (about 3 cups)

3 cups assorted fresh berries,
such as blueberries,
raspberries, and strawberries

Fresh mint (optional)

Thinly sliced nectarines or peaches make an excellent substitute for the plums. Make sure you have about 3 cups of sliced fruit.

Prep time: 15 minutes

DIRECTIONS

1. In a small mixing bowl stir together the yogurt, honey, and snipped mint. Cover and chill until ready to serve.

2. To serve, in a medium bowl combine the plums and assorted berries. Divide fruit mixture among 6 individual dessert dishes. Spoon yogurt mixture on top of each serving. If desired, garnish with additional fresh mint. Makes 6 servings.

NUTRITION FACTS PER SERVING:

144 calories
1 g total fat
0 g saturated fat
1 mg cholesterol
56 mg sodium
31 g carbohydrate
3 g fiber
5 g protein

Autumn Fruits with Cinnamon Custard

INGREDIENTS

- 6   Seckel or Forelle pears
- 6   Lady apples
- ⅔   cup white vermouth, apple cider,
      or apple juice
- 3   whole star anise
- 3   tablespoons sugar
- 1   recipe Cinnamon Custard

Lady apples and small Seckel pears combine for a comforting twosome, served with a cinnamony stirred custard. If Lady apples and Seckel pears aren't available, don't worry—this recipe works well with other varieties of these fruits.

Start to finish: 25 minutes

DIRECTIONS

1. If desired, core fruit. Quarter the pears lengthwise; halve the apples crosswise. Set aside. In a large skillet bring the vermouth, apple cider, or apple juice just to boiling; reduce heat. Gently add the pears, apples, and star anise to hot liquid. Sprinkle the sugar over the fruit. Cook, covered, about 5 minutes or until the fruit is just tender.

2. Using a slotted spoon, transfer fruit to 6 dessert dishes. Discard poaching liquid. Drizzle fruit with Cinnamon Custard. Serves 6.

Cinnamon Custard: In a small heavy saucepan combine 1 beaten egg, ⅔ cup milk, and 4 teaspoons sugar. Cook and stir over medium heat just until the mixture coats the back of a spoon. Stir in ½ teaspoon vanilla and a dash of ground cinnamon. Remove from heat. If desired, place in a pan of ice water to stop the cooking process.

To test the custard, dip a clean metal spoon into the cooked custard. The custard should coat the spoon. Using your finger, draw a line down the center of the back of the spoon. The edges of the custard along the path drawn should hold their shape.

NUTRITION FACTS PER SERVING:

188 calories
2 g total fat
1 g saturated fat
38 mg cholesterol
25 mg sodium
36 g carbohydrate
4 g fiber
3 g protein

243

Glazed Nectarines With Chocolate Sauce

Celebrate the sweet arrival of nectarines with this luscious dessert. Indulging is easy because it goes together in just minutes. Serve it with a frosty mug of sun-brewed tea.

INGREDIENTS

4 medium nectarines or peaches, peeled (about 1½ pounds total)

¼ cup orange marmalade or apricot or peach preserves

1 tablespoon margarine or butter

1 tablespoon orange liqueur, apricot brandy, or orange juice

Chocolate ice-cream topping

Prep time: 15 minutes
Cooking time: 7 minutes

To glaze the nectarines in the microwave oven, pit fruit as directed. For glaze, in a 1½-quart microwave-safe casserole, microwave margarine or butter, uncovered, on 100% power (high) for 30 to 40 seconds or until melted. Stir in marmalade or preserves and liqueur, brandy, or orange juice. Add fruit; spoon glaze over fruit. Cover and micro-cook on high for 3 to 4 minutes or until the fruit is tender, gently stirring once or twice. Serve as at right.

DIRECTIONS

1. Carefully remove and discard the pits from the nectarines or peaches, leaving fruit whole. Set aside.

2. For glaze, in a medium skillet combine the marmalade or preserves, margarine or butter, and liqueur, brandy, or orange juice; heat over medium heat just until margarine and marmalade are melted.

3. Add fruit. Spoon glaze over fruit. Bring to boiling; reduce heat. Cover and simmer for 7 to 9 minutes or until fruit is tender, gently stirring once.

4. To serve, divide fruit among 4 dessert dishes. Spoon glaze and chocolate topping over fruit. Makes 4 servings.

NUTRITION FACTS PER SERVING:

144 calories
3 g total fat
1 g saturated fat
0 mg cholesterol
41 mg sodium
30 g carbohydrate
2 g fiber
1 g protein

INGREDIENTS

⅓ cup apricot jam

¼ cup orange juice

4 small pears, halved, peeled, and
  cored

Whipped cream (optional)

Apricot-Glazed Pears

The sweetness of apricot jam brings out the juicy best in succulent fresh pears. Serve this simple, yet sophisticated, dessert as a fitting finale to a special meal.

Start to finish: 30 minutes

DIRECTIONS

1. In a 2-quart rectangular baking dish stir together the jam and orange juice. Place pears in dish, cut sides down; spoon sauce over top. Bake, covered, in a 350° oven about 25 minutes or until pears are tender.

2. Serve warm pears in 4 dessert dishes. Spoon sauce over pears. If desired, serve with whipped cream. Makes 4 servings.

NUTRITION FACTS PER SERVING:

178 calories
1 g total fat
0 g saturated fat
0 mg cholesterol
3 mg sodium
45 g carbohydrate
5 g fiber
1 g protein

Keep the kitchen cool by preparing this refreshing dessert in the microwave oven. Prepare fruit as directed, except decrease orange juice to 3 tablespoons. Stir together jam and juice; arrange pear halves in a 2-quart microwave-safe baking dish. Cover with plastic wrap; turn back a corner to vent steam. Microwave on 100% power (high) for 6 to 9 minutes or until pears are tender, rearranging pears once during cooking. Serve as directed.

Red-Wine-Marinated Peaches

Carpe diem, meaning "seize the day" in Latin, must refer to that much-anticipated though fleeting time in late summer when juicy peaches are at their peak. Embellish this golden fruit with red wine, cinnamon, and cloves.

INGREDIENTS

- 6 ripe medium peaches, peeled, pitted, and sliced, or pears, cored and sliced
- 1½ cups fruity red wine (such as Beaujolais) or dry white wine
- ¾ cup sugar
- ½ teaspoon ground cinnamon
- ⅛ teaspoon ground cloves

If you're short on time, dessert doesn't have to be a lost prospect. Try one of these super-simple ideas:
- Fresh fruit sliced and tossed with a little honey and sprinkled with toasted almonds.
- A tea bar set up with several kinds of tea bags, lemon, milk, honey, and sugar—and purchased tea biscuits.
- A cheese course featuring a selection of cheeses and fresh fruit. Ripe pears with blue cheese, berries and apples with brie, and oranges with thin wedges of Parmesan are great choices.

Prep time:15 minutes
Marinating time: 30 minutes

DIRECTIONS

1. Place peaches in a large bowl. For marinade, in a medium saucepan combine the wine, sugar, cinnamon, and cloves. Cook and stir over medium heat until sugar is dissolved.

2. Pour the marinade over peaches; toss gently to coat. Marinate at room temperature for 30 to 60 minutes, stirring occasionally. To serve, spoon the peaches and marinade into 6 dessert dishes. Makes 6 servings.

NUTRITION FACTS PER SERVING:

262 calories
0 g total fat
0 g saturated fat
0 mg cholesterol
6 mg sodium
51 g carbohydrate
3 g fiber
1 g protein

Autumn Apple Fritters

INGREDIENTS

- 2 tart medium cooking apples (such as Jonathan or Granny Smith)
- $\frac{2}{3}$ cup all-purpose flour
- 1 tablespoon powdered sugar
- $\frac{1}{2}$ teaspoon finely shredded lemon peel
- $\frac{1}{4}$ teaspoon baking powder
- 1 egg
- $\frac{1}{2}$ cup milk
- 1 teaspoon cooking oil
- Shortening or cooking oil for deep-fat frying
- Powdered sugar (optional)

You won't fritter away your time in the kitchen creating these batter-covered fruit slices. Simply leave on the apple peels (but do remove the core) to produce this homey treat perfect for dessert or a snack.

Start to finish: 20 minutes

DIRECTIONS

1. Core apples and cut each crosswise into 6 rings. In a medium bowl combine the flour, the 1 tablespoon powdered sugar, the lemon peel, and baking powder.

2. In a bowl use a wire whisk to combine the egg, milk, and the 1 teaspoon cooking oil. Add egg mixture all at once to flour mixture; beat until smooth.

3. Using a fork, dip apple rings into batter; drain off excess batter. Fry 2 to 3 fritters at a time in deep hot fat (365°) about 2 minutes or until golden, turning once with a slotted spoon. Drain on paper towels. Repeat with remaining apple rings. If desired, sprinkle fritters with powdered sugar. Cool on wire racks. Makes 12 fritters.

When deep-fat frying, don't overheat the melted shortening or cooking oil to the point that it smokes. By that time, it is already breaking down. Instead, invest in a deep-fat-frying thermometer and heat the fat or oil to the temperature called for in a recipe. For these fritters, the temperature is 365°.

NUTRITION FACTS PER SERVING:

91 calories
6 g total fat
1 g saturated fat
19 mg cholesterol
18 mg sodium
9 g carbohydrate
1 g fiber
2 g protein

247

Sweet and Spicy Peaches

Frozen peaches make it possible for you to enjoy this dessert year-round. Top it with yogurt as suggested, or spoon over a scoop of light ice cream.

INGREDIENTS

2 tablespoons brown sugar

1 tablespoon lime juice or lemon juice

½ teaspoon vanilla

¼ teaspoon ground allspice

1 pound peaches, peeled, pitted, and sliced (3 cups), or 3 cups frozen unsweetened peach slices

¼ cup vanilla low-fat yogurt or fat-free dairy sour cream

Lime peel strips (optional)

Micro-cook these juicy peaches by combining the brown sugar, lime or lemon juice, vanilla, and allspice in a 1-quart microwave-safe casserole. Stir in the peaches. Cover and microwave on 100% power (high) for 2 to 5 minutes (4 to 7 minutes if using frozen peaches) or until the peaches are tender and heated through, stirring once. Serve as directed.

Prep time: 10 minutes

Cooking time: 15 minutes

DIRECTIONS

1. In a medium saucepan combine the brown sugar, lime or lemon juice, vanilla, and allspice. Stir in the peaches.

2. Bring to boiling; reduce heat. Cover and simmer about 10 minutes or until peaches are tender and hot. Serve warm, topped with the yogurt or sour cream. If desired, garnish with lime peel strips. Makes 4 servings.

NUTRITION FACTS PER SERVING:

93 calories

0 g total fat

0 g saturated fat

1 mg cholesterol

11 mg sodium

23 g carbohydrate

2 g fiber

2 g protein

Fresh Fruit with Mocha Fondue

Dessert fondues encourage lingering over the dinner table with good conversation. For a truly memorable dessert, we added coffee crystals and coffee liqueur to a rich chocolate fondue.

INGREDIENTS

1　4-ounce package sweet baking chocolate, broken up

4　ounces semisweet chocolate, chopped

⅔　cup half-and-half, light cream, or milk

½　cup sifted powdered sugar

1　teaspoon instant coffee crystals

2　tablespoons coffee liqueur

　　Assorted fresh fruit (such as apricot wedges, pear wedges, plum wedges, strawberries, pineapple chunks, kiwi fruit wedges, and/or banana slices)

Start to finish: 15 minutes

DIRECTIONS

1. In a heavy medium saucepan combine sweet baking chocolate; semisweet chocolate; half-and-half, light cream, or milk; powdered sugar; and coffee crystals. Heat and stir over low heat until melted and smooth. Remove from heat; stir in liqueur.

2. Pour into a fondue pot; keep warm over low heat. Serve with fresh fruit as dippers. Makes 6 to 8 servings.

NUTRITION FACTS PER SERVING:

305 calories
16 g total fat
10 g saturated fat
10 mg cholesterol
13 mg sodium
43 g carbohydrate
2 g fiber
3 g protein

For attractive fruit pieces, dip the pear wedges and banana slices in a little lemon juice to keep them from turning brown.

249

Fresh Fruit with Honey-Lime Sauce

Sweet and juicy, fresh pineapple makes a wonderful addition to all kinds of fruit desserts. To simplify preparation, look for peeled and cored fresh pineapple in the produce section of your supermarket.

INGREDIENTS

- 2 cups cut-up fresh pineapple
- 3 kiwi fruit, peeled, halved lengthwise, and sliced
- 1 medium papaya, peeled, seeded, and sliced
- 1 medium banana, sliced
- ¼ of a small watermelon, sliced and cut into wedges
- 2 tablespoons lime juice
- 1 8-ounce carton vanilla low-fat yogurt
- 4 teaspoons honey
- ½ teaspoon finely shredded lime peel
- 1 tablespoon lime juice

Why throw away limes, lemons, or oranges when you can still use the peel? After squeezing out the juice, store the halved rinds in a storage container in the freezer. When a recipe calls for finely shredded peel, simply grate the frozen rind. That way, you get the fresh citrus flavor without having to keep the fresh fruits on hand.

Start to finish: 25 minutes

DIRECTIONS

1. Arrange pineapple, kiwi fruit, papaya, banana, and watermelon on 6 dessert plates. Sprinkle with the 2 tablespoons lime juice.

2. For sauce, in a medium bowl stir together the yogurt, honey, lime peel, and the 1 tablespoon lime juice.

3. Spoon sauce over fruit. Serve immediately. Makes 6 servings.

NUTRITION FACTS PER SERVING:

144 calories
1 g total fat
1 g saturated fat
2 mg cholesterol
26 mg sodium
33 g carbohydrate
3 g fiber
3 g protein

Chocolate-Cinnamon Angel Cake

INGREDIENTS

1½ cups egg whites (10 to 12 large eggs)

1½ cups sifted powdered sugar

1 cup sifted cake flour or sifted all-purpose flour

3 tablespoons unsweetened cocoa powder

¼ teaspoon ground cinnamon

1½ teaspoons cream of tartar

1 teaspoon vanilla

1 cup granulated sugar

Chocolate-flavored syrup (optional)

Strawberries (optional)

A mild chocolate flavor accented with cinnamon sets this angel cake apart from others. However, it's still low in calories and fat-free. Chocolate purists can omit the cinnamon.

Prep time: 50 minutes

Baking time: 40 minutes

Cooling time: 3 hours

DIRECTIONS

1. In an extra-large mixing bowl allow the egg whites to stand at room temperature for 30 minutes.

2. Meanwhile, sift the powdered sugar, flour, cocoa powder, and cinnamon together 3 times. Set aside.

3. Add the cream of tartar and vanilla to the egg whites. Beat with an electric mixer on medium speed until soft peaks form (tips curl).

4. Gradually add granulated sugar, about 2 tablespoons at a time, beating on high speed until stiff peaks form (tips stand straight).

5. Sift about one-fourth of the dry mixture over the beaten egg whites; fold in gently. Repeat, folding in the remaining dry mixture by fourths. Pour into an ungreased 10-inch tube pan. Using a narrow metal spatula or knife, gently cut through the batter to remove any large air pockets.

6. Bake in a 350° oven on the lowest rack for 40 to 45 minutes or until the top of the cake springs back when lightly touched.

7. Immediately invert cake (leave in pan); cool completely. When cool, loosen sides of cake from pan. Remove cake from pan. To serve, slice into wedges. If desired, serve cake drizzled with chocolate-flavored syrup and garnish with strawberries. Makes 16 servings.

NUTRITION FACTS PER SERVING:

125 calories
0 g total fat
0 g saturated fat
0 mg cholesterol
35 mg sodium
28 g carbohydrate
0 g fiber
3 g protein

251

Strawberry-Topped Cheesecake

To test for a perfectly baked, creamy cheesecake, gently shake the pan after the minimum baking time. The center should appear nearly set. If it still jiggles, bake it 5 minutes longer and test again.

INGREDIENTS

- ½ cup graham cracker crumbs
- 4 teaspoons margarine or butter, melted
- 2 8-ounce packages fat-free cream cheese (block style)
- 1 cup fat-free cottage cheese
- ¼ cup fat-free milk
- ¾ cup sugar
- 2 tablespoons all-purpose flour
- 1¼ teaspoons vanilla
- ½ teaspoon finely shredded lemon peel
- 3 eggs or ¾ cup refrigerated or frozen egg product, thawed
- ¼ cup fat-free or light dairy sour cream
- 2 teaspoons fat-free milk
- 1 teaspoon sugar
- 1 cup sliced strawberries

Prep time: 20 minutes
Baking time: 35 minutes
Cooling time: 2 hours
Chilling time: 4 hours

DIRECTIONS

1. In a small bowl stir together the graham cracker crumbs and melted margarine or butter. Press onto the bottom of an 8-inch springform pan. Set aside.

2. Cut up the cream cheese. In a large food processor bowl place the undrained cottage cheese and the ¼ cup milk. Cover and process until smooth. Add cream cheese, the ¾ cup sugar, the flour, 1 teaspoon of the vanilla, and the lemon peel. Cover; process until smooth. Add the eggs or egg product and process just until combined. Do not overprocess. Pour mixture into pan. Place on a baking sheet.

3. Bake in a 375° oven for 35 to 40 minutes or until set. Cool for 15 minutes. Using a narrow metal spatula, loosen the side of the cheesecake from the pan. Cool 30 minutes more, then remove the side of the pan. Cool completely. Cover and chill for at least 4 hours.

4. In a small bowl combine the sour cream, the 2 teaspoons milk, the 1 teaspoon sugar, and the remaining vanilla. To serve, arrange berries on top of cheesecake; drizzle with sour cream mixture. Serves 12.

NUTRITION FACTS PER SERVING:

163 calories
3 g total fat
1 g saturated fat
62 mg cholesterol
92 mg sodium
22 g carbohydrate
0 g fiber
11 g protein

INGREDIENTS

Nonstick cooking spray

⅓ cup crushed vanilla wafers
   (8 wafers)

1½ 8-ounce tubs fat-free cream
   cheese, softened
   (12 ounces total)

½ cup sugar

1 tablespoon all-purpose flour

1 teaspoon vanilla

¼ cup frozen egg product, thawed

¾ cup fresh raspberries;
   blueberries; sliced, peeled
   kiwi fruit; sliced strawberries;
   sliced, pitted plums; and/or
   orange sections

Mini Cheesecakes

Top these tiny cheesecakes with whatever fruit strikes your fancy. The small size makes perfect light desserts or party treats.

Prep time: 20 minutes

Baking time: 18 minutes

Chilling time: 4 hours

DIRECTIONS

1. Coat ten 2½-inch muffin cups with cooking spray. Sprinkle bottom and side of each cup with about 1 teaspoon of the crushed vanilla wafers. Set aside.

2. In a medium mixing bowl beat the cream cheese with an electric mixer on medium speed until smooth. Add the sugar, flour, and vanilla. Beat on medium speed until smooth. Add the egg product and beat on low speed just until combined. Divide mixture evenly among muffin cups.

3. Bake in a 325° oven for 18 to 20 minutes or until set. Cool in pan on a wire rack for 5 minutes. Cover pan and chill for 4 to 24 hours. Remove the cheesecakes from the muffin cups. Just before serving, top the cheesecakes with fresh fruit. Makes 10 cheesecakes.

NUTRITION FACTS PER SERVING:

124 calories
4 g total fat
1 g saturated fat
5 mg cholesterol
25 mg sodium
16 g carbohydrate
0 g fiber
6 g protein

Citrus-Hazelnut Bars

Definitely a bar cookie with lots of appeal—these double citrus and nutty delights are not overly sweet. They make a great accompaniment to an afternoon tea break.

INGREDIENTS

⅓ cup butter

¼ cup granulated sugar

1 cup all-purpose flour

⅓ cup chopped toasted hazelnuts
   (filberts) or chopped almonds

2 eggs

¾ cup granulated sugar

2 tablespoons all-purpose flour

1 teaspoon finely shredded
   orange peel

1 teaspoon finely shredded
   lemon peel

2 tablespoons orange juice

1 tablespoon lemon juice

½ teaspoon baking powder

Powdered sugar (optional)

Prep time: 20 minutes
Baking time: 30 minutes

DIRECTIONS

1. For the crust, beat the butter in a medium mixing bowl with an electric mixer on medium to high speed for 30 seconds. Add the ¼ cup granulated sugar. Beat until thoroughly combined. Beat in the 1 cup flour and about half of the nuts until mixture is crumbly.

2. Press mixture into the bottom of an ungreased 8×8×2-inch baking pan. Bake in a 350° oven for 10 minutes or until lightly browned.

3. Meanwhile, in a mixing bowl stir together the eggs, the ¾ cup granulated sugar, the 2 tablespoons flour, the orange peel, lemon peel, orange juice, lemon juice, and baking powder. Beat for 2 minutes at medium speed or until combined. Pour over hot baked layer. Sprinkle with remaining nuts.

4. Bake about 20 minutes more or until light brown around the edges and the center is set. Cool on a rack. If desired, sifted powdered sugar over the top. Cut into bars. Store bars, covered, in the refrigerator. Makes 20 bars.

NUTRITION FACTS PER BAR:

111 calories
5 g total fat
1 g saturated fat
25 mg cholesterol
43 mg sodium
16 g carbohydrate
0 g fiber
2 g protein

Lemon Bars with Raspberries

Impressive and easy to make, this refreshingly tart dessert is a great ending to any meal.

INGREDIENTS

Nonstick cooking spray

¾ cup all-purpose flour

3 tablespoons sugar

¼ cup margarine or butter

1 egg

1 egg white

⅔ cup sugar

2 tablespoons all-purpose flour

1 teaspoon finely shredded lemon
   peel (set aside)

2 tablespoons lemon juice

1 tablespoon water

¼ teaspoon baking powder

1½ cups fresh raspberries

2 tablespoons red currant
   jelly, melted

Prep time: 25 minutes
Baking time: 35 minutes
Cooling time: 1 hour

DIRECTIONS

1. Coat an 8×8×2-inch baking pan with cooking spray. Set aside. In a small mixing bowl combine the ¾ cup flour and the 3 tablespoons sugar. Cut in the margarine or butter until crumbly. Pat the mixture onto the bottom of the prepared pan. Bake in a 350° oven for 15 minutes.

2. Meanwhile, for filling, in a small mixing bowl combine the egg and egg white. Beat with an electric mixer on medium speed until frothy. Add the ⅔ cup sugar, the 2 tablespoons flour, the lemon juice, water, and baking powder. Beat on medium speed about 3 minutes or until slightly thickened. Stir in lemon peel.

3. Pour over hot baked layer in pan. Bake for 20 to 25 minutes more or until edges are light brown and center is set. Cool completely in pan on a wire rack. Cut into 9 squares; cut each square diagonally to make a triangle. Top triangles with raspberries. Drizzle with the jelly. Makes 18 servings.

NUTRITION FACTS PER SERVING:

96 calories
3 g total fat
1 g saturated fat
12 mg cholesterol
42 mg sodium
17 g carbohydrate
1 g fiber
1 g protein

Apricot-Cardamom Bars

Applesauce and apricot nectar replace some of the fat in these moist snack bars.

INGREDIENTS

1 cup all-purpose flour

½ cup packed brown sugar

½ teaspoon baking powder

¼ teaspoon baking soda

¼ teaspoon ground cardamom or

⅛ teaspoon ground cloves

1 slightly beaten egg

½ cup apricot nectar or

orange juice

¼ cup unsweetened applesauce

2 tablespoons cooking oil

½ cup finely snipped dried apricots

1 recipe Apricot Icing

Experiment with cardamom for a new change of spice. Cardamom has a pungent and aromatic flowery sweetness that's a little like ginger but is much more subtle. Try it in place of some of your favorite spices, such as cinnamon, nutmeg, or ginger.

Prep time: 20 minutes

Baking time: 25 minutes

Cooling time: 2 hours

DIRECTIONS

1. In a medium mixing bowl stir together the flour, brown sugar, baking powder, baking soda, and cardamom or cloves; set aside. In a small mixing bowl stir together the egg, apricot nectar or orange juice, applesauce, and oil until combined. Add to dry ingredients, stirring just until moistened. Stir in apricots.

2. Spread batter in an ungreased 11×7×1½-inch baking pan. Bake in a 350° oven about 25 minutes or until a toothpick inserted near the center comes out clean. Cool in pan on a rack. Drizzle with Apricot Icing. Cut into bars. Makes 24 bars.

Apricot Icing: In a small bowl stir together ½ cup sifted powdered sugar and 1 to 2 teaspoons apricot nectar or orange juice. Stir in enough additional apricot nectar or orange juice, 1 teaspoon at a time, to make of drizzling consistency.

NUTRITION FACTS PER BAR:

63 calories

1 g total fat

0 g saturated fat

9 mg cholesterol

25 mg sodium

12 g carbohydrate

1 g fiber

1 g protein

INGREDIENTS

- 1 **cup all-purpose flour**
- 1 **cup sliced almonds, finely chopped**
- ¾ **cup packed dark brown sugar**
- ½ **cup light-colored corn syrup**
- ½ **cup butter**
- 1 **teaspoon vanilla**
- 3 **cups raspberry and/or lemon sorbet**
- **Fresh raspberries**

Almond Cookie Cups with Sorbet

Like pastel eggs in an Easter basket, scoops of sorbet are nestled prettily in crisp, almond-flavored cups. In addition to raspberry and lemon sorbet, try other flavors, such as lime, grapefruit, peach, and pear.

Prep time: 15 minutes
Baking time: 10 minutes per batch

DIRECTIONS

1. In a small bowl combine the flour and almonds; set aside. In a medium saucepan bring the brown sugar, corn syrup, and butter to a full boil over medium heat. Remove from heat. Stir in the flour mixture and vanilla.

2. Line a large cookie sheet with parchment paper. For each cookie cup, drop about 3 tablespoonfuls of batter about 5 inches apart onto prepared cookie sheet (bake 3 or 4 at a time). Bake in a 350° oven for 10 to 12 minutes or until bubbly and deep golden brown (cookies will form irregular shapes). Let stand on cookie sheet about 2 minutes. When firm but still pliable, place on top of inverted custard cups to form small bowls. Cool to room temperature.

3. To serve, fill 6 of the cups with scoops of sorbet. Garnish with raspberries. Serve immediately. Store the remaining cups in an airtight container in the freezer for up to 3 months. Makes 6 servings.

NUTRITION FACTS PER SERVING:

380 calories
15 g total fat
6 g saturated fat
25 mg cholesterol
121 mg sodium
60 g carbohydrate
1 g fiber
4 g protein

257

Brownie-Fruit Pizza

To make the brownie crust easier to cut, spray a pizza cutter or knife with nonstick cooking spray.

INGREDIENTS

Nonstick cooking spray

½ cup sugar

3 tablespoons margarine or butter, softened

¼ cup refrigerated or frozen egg product, thawed

¾ cup chocolate-flavored syrup

⅔ cup all-purpose flour

3 cups fresh fruit, such as sliced, peeled, and quartered kiwi fruit; sliced, peeled peaches; sliced nectarines or strawberries; raspberries; or blueberries

½ cup chocolate-flavored syrup

Prep time: 15 minutes
Baking time: 20 minutes
Cooling time: 2 hours

DIRECTIONS

1. Coat a 12-inch pizza pan with cooking spray. Set aside.

2. For crust, in a medium mixing bowl combine the sugar and margarine or butter. Beat with an electric mixer on medium speed until creamy. Add the egg product; beat well. Alternately add the ¾ cup chocolate syrup and the flour, beating after each addition on low speed until combined. Spread in the prepared pizza pan.

3. Bake in a 350° oven about 20 minutes or until the top springs back when lightly touched. Cool in the pan on a wire rack.

4. To serve, cut the brownie into 12 wedges. Top each wedge with fruit and drizzle with the ½ cup chocolate syrup. Makes 12 servings.

NUTRITION FACTS PER SERVING:

169 calories
4 g total fat
1 g saturated fat
0 mg cholesterol
60 mg sodium
35 g carbohydrate
1 g fiber
2 g protein

Cookies And Cream

INGREDIENTS

- ¼ of an 18-ounce roll refrigerated sugar cookie dough, sliced ¼ inch thick (8 slices)
- ½ cup frozen light whipped dessert topping, thawed
- ½ cup fat-free dairy sour cream
- 1 teaspoon finely shredded orange peel
- 3 cups fresh or frozen berries (such as raspberries, blackberries, or sliced strawberries), thawed and drained
- Sifted unsweetened cocoa powder (optional)
- Orange peel twists (optional)
- Edible flowers (optional)

This Italian dessert is usually laden with whipped cream and yogurt. To lighten the calorie load, we skipped the cream and yogurt and added fat-free sour cream to light dessert topping instead. We also used slice-and-bake cookies instead of a homemade dough to save you time.

Prep time: 20 minutes
Baking time: 8 minutes

DIRECTIONS

1. Bake sugar cookies according to package directions. Set aside to cool.

2. Meanwhile, combine the whipped topping and sour cream. Stir in the shredded orange peel. Cover and chill until serving time.

3. To assemble, place a cookie on each of 4 dessert plates. Top each cookie with about one-fourth of the berries, one-fourth of the sour cream mixture, another cookie, the remaining sour cream mixture, and the remaining berries. If desired, dust with cocoa powder and garnish with orange peel and edible flowers. Makes 4 servings.

NUTRITION FACTS PER SERVING:

222 calories
7 g total fat
3 g saturated fat
5 mg cholesterol
154 mg sodium
36 g carbohydrate
4 g fiber
3 g protein

Strawberry Bavarian Pie

Naturally low-fat ladyfinger sponge cakes form the crust for this light, strawberry-flavored pie. Shop for soft ladyfingers at bakeries or grocery stores; the crispy ones will not work as well.

INGREDIENTS

- 3 cups fresh strawberries
- ¼ cup sugar
- 1 envelope unflavored gelatin
- 3 slightly beaten egg whites
- 1 3-ounce package ladyfingers, split
- 2 tablespoons orange juice
- ½ of an 8-ounce container frozen light whipped dessert topping, thawed (about 1⅔ cups)
- Frozen light whipped dessert topping, thawed (optional)
- Strawberry fans (optional)

Prep time: 20 minutes
Chilling time: 2½ hours

DIRECTIONS

1. Place the 3 cups strawberries in a blender container or food processor bowl. Cover; blend or process until smooth. Measure the strawberries (you should have about 1¾ cups).

2. In a medium saucepan combine the sugar and gelatin. Stir in the blended strawberries. Cook and stir over medium heat until the mixture bubbles and the gelatin is dissolved.

3. Gradually stir about half of the gelatin mixture into the slightly beaten egg whites.

Return all of the mixture to the saucepan. Cook, stirring constantly, over low heat for 2 to 3 minutes or until slightly thickened. Do not boil. Pour into a mixing bowl. Chill just until the mixture mounds when dropped from a spoon, stirring occasionally.

4. Meanwhile, cut about half of the split ladyfingers in half crosswise; stand these on end around the outside edge of a 9- or 9½-inch tart pan with removable bottom or a 9-inch springform pan. Arrange the remaining split ladyfingers in bottom of pan. Slowly drizzle the orange juice over the ladyfingers.

5. Fold the whipped topping into the strawberry

mixture; spoon into the ladyfinger-lined pan. Cover and chill for at least 2 hours or until set. If desired, garnish with additional whipped topping and strawberry fans. Makes 10 servings.

NUTRITION FACTS PER SERVING:

98 calories
2 g total fat
2 g saturated fat
31 mg cholesterol
39 mg sodium
16 g carbohydrate
1 g fiber
3 g protein

Deep-Dish Apple Pie

INGREDIENTS

- 6 cups thinly sliced, peeled cooking apples (about 2 pounds total)
- ¼ cup sugar
- 1 teaspoon ground cinnamon
- 1 tablespoon cornstarch
- ⅛ teaspoon salt
- ¾ cup all-purpose flour or ½ cup all-purpose flour plus ¼ cup whole wheat flour
- Dash ground nutmeg
- 3 tablespoons margarine or butter
- 2 to 3 tablespoons cold water
- Fat-free milk

Bite into this all-American dessert and you'll experience some of our country's best from the past. Each forkful boasts a luscious cinnamon-apple filling and flaky pastry.

Prep time: 30 minutes
Baking time: 40 minutes

DIRECTIONS

1. Place apples in a 2-quart square baking dish.

2. In a small bowl combine the sugar and cinnamon; set aside 1 teaspoon of the mixture. Stir the cornstarch and salt into the remaining sugar mixture; sprinkle evenly over the apples in the baking dish.

3. In a medium bowl stir together the flour and nutmeg. Using a pastry blender, cut in the margarine or butter until mixture resembles coarse crumbs. Sprinkle 1 tablespoon of the water over part of the mixture; gently toss with a fork. Add the remaining water, 1 tablespoon at a time, until the dough is moistened. Form into a ball.

4. On a lightly floured surface, roll the dough into a 10-inch square. Cut decorative vents in pastry. Carefully place pastry over apples. Using the tines of a fork, press edges to sides of dish. Brush pastry with milk and sprinkle with the reserved sugar mixture.

5. Bake in a 375° oven about 40 minutes or until the apples are tender and the crust is golden brown. Serve warm. Makes 8 servings.

NUTRITION FACTS PER SERVING:

171 calories
5 g total fat
1 g saturated fat
0 mg cholesterol
85 mg sodium
33 g carbohydrate
2 g fiber
1 g protein

Country Apricot Tart

The flavor of this cornmeal crust is outstanding and—better yet—it's great for those who haven't mastered the art of making beautifully crimped pie edges. You simply fold the crust over the filling.

INGREDIENTS

1 recipe Cornmeal Crust

⅓ cup sugar

3 tablespoons all-purpose flour

¼ teaspoon ground nutmeg
    or cinnamon

3 cups sliced, pitted fresh apricots
    or 3 cups frozen,
    unsweetened peach slices,
    thawed (do not drain)

1 tablespoon lemon juice

2 teaspoons fat-free milk

Prep time: 30 minutes
Baking time: 40 minutes

DIRECTIONS

1. Grease and lightly flour a large baking sheet. Prepare the Cornmeal Crust. Place on the baking sheet; flatten the dough. Roll into a 12-inch circle. Set aside.

2. For filling, in a large bowl stir together the sugar, flour, and nutmeg or cinnamon. Stir in the apricots or peaches and the lemon juice. Mound the filling in center of crust, leaving a 2-inch border. Fold the border up over filling. Brush edge of crust with the 2 teaspoons milk.

3. Bake in a 375° oven about 40 minutes or until the crust is golden and the filling is bubbly. Loosely cover the edge of crust with foil the last 10 to 15 minutes of baking to prevent overbrowning. Serve warm. Makes 8 servings.

Cornmeal Crust: In a medium bowl stir together ¾ cup all-purpose flour, ⅓ cup cornmeal, 2 tablespoons sugar, 1 teaspoon baking powder, and ⅛ teaspoon salt. Cut in 3 tablespoons butter or margarine until the size of small peas. Sprinkle 1 tablespoon cold fat-free milk over part of mixture; gently toss with a fork. Add 3 to 4 tablespoons more fat-free milk, 1 tablespoon at a time, until dough is moistened (dough will be crumbly). On a lightly floured surface, knead gently 7 to 8 strokes or just until the dough clings together. Form into a ball.

NUTRITION FACTS PER SERVING:

176 calories
5 g total fat
3 g saturated fat
12 mg cholesterol
128 mg sodium
32 g carbohydrate
2 g fiber
3 g protein

INGREDIENTS

Nonstick cooking spray

½ cup water

2 tablespoons margarine or butter

½ cup all-purpose flour

2 eggs

1 4-serving-size package fat-free
  instant chocolate pudding mix
  or reduced-calorie chocolate
  pudding mix

⅛ teaspoon peppermint extract

1 cup sliced strawberries

Sifted powdered sugar (optional)

Fresh mint (optional)

Mint-Chocolate Cream Puffs

Watching your diet doesn't mean giving up chocolate. These minty chocolate puffs have loads of flavor—and only 126 calories and 4 grams of fat per serving.

Prep time: 25 minutes
Baking time: 30 minutes
Cooling time: 1 hour

DIRECTIONS

1. Coat a baking sheet with cooking spray. Set aside. In a small saucepan combine the water and margarine or butter. Bring to boiling. Add the flour all at once, stirring vigorously. Cook and stir until mixture forms a ball. Remove from heat. Cool for 5 minutes.

2. Add the eggs, one at a time, beating after each addition. Drop the mixture into 8 mounds, about 3 inches apart, onto the prepared baking sheet.

3. Bake in a 400° oven about 30 minutes or until golden brown. Remove from oven. Split puffs and remove any soft dough from inside. Cool well on a wire rack.

4. Meanwhile, for filling, prepare the pudding mix according to package directions. Stir in peppermint extract. Cover the surface of pudding with plastic wrap and chill thoroughly.

5. To serve, spoon about ¼ cup of the filling into the bottom half of each cream puff. Top with the sliced strawberries. Replace the tops. If desired, dust with powdered sugar and garnish with fresh mint. Makes 8 servings.

After adding the flour, stir the dough vigorously until the mixture forms a ball that doesn't separate. Cool as directed. Add the eggs, one at a time. After each addition, use a wooden spoon to beat the dough until it is smooth.

NUTRITION FACTS PER SERVING:

126 calories
4 g total fat
1 g saturated fat
53 mg cholesterol
225 mg sodium
20 g carbohydrate
1 g fiber
2 g protein

Fresh Pear Custard Tart

Be sure to use ripe pears for this tart. Pears that are too firm or unripe will make it difficult to eat. If you're really in a pinch, substitute sliced, well-drained canned pears.

INGREDIENTS

- 1 recipe Single-Crust Pastry
- ½ cup granulated sugar
- 2 tablespoons cornstarch
- 2 cups fat-free milk
- 2 beaten eggs
- 4 teaspoons finely chopped crystallized ginger
- 1 teaspoon vanilla
- ⅔ cup pear nectar
- 1½ teaspoons cornstarch
- 3 small ripe pears
- ½ cup fresh berries (such as raspberries, blackberries, and/or blueberries)
- Sifted powdered sugar (optional)
- Fresh mint (optional)
- Edible flowers (optional)

Prep time: 1 hour
Chilling time: 1 hour

DIRECTIONS

1. Prepare the Single-Crust Pastry. For filling, in a medium heavy saucepan combine the granulated sugar and the 2 tablespoons cornstarch. Stir in milk. Cook and stir over medium heat until thickened and bubbly. Cook and stir for 2 minutes more. Remove from heat.

2. Gradually stir about 1 cup of the hot mixture into beaten eggs. Return all of the mixture to the saucepan. Stir in the ginger. Cook and stir until thickened and bubbly. Reduce heat. Cook and stir for 2 minutes more. Remove from heat. Stir in the vanilla. Pour into the baked tart shell. Cover and chill until ready to assemble.

3. Meanwhile, for glaze, in a small saucepan combine the pear nectar and the 1½ teaspoons cornstarch. Cook and stir until thickened and bubbly. Cook and stir for 2 minutes more. Remove from heat. Cover and cool to room temperature.

4. To assemble the tart, peel, core, and thinly slice the pears. Arrange in a concentric pattern over the filling. Pour the cooled glaze over the pears, spreading evenly. Cover and chill for 1 to 4 hours. To serve, top with berries. If desired, dust with powdered sugar and garnish with fresh mint and edible flowers. Makes 10 servings.

Single-Crust Pastry: In a medium bowl stir together 1¼ cups all-purpose flour and ¼ teaspoon salt. In a small bowl combine ¼ cup fat-free milk and 3 tablespoons cooking oil; add all at once to flour mixture. Stir with a fork until a dough forms. Form into a ball.

On a lightly floured surface, roll dough from center to edge into a 13-inch circle. Ease into an 11-inch tart pan with removable bottom. Trim to edge of pan. Prick bottom and side well with tines of a fork. Bake in a 450° oven for 10 to 12 minutes or until golden brown. Cool in pan on a wire rack.

NUTRITION FACTS PER SERVING:

- 216 calories
- 6 g total fat
- 1 g saturated fat
- 44 mg cholesterol
- 96 mg sodium
- 37 g carbohydrate
- 2 g fiber
- 5 g protein

Cranberry Tart

Tissue-thin layers of phyllo pastry form the crispy crust of this tart. Packaged frozen phyllo dough, readily available in supermarkets, is easy to use.

INGREDIENTS

1 cup cranberries

¼ cup sugar

1 tablespoon orange juice

1 8-ounce package reduced-fat cream cheese (Neufchâtel)

¼ cup sugar

1 egg

1 egg white

1 teaspoon vanilla

Butter-flavored nonstick cooking spray

4 sheets frozen phyllo dough, thawed

1 ounce white chocolate, melted (optional)

Prep time: 20 minutes
Baking time: 25 minutes
Cooling time: 1 hour
Chilling time: 4 hours

DIRECTIONS

1. In a small saucepan combine the cranberries, the ¼ cup sugar, and the orange juice. Cook, uncovered, over medium heat until the cranberries pop and the mixture thickens slightly, stirring frequently. Remove from heat. Set aside.

2. In a food processor bowl combine the cream cheese, the ¼ cup sugar, the egg, egg white, and vanilla. Cover and process until smooth. Set the mixture aside.

3. Coat a 9-inch tart pan or pie plate with cooking spray. Coat 1 phyllo sheet with cooking spray. Fold the sheet in half crosswise to form a rectangle (about 13×9 inches). Gently press the folded sheet of phyllo into the prepared tart pan, allowing ends to extend over edge of pan. Coat with cooking spray. Coat and fold another sheet of phyllo; place across first sheet in a crisscross fashion. Coat with cooking spray. Repeat with remaining 2 sheets of phyllo. (If desired, turn under edges of phyllo to form a crust.) Bake, uncovered, in a 350° oven for 5 minutes.

4. Spoon the cream cheese mixture into the phyllo crust, spreading evenly. Spoon the cranberry mixture over the cream cheese mixture. Using a knife, marble the mixtures together slightly.

5. Bake tart for 20 to 25 minutes or until the phyllo is lightly browned and the filling is set. Cool on a wire rack for 1 hour. Cover and chill for 4 to 24 hours. If desired, drizzle edges of phyllo with white chocolate before serving. Makes 10 servings.

NUTRITION FACTS PER SERVING:

192 calories
7 g total fat
4 g saturated fat
40 mg cholesterol
142 mg sodium
18 g carbohydrate
1 g fiber
4 g protein

Summer Fruit Tart

A pudding-like mixture fills this fruit-topped tart. Use any type of in-season fruit you like.

INGREDIENTS

1   recipe Tart Pastry
¼   cup sugar
2   tablespoons cornstarch
1   12-ounce can evaporated
    fat-free milk
¼   cup refrigerated or frozen egg
    product, thawed
½   teaspoon vanilla
2   medium fresh nectarines or
    peeled peaches, thinly sliced
2   fresh plums, thinly sliced
2   kiwi fruit, peeled and sliced

½   cup fresh blueberries,
    raspberries, and/or
    blackberries
2   tablespoons honey
1   tablespoon rum or orange juice

Prep time: 35 minutes
Chilling time: 2 hours

DIRECTIONS

1. Prepare Tart Pastry. For filling, in a medium heavy saucepan combine sugar and cornstarch. Stir in evaporated milk and egg product. Cook and stir over medium heat until thickened and bubbly. Cook and stir for 2 minutes more. Remove from heat. Stir in vanilla. Cover surface with plastic wrap; chill for 1 hour.

2. Spread the filling in the baked tart shell. Arrange the nectarines, plums, and kiwi fruit on top of filling. Sprinkle with the berries. Combine the honey and rum or orange juice; brush over fruit. Cover and chill for up to 1 hour. Makes 10 servings.

Tart Pastry: In a medium bowl stir together 1¼ cups all-purpose flour and ¼ teaspoon salt. Using a pastry blender, cut in ¼ cup shortening until the mixture resembles fine crumbs. Sprinkle 1 tablespoon cold water over part of mixture; gently toss with a fork. Add 3 to 4 tablespoons more cold water, 1 tablespoon at a time, until the mixture is moistened. Form into a ball.

On a lightly floured surface, roll dough from center to edge into a 13-inch circle. Ease into an 11-inch tart pan with removable bottom. Trim to edge of pan. Prick bottom and side well with fork. Bake in a 450° oven for 10 to 12 minutes or until golden. Cool in pan on a wire rack.

NUTRITION FACTS PER SERVING:

187 calories
6 g total fat
1 g saturated fat
1 mg cholesterol
84 mg sodium
31 g carbohydrate
2 g fiber
4 g protein

Flan

INGREDIENTS

- ⅓ cup sugar
- 3 beaten eggs
- 1 12-ounce can (1½ cups) evaporated milk
- ⅓ cup sugar
- 1 teaspoon vanilla
- Fresh fruit (optional)
- Edible flowers (optional)

Flan was imported directly from Spain. The inverted caramel custard is so well loved it's found on restaurant dessert menus everywhere. Canned evaporated milk gives the custard a rich flavor.

Prep time: 30 minutes
Baking time: 30 minutes
Chilling time: 4 hours

DIRECTIONS

1. To caramelize sugar, in a heavy skillet cook ⅓ cup sugar over medium-high heat until the sugar begins to melt, shaking skillet occasionally. Do not stir. Once the sugar starts to melt, reduce heat to low and cook about 5 minutes more or until all of the sugar melts and is golden brown, stirring as needed with a wooden spoon.

2. Remove skillet from heat. Immediately pour the caramelized sugar into an 8-inch flan pan or an 8×1½-inch round baking pan (or divide caramelized sugar among six 6-ounce custard cups). Working quickly, rotate pan or cups so sugar coats the bottom as evenly as possible. Cool.

3. In a medium mixing bowl combine the eggs, evaporated milk, ⅓ cup sugar, and vanilla. Place the pan or custard cups in a 13×9×2-inch baking pan on an oven rack. Pour the egg mixture into pan or custard cups. Pour the hottest tap water available into the 13×9×2-inch pan around the flan or 8-inch baking pan or custard cups to a depth of about ½ inch.

4. Bake in a 325° oven for 30 to 35 minutes for flan or 8-inch baking pan (35 to 40 minutes for custard cups) or until a knife inserted near the center comes out clean. Immediately remove pan or custard cups from hot water. Cool on a wire rack. Cover and chill for 4 to 24 hours.

5. To unmold flan, loosen edges with a knife, slipping end of knife down sides of pan to let in air. Invert a serving platter over the pan or dessert plates over each custard cup; turn dishes over together to release custard. Spoon any caramelized sugar that remains in pan or cups over top(s). If desired, serve with fresh fruit and garnish with edible flowers. Makes 6 servings.

Before the sugar begins to melt, shake the pan occasionally, but do not stir until melting begins. The sugar is caramelized when it is syrupy and golden brown.

NUTRITION FACTS PER SERVING:

202 calories
7 g total fat
3 g saturated fat
123 mg cholesterol
92 mg sodium
28 g carbohydrate
0 g fiber
7 g protein

Mango Mousse

For this recipe, look for mangoes that have a healthy red blush and feel slightly soft to the touch like a ripe tomato.

INGREDIENTS

2 ripe mangoes, seeded, peeled, and chopped

1 envelope unflavored gelatin

2 tablespoons sugar

2 teaspoons lemon juice

1 8-ounce container frozen light whipped dessert topping, thawed

Mango and/or kiwi fruit slices (optional)

Removing a mango seed takes a little cutting know-how. Place the fruit on its blossom end and align a sharp knife slightly off-center of the stemmed end. Slice down through the peel and flesh, next to the seed. Repeat on the other side. Cut off the remaining flesh around the seed. Cut off the peel, then cut the mango into pieces as directed.

Prep time: 20 minutes
Freezing time: 45 minutes
Chilling time: 4 hours

DIRECTIONS

1. Place the chopped mangoes in a food processor bowl or blender container. Cover and process or blend until smooth. Add enough water to make 2 cups puree. Transfer the mango mixture to a medium saucepan and bring to boiling.

2. In a large mixing bowl stir together the gelatin and sugar. Pour mango mixture over gelatin mixture and stir until gelatin dissolves. Stir in the lemon juice. Cover and freeze for 45 to 60 minutes or until the mixture mounds when dropped from a spoon, stirring occasionally.

3. Beat the mango mixture with an electric mixer for 2 to 3 minutes or until mixture is thick and light. Fold in the whipped topping.

4. Pipe or spoon the mango mixture into 6 dessert dishes or parfait glasses. Cover and chill until set. If desired, garnish with mango and/or kiwi fruit slices. Makes 6 servings.

NUTRITION FACTS PER SERVING:

149 calories
5 g total fat
0 g saturated fat
1 mg cholesterol
31 mg sodium
25 g carbohydrate
2 g fiber
1 g protein

INGREDIENTS

- ⅓ cup granulated sugar
- 3 tablespoons all-purpose flour
- ⅔ cup milk
- 1 egg
- 1 egg yolk
- ¼ cup ground toasted almonds
- 1 tablespoon butter or margarine
- 1 teaspoon vanilla
- ¼ teaspoon almond extract
- 3 egg yolks
- ¼ teaspoon vanilla

- ½ cup milk
- 3 tablespoons butter or margarine, melted
- ½ cup all-purpose flour
- ¼ cup granulated sugar
- 3 egg whites
- Cooking oil
- Sliced almonds, toasted
- Sifted powdered sugar
- Mixed fresh berries (optional)

Almond Cream Crepes

In France, it's customary to touch the handle of the pan during cooking and make a wish while the crepe is turned.

Prep time: 1 hour
Baking time: 10 minutes

DIRECTIONS

1. For filling, in a small saucepan combine the ⅓ cup granulated sugar and the 3 tablespoons flour. Add the ⅔ cup milk; cook and stir until thickened and bubbly. Cook and stir for 1 minute more. Beat the whole egg and the 1 egg yolk together slightly. Gradually stir half of the hot mixture into the beaten eggs. Return all of the mixture to the saucepan. Cook and stir over low heat for 2 minutes (do not boil). Remove from heat. Stir in the ground almonds, the 1 tablespoon butter or margarine, the 1 teaspoon vanilla, and the almond extract. Cover and set aside.

2. Meanwhile, for crepes, in a small mixing bowl stir together the 3 egg yolks and the ¼ teaspoon vanilla; stir in the ½ cup milk and the 3 tablespoons melted butter or margarine. Stir in the ½ cup flour and the ¼ cup granulated sugar until smooth. In a medium mixing bowl beat the egg whites with an electric mixer until stiff peaks form (tips stand straight). Gently fold the batter into beaten egg whites.

3. Brush a 6-inch skillet with cooking oil; heat over medium heat. Spoon a generous tablespoon of batter into the skillet; spread with the back of a spoon into a 4- to 5-inch circle. Cook over medium heat for 30 to 45 seconds or until the underside is brown. Turn and cook just until the other side is light brown. Invert onto paper towels. Cover; keep warm. Repeat with remaining batter to make 24 crepes.

4. To assemble, spread about 2 teaspoons of the filling onto each crepe; fold in half, then fold in half again to form a triangle. Place the crepes in an ungreased 3-quart rectangular baking dish. Bake, uncovered, in a 350° oven about 10 minutes or until heated through. Sprinkle with sliced almonds and powdered sugar. If desired, serve with fresh berries. Makes 12 servings.

NUTRITION FACTS PER SERVING:

152 calories
8 g total fat
2 g saturated fat
90 mg cholesterol
78 mg sodium
17 g carbohydrate
0 g fiber
4 g protein

269

Caramel Crunch Ice-Cream Sauce

Surprise—cereal adds crunch to this sauce, which is ready in 15 minutes.

Start to finish: 15 minutes

INGREDIENTS

- ¼ cup margarine or butter
- ⅓ cup chopped or sliced almonds
- ⅓ cup light-colored corn syrup
- ⅓ cup packed brown sugar
- 1 tablespoon water
- ⅓ cup crisp rice cereal, coarsely crushed
- Ice cream

DIRECTIONS

1. In a medium skillet melt margarine or butter. Add the almonds; cook and stir over medium-low heat about 5 minutes or until almonds are browned.

2. Add the corn syrup, brown sugar, and water to the skillet. Cook and stir until bubbly and the brown sugar is dissolved (about 4 minutes). Stir in the rice cereal. Serve immediately over ice cream. Makes about 1 cup sauce.

NUTRITION FACTS PER SERVING:

159 calories
9 g total fat
1 g saturated fat
0 mg cholesterol
92 mg sodium
21 g carbohydrate
1 g fiber
1 g protein

INGREDIENTS

- ¼ cup low-calorie orange marmalade spread
- ¼ cup orange juice
- 2 teaspoons cornstarch
- 1 teaspoon margarine or butter
- ¼ teaspoon ground cardamom or ground cinnamon
- 2 cups sliced, peeled peaches or nectarines or frozen unsweetened peach slices
- 1 cup pitted dark sweet cherries or frozen unsweetened pitted dark sweet cherries
- ½ cup frozen yogurt or low-fat or light ice cream

Peachy Cherry Sauce

This luscious fruit dessert boasts only 2 grams of fat per serving.

Prep time: 20 minutes
Cooking time: 10 minutes

DIRECTIONS

1. In a medium saucepan combine the marmalade spread, orange juice, cornstarch, margarine or butter, and cardamom or cinnamon. Cook and stir until thickened and bubbly. Stir in the peaches and cherries. Cover and cook over medium heat for 10 to 12 minutes or until fruits are just tender, stirring once. Cool slightly.

2. To serve, spoon sauce into dessert dishes. Top each serving with a small spoonful of the frozen yogurt. Makes 5 servings.

NUTRITION FACTS PER SERVING:

117 calories
2 g total fat
1 g saturated fat
2 mg cholesterol
21 mg sodium
24 g carbohydrate
2 g fiber
2 g protein

To remove the peel from a peach,
dip the peach into boiling water for 20 seconds. Then use a paring knife to remove the skin. If the skin doesn't peel easily, return the peach to the boiling water for a few more seconds.

Pineapple-Topped Ice Cream

Present this versatile dessert as flashy or as humbly as you like. Ignite the rum and serve as a sensational flambé. Or skip the rum and crown it with light whipped dessert topping and a maraschino cherry.

INGREDIENTS

- ½ teaspoon finely shredded orange peel
- ¼ cup orange juice
- 2 teaspoons cornstarch
- ½ teaspoon ground ginger
- 1 20-ounce can crushed pineapple (juice pack), undrained
- 2 tablespoons light rum (optional)
- 1½ cups vanilla low-fat or light ice cream or frozen yogurt
- Orange peel strips (optional)

The freezer section is brimming with a variety of ice-cream-like treats in a multitude of tempting flavors. Which one is best for a healthy diet? Check out the fat contents listed on the packages of ice cream, ice milk, frozen yogurt, and sherbet to help you decide.

Start to finish: 12 minutes

DIRECTIONS

1. In a large skillet stir together the shredded orange peel, the orange juice, cornstarch, and ground ginger. Stir in undrained pineapple. Cook and stir until slightly thickened and bubbly. Cook and stir for 2 minutes more. Remove from heat.

2. If desired, in a small saucepan heat the rum over low heat just until warm. Using a long match, carefully ignite the rum. While it's still flaming, carefully pour the rum over the pineapple mixture. When the flame dwindles, serve immediately over the ice cream or frozen yogurt. If desired, garnish with orange peel strips. Makes 6 servings.

NUTRITION FACTS PER SERVING:

111 calories
2 g total fat
1 g saturated fat
5 mg cholesterol
30 mg sodium
24 g carbohydrate
1 g fiber
2 g protein

Rum-Sauced Bananas

Shop for the best nutritional bargain when selecting low-fat or light ice cream. Compare the nutrition content of several brands and choose the one that's lowest in calories and fat.

INGREDIENTS

- ¼ cup apple cider or apple juice
- 4 teaspoons brown sugar
- 1 teaspoon margarine or butter
  Dash ground nutmeg
- 2 large bananas, sliced (about 1¾ cups)
- 1 tablespoon rum
- 1 cup vanilla or coffee low-fat or light ice cream or frozen yogurt

Start to finish: 10 minutes

DIRECTIONS

1. In a medium saucepan combine the apple cider or apple juice, brown sugar, margarine or butter, and nutmeg. Heat just to boiling.

2. Add sliced bananas; toss to coat. Heat through. Stir in the rum.

3. Serve banana mixture over the ice cream. Makes 4 servings.

NUTRITION FACTS PER SERVING:

163 calories
3 g total fat
1 g saturated fat
5 mg cholesterol
41 mg sodium
33 g carbohydrate
2 g fiber
2 g protein

If you prefer, prepare the banana mixture in the microwave oven. In a 1-quart microwave-safe bowl combine the apple cider, brown sugar, margarine or butter, and nutmeg. Microwave, uncovered, on 100% power (high) for 1 minute. Add the sliced bananas; toss to coat. Micro-cook on 100% power (high) for 1½ to 2 minutes or until the bananas are heated through; stir in the rum. Serve over the ice cream.

Grilled Banana Sundaes

Even if you can't vacation in the tropics, you can enjoy the taste of the tropics. Cook bananas and a quick caramel sauce on the grill, then spoon over ice cream.

INGREDIENTS

- 3 large firm bananas
- 1 tablespoon margarine or butter, melted
- 2 teaspoons lime juice or orange juice
- ½ cup caramel ice-cream topping
- ¼ teaspoon ground cinnamon
- 1 pint vanilla ice cream
- Toasted coconut (optional)
- Sliced almonds, toasted (optional)

Start to finish: 20 minutes

DIRECTIONS

1. Cut bananas in half lengthwise, then cut each piece in half crosswise. (You should have 12 pieces.) Stir together margarine or butter and 1 teaspoon of the lime or orange juice. Brush mixture on all sides of banana pieces.

2. Place bananas directly on the grill rack over medium-hot coals. Grill, uncovered, for 2 minutes; turn over and grill for 2 minutes more or until heated through.

3. Meanwhile, in a heavy, medium skillet or saucepan combine the caramel topping and the remaining lime or orange juice. Heat on the grill rack alongside bananas directly over the coals until bubbly, stirring frequently. (Or, heat on range top over medium heat until bubbly, stirring frequently.) Stir in cinnamon. Add bananas and stir gently to coat.

4. To serve, scoop ice cream into 4 dessert dishes. Spoon sauce and bananas over ice cream. If desired, sprinkle with coconut and/or almonds. Makes 4 servings.

NUTRITION FACTS PER SERVING:

367 calories
11 g total fat
5 g saturated fat
29 mg cholesterol
231 mg sodium
70 g carbohydrate
2 g fiber
4 g protein

INGREDIENTS

1 12-ounce jar caramel ice-cream
topping

⅓ cup pure maple syrup or
maple-flavored syrup

1 quart (4 cups) macadamia
brittle, butter brickle, or
butter-pecan ice cream

2 cups sliced mango or papaya or
fresh pineapple chunks

Shredded coconut, toasted
(optional)

Tropicana Delight

Indulge in this irresistible sundae topped with mango, papaya, or pineapple and experience the romance of the tropics.

Start to finish: 10 minutes

DIRECTIONS

1. Stir together the caramel ice-cream topping and maple syrup.

2. Layer scoops of ice cream and caramel mixture into 8 sundae glasses. Top with sliced mango, papaya, or pineapple chunks. If desired, sprinkle with toasted coconut. Makes 8 servings.

NUTRITION FACTS PER SERVING:

343 calories
9 g total fat
5 g saturated fat
30 mg cholesterol
211 mg sodium
63 g carbohydrate
2 g fiber
2 g protein

For a raspberry delight, combine some unsweetened raspberries (thawed, if frozen) and a few spoonfuls of sugar. Mash some of the raspberries slightly. Let stand at room temperature until syrupy. Layer scoops of raspberry sherbet and the raspberries in sundae glasses. Sprinkle generously with white chocolate shavings. If desired, garnish with fresh mint.

Towering Brownie Sundaes

The smaller the brownies, the quicker they bake. The individual mini brownies used in this recipe bake in just 15 minutes.

INGREDIENTS

Nonstick cooking spray

¼ cup butter

1 ounce unsweetened chocolate, cut up

½ cup sugar

1 egg

½ teaspoon vanilla

⅓ cup all-purpose flour

¼ cup coarsely chopped peanuts

1 cup chocolate-fudge ice-cream topping

2 tablespoons peanut butter

1 quart (4 cups) tin roof sundae ice cream or vanilla ice cream

Banana slices (optional)

Chocolate-covered peanut butter cups, chopped (optional)

Peanuts (optional)

Start to finish: 30 minutes

DIRECTIONS

1. Lightly coat twelve 1¾ inch muffin cups with nonstick spray; set aside.

2. In a medium saucepan melt the butter and unsweetened chocolate over low heat. Remove from heat. Cool for 3 minutes. Stir in sugar. Add egg and vanilla, beating lightly with a spoon just until combined. (Don't overbeat.) Stir in flour and the ¼ cup peanuts.

3. Divide batter evenly among prepared muffin cups, filling each nearly full. Bake in a 350° oven 15 minutes or until set (toothpick will not come out clean, nor will brownies spring back). Cool brownies 3 minutes in pan; remove to a wire rack to cool.

4. Meanwhile, in a small heavy saucepan heat and stir ice-cream topping and peanut butter over medium-low heat until smooth. Remove saucepan from heat.

5. Spoon ice cream into 6 dessert dishes. Top each serving with 2 brownies and, if desired, banana slices. Drizzle with the warm peanut butter mixture. If desired, top with peanut butter cups and additional peanuts. Makes 6 servings.

NUTRITION FACTS PER SERVING:

640 calories
36 g total fat
18 g saturated fat
95 mg cholesterol
299 mg sodium
77 g carbohydrate
1 g fiber
12 g protein

Frozen Berry Yogurt

Kick off the ice-cream-making season with this frosty treat.

INGREDIENTS

1¼ cups sugar

1 cup water

3 cups fresh raspberries, blackberries, and/or strawberries

3 8-ounce cartons vanilla yogurt

1 teaspoon vanilla

Fresh melon or other fruit, cut into thin slices (optional)

Prep time: 25 minutes
Chilling time: 8 minutes
Freezing time: 45 minutes
Ripening time: 4 hours

DIRECTIONS

1. In a medium saucepan combine the sugar and water. Cook and stir over high heat until the mixture comes to a boil and the sugar dissolves. Remove from heat; cool.

2. In a blender container combine half of the sugar mixture and half of the berries. Cover and blend until almost smooth. Pour into a fine mesh sieve set over a bowl. Press the berry mixture through sieve; discard seeds. Transfer the berry mixture to a large mixing bowl. Repeat with the remaining sugar mixture and the remaining berries. Stir in the yogurt and vanilla; mix until well combined. Cover and chill for at least 8 hours or overnight.

3. Freeze the mixture in a 2-quart ice-cream freezer according to manufacturer's directions. Ripen for 4 hours. If desired, cut melon or other fruit into long, thin ribbons with a vegetable peeler. Serve with scoops of frozen yogurt. Makes 6 to 8 servings.

Homemade frozen yogurt and ice cream taste better and melt more slowly if they are ripened before serving. To ripen, follow the manufacturer's directions for your ice-cream freezer.

NUTRITION FACTS PER SERVING:

298 calories
2 g total fat
1 g saturated fat
6 mg cholesterol
67 mg sodium
67 g carbohydrate
3 g fiber
5 g protein

It you don't have:	Substitute:
Bacon, 1 slice, crisp-cooked, crumbled	1 tablespoon cooked bacon pieces
Baking powder, 1 teaspoon	½ teaspoon cream of tartar plus ¼ teaspoon baking soda
Balsamic vinegar, 1 tablespoon	1 tablespoon cider vinegar or red wine vinegar plus ½ teaspoon sugar
Bread crumbs, fine dry, ¼ cup	¾ cup soft bread crumbs, or ¼ cup cracker crumbs, or ¼ cup cornflake crumbs
Broth, beef or chicken, 1 cup	1 teaspoon or 1 cube instant beef or chicken bouillon plus 1 cup hot water
Butter, 1 cup	1 cup shortening plus ¼ teaspoon salt, if desired
Buttermilk, 1 cup	1 tablespoon lemon juice or vinegar plus enough milk to make 1 cup (let stand 5 minutes before using) or 1 cup plain yogurt
Chocolate, semisweet, 1 ounce	3 tablespoons semisweet chocolate pieces, or 1 ounce unsweetened chocolate plus 1 tablespoon granulated sugar, or 1 tablespoon unsweetened cocoa powder plus 2 teaspoons sugar and 2 teaspoons shortening
Chocolate, sweet baking, 4 ounces	¼ cup unsweetened cocoa powder plus ⅓ cup granulated sugar and 3 tablespoons shortening
Chocolate, unsweetened, 1 ounce	3 tablespoons unsweetened cocoa powder plus 1 tablespoon cooking oil or shortening, melted (for thickening)
Cornstarch, 1 tablespoon	2 tablespoons all-purpose flour
Corn syrup (light), 1 cup	1 cup granulated sugar plus ¼ cup water
Egg, 1 whole	2 egg whites, or 2 egg yolks, or ¼ cup refrigerated or frozen egg product, thawed
Flour, cake, 1 cup	1 cup minus 2 tablespoons all-purpose flour
Flour, self-rising, 1 cup	1 cup all-purpose flour plus 1 teaspoon baking powder, ½ teaspoon salt, and ¼ teaspoon baking soda
Garlic, 1 clove	½ teaspoon bottled minced garlic or ⅛ teaspoon garlic powder
Ginger, grated fresh, 1 teaspoon	¼ teaspoon ground ginger
Half-and-half or light cream, 1 cup	1 tablespoon melted butter or margarine plus enough whole milk to make 1 cup
Molasses, 1 cup	1 cup honey
Mustard, dry, 1 teaspoon	1 tablespoon prepared (in cooked mixtures)
Mustard, prepared, 1 tablespoon	½ teaspoon dry mustard plus 2 teaspoons vinegar
Onion, chopped, ½ cup	2 tablespoons dried minced onion or ½ teaspoon onion powder
Sour cream, dairy, 1 cup	1 cup plain yogurt
Sugar, granulated, 1 cup	1 cup packed brown sugar or 2 cups sifted powdered sugar
Sugar, brown, 1 cup packed	1 cup granulated sugar plus 2 tablespoons molasses
Tomato juice, 1 cup	½ cup tomato sauce plus ½ cup water
Tomato sauce, 2 cups	¾ cup tomato paste plus 1 cup water
Vanilla bean, 1 whole	2 teaspoons vanilla extract
Wine, red, 1 cup	1 cup beef or chicken broth in savory recipes; cranberry juice in desserts
Wine, white, 1 cup	1 cup chicken broth in savory recipes; apple juice or white grape juice in desserts
Yeast, active dry, 1 package	about 2¼ teaspoons active dry yeast

seasonings

Apple pie spice, 1 teaspoon	½ teaspoon ground cinnamon plus ¼ teaspoon ground nutmeg, ⅛ teaspoon ground allspice, and dash ground cloves or ginger
Cajun seasoning, 1 tablespoon	½ teaspoon white pepper, ½ teaspoon garlic powder, ½ teaspoon onion powder, ½ teaspoon ground red pepper, ½ teaspoon paprika, and ½ teaspoon black pepper
Herbs, snipped fresh, 1 tablespoon	½ to 1 teaspoon dried herb, crushed, or ½ teaspoon ground herb
Poultry seasoning, 1 teaspoon	¾ teaspoon dried sage, crushed, plus ¼ teaspoon dried thyme or marjoram, crushed
Pumpkin pie spice, 1 teaspoon	½ teaspoon ground cinnamon plus ¼ teaspoon ground ginger, ¼ teaspoon ground allspice, and ⅛ teaspoon ground nutmeg

G-K

Metric Information

The charts on this page provide a guide for converting measurements from the U.S. customary system, which is used throughout this book, to the metric system.

Product Differences: Most of the ingredients called for in the recipes in this book are available in most countries. However, some are known by different names. Here are some common American ingredients and their possible counterparts.

• Sugar (white) is granulated, fine granulated, or castor sugar.

• Powdered sugar is icing sugar.

• All-purpose flour is enriched, bleached or unbleached white household flour. When self-rising flour is used in place of all-purpose flour in a recipe that calls for leavening, omit the leavening agent (baking soda or baking powder) and salt.

• Light-color corn syrup is golden syrup.

• Cornstarch is cornflour.

• Baking soda is bicarbonate of soda.

• Vanilla or vanilla extract is vanilla essence.

• Green, red, or yellow sweet peppers are capsicums or bell peppers.

• Golden raisins are sultanas.

Volume and Weight: The United States traditionally uses cup measures for liquid and solid ingredients. The chart below shows the approximate imperial and metric equivalents. If you are accustomed to weighing solid ingredients, the following approximate equivalents will be helpful.

• 1 cup butter, castor sugar, or rice = 8 ounces = ½ pound = 250 grams

• 1 cup flour = 4 ounces = ¼ pound = 125 grams

• 1 cup icing sugar = 5 ounces = 150 grams

Canadian and U.S. volume for a cup measure is 8 fluid ounces (237 ml), but the standard metric equivalent is 250 ml.

1 British imperial cup is 10 fluid ounces.

In Australia, 1 tablespoon equals 20 ml, and there are 4 teaspoons in the Australian tablespoon.

Spoon measures are used for smaller amounts of ingredients. Although the size of the tablespoon varies slightly in different countries, for practical purposes and for recipes in this book, a straight substitution is all that's necessary. Measurements made using cups or spoons always should be level unless stated otherwise.

U.S. STANDARD METRIC EQUIVALENTS

⅛ teaspoon = 0.5 ml	⅓ cup = 3 fluid ounces = 75 ml
¼ teaspoon = 1 ml	½ cup = 4 fluid ounces = 125 ml
½ teaspoon = 2 ml	⅔ cup = 5 fluid ounces = 150 ml
1 teaspoon = 5 ml	¾ cup = 6 fluid ounces = 175 ml
1 tablespoon = 15 ml	1 cup = 8 fluid ounces = 250 ml
2 tablespoons = 25 ml	2 cups = 1 pint = 500 ml
¼ cup = 2 fluid ounces = 50 ml	1 quart = 1 litre

BAKING PAN SIZES

Imperial/U.S.	Metric
9x1½-inch round cake pan	22- or 23x4-cm (1.5 L)
9x1½-inch pie plate	22- or 23x4-cm (1 L)
8x8x2-inch square cake pan	20x5-cm (2 L)
9x9x2-inch square cake pan	22- or 23x4.5-cm (2.5 L)
11x7x1½-inch baking pan	28x17x4-cm (2 L)
2-quart rectangular baking pan	30x19x4.5-cm (3 L)
13x9x2-inch baking pan	34x22x4.5-cm (3.5 L)
15x10x1-inch jelly roll pan	40x25x2-cm
9x5x3-inch loaf pan	23x13x8-cm (2 L)
2-quart casserole	2 L

OVEN TEMPERATURE EQUIVALENTS

Fahrenheit Setting	Celsius Setting*	Gas Setting
300°F	150°C	Gas Mark 2 (very low)
325°F	160°C	Gas Mark 3 (low)
350°F	180°C	Gas Mark 4 (moderate)
375°F	190°C	Gas Mark 5 (moderate)
400°F	200°C	Gas Mark 6 (hot)
425°F	220°C	Gas Mark 7 (hot)
450°F	230°C	Gas Mark 8 (very hot)
475°F	240°C	Gas Mark 9 (very hot)
500°F	260°C	Gas Mark 10 (extremely hot)
Broil		Grill

*Electric and gas ovens may be calibrated using Celsius. However, for an electric oven, increase Celsius setting 10 to 20 degrees when cooking above 160°C. For convection or forced-air ovens (gas or electric), lower the temperature setting 25°F/10°C when cooking at all heat levels.

COMMON WEIGHT RANGE REPLACEMENTS

Imperial/U.S.	Metric
½ ounce	15 g
1 ounce	25 g or 30 g
4 ounces (¼ pound)	115 g or 125 g
8 ounces (½ pound)	225 g or 250 g
16 ounces (1 pound)	450 g or 500 g
1¼ pounds	625 g
1½ pounds	750 g
2 pounds or 2¼ pounds	1,000 g or 1 Kg